THE OTHER PANDEMIC

THE OTHER PANDEMIC

How QAnon Contaminated the World

James Ball

BLOOMSBURY PUBLISHING
LONDON • OXFORD • NEW YORK • NEW DELHI • SYDNEY

BLOOMSBURY PUBLISHING
Bloomsbury Publishing Plc
50 Bedford Square, London, WC1B 3DP, UK
29 Earlsfort Terrace, Dublin 2, Ireland

BLOOMSBURY, BLOOMSBURY PUBLISHING and the Diana logo are
trademarks of Bloomsbury Publishing Plc

First published in Great Britain 2023

A catalogue record for this book is available from the British Library

ISBN: HB: 978-1-5266-4255-4; TPB: 978-1-5266-4253-0;
EBOOK: 978-1-5266-4250-9; EPDF: 978-1-5266-7185-1

2 4 6 8 10 9 7 5 3 1

Typeset by Newgen KnowledgeWorks Pvt. Ltd., Chennai, India
Printed and bound in Great Britain by CPI Group (UK) Ltd, Croydon CR0 4YY

To find out more about our authors and books visit www.bloomsbury.com
and sign up for our newsletters

'Whoever fights monsters should see to it that in the process he does not become a monster. And if you gaze long enough into an abyss, the abyss will gaze back into you.'

– Friedrich Nietzsche, 1886

Contents

Introduction

It doesn't take long browsing the messageboard of 4chan to realise that you're not in Kansas anymore, Toto. The structure might look similar to mainstream forums like Reddit, or even Mumsnet, but differences quickly jump out.

No one has a username – everyone is anonymous. Posts leap from the pornographic, to discussions of obscure anime, to far-right politics and back. Looking for some common thread of coherence is an exercise in futility. Conversations don't stay around for long, either – as new topics come to the fore, the old ones vanish into the memory hole, gone forever. Where other boards look to build a community through a sense of identity and cohesiveness, 4chan's anarchic culture is built on almost the opposite.

That means the boards move at pace. One day, 4chan's users might be obsessed with finding a way to troll the discourse on Pride parades[1] – creating supposedly earnest Twitter accounts arguing they should be 'family friendly' and exclude kink subcultures, simply to start a fight – while the next day that's all history and the discussion is about how Ukraine shouldn't have bothered fighting its Russian invaders. It's generally a fast-moving nihilistic place that's all about 'the lulz'.

Some posts, though, have an impact that lasts long after the post itself has disappeared – perhaps none more so than a message posted on 28 October 2017 in a thread entitled 'Calm Before The Storm'. It opened: 'HRC extradition already in motion effective yesterday with several countries in case of cross border run.'

This was a big claim for a one-off post from a new 4chan user (the site gives each anonymous user a random code, so that you can see when the anonymous person replying is the same one who wrote a particular post). It claimed that the extradition of Hillary Clinton – HRC – was underway, and that her passport would be flagged within days. It went on to predict riots in response to the action, staged by some unnamed behind-the-scenes power. Tantalisingly, it also offered a form of 'proof', suggesting readers find someone they know who had signed up to the National Guard and ask if they had been 'activated for duty'.[2]

A few days and a few dozen posts later, the anonymous account offered an identity of sorts for himself: 'Q Clearance Patriot'.[3] 'Q' is a term for a high level of security clearance in the US Department of Energy, which among other duties oversees the USA's nuclear stockpiles. 'Q Clearance Patriot' quickly became known as Q for short among the community dissecting and analysing his posts.

Why someone with such high-level clearance and access to such explosive and sensitive information would choose 4chan to reveal it – and why they would risk compromising such a sensitive operation – was a question left unanswered. The same user posted cryptic but compelling follow-up messages in the hours and days following, but 30 October 2017 came and went and Hillary Clinton remained free, and the predicted riots failed to materialise.

Despite this failed prophecy, Q's posts started something – a sprawling online conspiracy theory that became a new cult, one with no clear leader and no clear agenda, one into which people across the globe self-radicalised, aided and abetted by the algorithms created by and the lax regulation of the world's largest companies. Given its birth on 4chan's anonymous bulletin boards and its initial devotion to the posts of Q, the movement came to be known by a catchy portmanteau: QAnon.

The QAnon conspiracy is a hard one to fully define – we will be doing that throughout the book. But at its core is the concept that the world is run by a satanic, paedophilic elite led by Hillary Clinton. The presidency of Donald Trump waged a heroic battle to stop that elite, all behind the scenes. And it was cut short by the 'stolen' US presidential election of 2020.

To most people, that whole concept will look like nonsense (or so I hope). But, from a tiny following among the already somewhat fringe community of 4chan users, it snowballed. Via QAnon influencers it reached a much larger audience through Facebook, YouTube and other social media sites.

The conspiracy theory was perhaps not as unbelievable as it should be. Over the years between 2017 and the present day, as QAnon rose and spread, people across the world watched as an elite continued to get vastly richer even as normal families struggled through first a pandemic and then a global economic crisis.

People also saw reports of elite crime rings based on sexual violence. Jeffrey Epstein, one of the leaders of such a criminal enterprise, had an air of credibility having been photographed with the Clintons, Trumps, celebrities and politicians around the world.[4] In a turn of events regarded as suspicious by many, he was found dead in his cell of an apparent suicide before he could stand trial. Ghislaine Maxwell, daughter of the media mogul Robert Maxwell, was later convicted of securing underage girls for Epstein. If that kind of elite crime ring could be real and come to light, what darker secrets might be being kept? The real world provided a tantalising way into the madness of QAnon.

In time the QAnon movement was embraced in the US by Congressional candidates, White House aides and perhaps even the president himself. But that's not where it stopped. From its genesis in 2017, QAnon caught on among millions in the US – and then around the world. It grew ever more active in the real world and sparked violent incidents and confrontations, leading directly and spectacularly, on 6 January 2021, to a poorly organised but dangerous mob invading the US Capitol Building in a bid to change the election results.

This was a moment that shocked a nation and stunned the world as a country supposed to be the world's leading democracy came within just metres of disaster.[5] It was only thanks to luck and the bravery of a few Capitol police officers that the insurrectionists didn't come into contact with representatives or senators.

It also, according to conventional wisdom, marked the high (or low) moment of QAnon. Following the riot, those physically present were arrested, while sluggish social networks finally banned its users from their online services. Couple this with yet another failure of prophecy – Biden was inaugurated two weeks later, contrary to the group's expectations, and Trump did not remain president – and the received wisdom, even among seasoned QAnon watchers, was that the movement was over.

But the conventional wisdom was wrong. Dangerously, complacently wrong. Those who thought the QAnon moment could pass so easily failed to see that QAnon did not come from nowhere and nothing – it had precursors that had built over at least a decade. They failed to see that unfulfilled prophecies rarely end cults, online or offline. And they failed to see that QAnon was already mutating into something new, even before the 6 January riots.

The reality is that as the months of 2021 rolled on, you rarely needed to look far to see that QAnon's influence was alive and well – a fact that should have been unsurprising: once you believe a murderous cabal is running the world, it takes quite a lot to shift you back to mainstream positions.

One huge opportunity for QAnon believers came through the Covid-19 pandemic, which necessarily required governments to take huge steps that would have seemed draconian just weeks earlier. It is, of course, not necessarily irrational or beyond the pale to oppose lockdown restrictions, or to have concerns about vaccines, but the anti-lockdown movements proved great fodder for QAnon and related groups, and became merged with its ethos.

The boots-on-the-ground proof came on 24 July (24/7: conspiracies thrive on catchy dates), with protests in London, Washington, DC, Mexico City, Paris, Rome, cities in Australia and beyond. It was branded the 'WORLD WIDE RALLY FOR FREEDOM'.[6] In total the protests were held in 129 towns and cities across the planet.[7]

The London rally put to bed any notion that the protests were just a series of coordinated anti-Covid-restriction marches – the content was far, far more extreme. From a stage in Trafalgar Square, Kate Shemirani, a former nurse, told the crowd the Covid vaccines were 'satanic' and contained the number of the devil.

Another speaker told the audience that 'Parliament are doing the bidding of evil.' Mark Steele, who campaigns against 5G, was given space on the stage to say that the UK's Scientific Advisory Group for Emergencies (the panel advising the government on Covid response) was 'a terrorist organisation' and that 'the virus is a hoax'.

The son of well-known conspiracy theorist David Icke was allowed on stage to cite 'the Great Reset' – a longstanding theory adopted by QAnon which holds that the global elite want to kill off most of the population, possibly for environmental reasons. Piers Corbyn, brother of the former Labour leader, told the protestors there were 'four legs and a tail' to the 'new world order', implying not only that there was a secret agenda for a one-world government, but that this agenda was also demonic.[8]

A mainstream protest against government overreach this was not. This was the stuff of the most extreme conspiracy movements, mobilised online by QAnon groups, even if not everyone in each crowd had heard of Q or QAnon.

On the very same day as the global protests, the onetime hero of the QAnon movement was holding a rally in Arizona, which did not exactly serve to tamp down the conspiratorial flames. Speaking on stage, former US president Donald J. Trump told his supporters that 'the cabal' was running Joe Biden's presidency and had campaigned for him to win in 2020.[9]

Whether the reference was deliberate or not is impossible to say – especially given Trump's chaotic speaking style – but the use of 'the cabal', a key QAnon phrase used to describe the conspiracy secretly running the world, re-energised the movement on a day it had shown its continuing worldwide influence. Those who think it's all over were, and are, sorely mistaken.

It's tempting to think of QAnon as something that began with Q's first post and ended alongside the presidency of Donald Trump. The truth is stranger and far more disturbing. QAnon was an inevitable product of the way the internet works, something that grew out of previous movements, absorbing the ideas that worked and evolving as it went.

More disturbingly, QAnon is still evolving. It has already merged with the anti-vaccine and anti-lockdown movements and continues to change. It is the conspiracy theory that has eaten all other conspiracy theories, having grown far beyond 4chan and even beyond the mysterious Q and their posts. Many of the millions of people devoting hours of every day to the movement have never read a single post by Q or even heard of 4chan – but they have signed up to a dangerous fringe movement that was born right there.

QAnon is not a cult in the classical sense, though it shares many characteristics with cults. It doesn't have set beliefs or a set leader. It is not just a conspiracy theory – it is something that consumes and combines conspiracy theories, joining ever more dots into an ever-larger plot.

Instead, QAnon is best thought of as our first digital pandemic – a threat to humanity that has evolved and gone global. It is the online equivalent of the viruses and bacteria that have (literally) plagued society for as long as society has existed. QAnon is not a digital virus in the sense of a computer virus, something that can damage our data or give a hacker access to our data. It is a pathogen that affects us, but instead of transmitting by bodily contact or breath, it transmits online – the ultimate form of social contagion. Social media is engineered to make things go viral. This mechanism inevitably gives rise to viral phenomena far beyond any individual meme or idea, and far more dangerous.

Just as we developed public health, vaccination, antibiotics and more to tackle real-world pandemics, we need to develop a toolkit to tackle the online equivalents – because while QAnon is the first digital pandemic, it won't be the last.

Digital viral reservoirs

Rabies. Smallpox. Ebola. Bird flu. Leprosy. Tuberculosis. Zika. Lassa fever. MERS.

What do the above have in common? All are infectious diseases, and none of them sound like much fun. But beyond that they don't have too many obvious similarities. Some are bacterial, some are viral. Some have effective treatments or vaccines, others don't. One of them, smallpox, is even eradicated in humans.

What all of them share in common is that they have what is known as a 'natural reservoir', a term used by epidemiologists to describe diseases that are common in certain animal populations, and which then can pass to humans. These animal reservoirs can lead to the emergence of new diseases or the re-emergence of diseases that had previously been thought extinct. The World Health Organization estimates that more than two-thirds of such diseases come via this route, and say that proportion is only growing. What is especially troubling to epidemiologists is that they don't fully understand how new diseases cross the species barrier from animal to human.[10]

The MERS (Middle East respiratory syndrome) outbreak of 2012 eventually affected 27 countries. This new and deadly virus – much deadlier than Covid-19 – took more than a year to trace back to its animal origin, which turned out to be the dromedary camel.[11] Thankfully, while MERS was dangerous, it was not especially infectious, meaning that in the decade since its discovery, it has killed fewer than 1,000 people.

We are not, at the time of writing, entirely certain that Covid-19 emerged from an animal reservoir, but researchers suspect that the virus may have emerged from bat populations. Even the 'lab leak' theory, which argues that the disease may have escaped from an infectious disease facility in Wuhan, doesn't rule out the pathogen having originated in animals.

The challenge of animal reservoirs is that we can neither control them nor predict what will emerge from them. The next disease to cross the barrier might be relatively innocuous (on a global scale, though not an individual one), like MERS, or a global catastrophe, like Covid-19. And while we can vaccinate human populations, and encourage people to wear masks and wash their hands, persuading rats, bats or mosquitos to mask up has proven somewhat fruitless.

Natural reservoirs are the perfect breeding grounds for viruses and bacteria to change and evolve, and from which to then emerge. Our problem is that we have created digital reservoirs too, from which QAnon and its precursors – some benign and some deadly – emerged, and from which future movements will also come.

Understanding those digital reservoirs and the lack of control we seem to have over them is key to understanding these new digital movements. And while we do not yet know how real-world viruses move from animals to humans, discovering how digital movements evolve and emerge should be an easier task – and an urgent one.

Most efforts to tackle online conspiracies do so through the lens of misinformation or disinformation, imagining that fact-checks, better moderation or better-managed social networks could go a long way towards fixing our issues. But thinking of QAnon and similar movements as biological entities that evolve in dark corners of the internet and then spread across the mainstream – and figuring out why this happens – reshapes our understanding of what's gone wrong and how to tackle it. If we're going to have any hope of returning to a saner public discourse, we don't have much time.

But, even though it's getting worse, the problem is anything but new.

Old ideas, new environments

On an ill-fated day in 1144 – almost a millennium ago – the body of an eight-year-old boy, William of Norwich, an apprentice skinner, was found on Mousehold Heath, an area of wood and scrubland just outside the city boundaries.

The death might have been forgotten but for an account from the monk Thomas of Monmouth, who recounted that the boy had been tortured and had a torture device left in his mouth. His injuries were such, the account noted, 'that no Christian but only a Jew could have taken it upon himself to kill the innocent in such way'.

Monmouth was no eyewitness to the crime, nor was he even in Norwich at the time of William's murder. His grisly and inflammatory 45,000-word account of the killing was written at least six years after the event, based on some dark rumours that had circulated at the time of the killing and then subsided.

Monmouth's text appears to have been fabricated in a bid to create a saint's cult to attract pilgrims and others to Norwich Cathedral. His account claimed that various miracles had happened at the original gravesite of William of Norwich, and he lobbied for martyrdom status for the boy and a Catholic cult celebrating St William. Such cults could prove lucrative for the clergy concerned.[12] Yet the rise in William's reputation came at the cost of that of the Jews – to the extent that Norwich's tiny medieval Jewish community had to be given shelter and then helped to flee by the local baron, for a crime there was no evidence they had any involvement with.

The consequences of Thomas of Monmouth's fake account have ricocheted through the centuries: the tale of William's murder is believed to be the origin of 'blood libel', the centuries-running falsehood that Jews engage in ritual child abuse and murder. The lie has been used to justify murder, exile, persecution and even the Holocaust.

It is also, essentially, the core of the QAnon conspiracy, but is completely missed even by some of those who get taken into the conspiracy. While the movement may have substituted a generalised 'global elite' for 'Jews', the core idea of a powerful and secretive cabal engaging in child murder and sexual abuse doesn't just predate the internet by centuries – it predates the printing press by centuries, too.[13]

Blood libel is one of the enduring conspiracy theories of modern and pre-modern society and had no trouble surviving and spreading before the internet. But the emergence of the internet has let it change form at a pace never seen before.

While anyone who knows the origin of the conspiracy will be aware of its inherent antisemitism, this is not true of everyone. QAnon, like many other online groups, is not always overtly antisemitic – instead, it is often just one scratch below the surface. The group talks about the Rothschilds, or Soros, or the 'global elite'. Like all dog whistles, to those who know what they are listening for it is loud and clear, but is completely missed even by some of those who get taken into the conspiracy, who don't share those antisemitic views.

QAnon demonstrates the ability of online culture to repurpose old ideas, old conspiracies, old plots, to new audiences and new times. Tropes and narratives that have held for a long time are given new protagonists – whether Antifa, Soros, hedge funds or something else. The stories are also combined in new ways to create a deep rabbit hole, one that is so compelling people can't help but crawl down it.

When you're battling narratives that have captured people for centuries, taking down the odd detail won't work. When we try to tackle phenomena like QAnon through reporting, debunking or fact-checking, we make a category error – followers of Q saw prediction after prediction fail, and reformed their beliefs and the story to fit it.

Someone in the mainstream media or mainstream politics – someone whom followers of Q will likely believe is wittingly or otherwise part of the conspiracy – is not going to derail those beliefs. We keep redoubling our efforts to chop at branches while letting the roots establish themselves ever more widely and deeply.

Intermeshing online subcultures have become an ecosystem – one which fosters extreme movements that often blur into one another. More than a decade ago, the online collective Anonymous sprang forth from 4chan and became one of the first online movements to mobilise people in the real world, in a loud public clash with the Church of Scientology. Many of us cheered on Anonymous as the 'good guys' in this fight (doubtless Scientologists felt differently). But later movements growing out of the 4chan and Anonymous breeding grounds tacked increasingly to the right, and became intrinsically far nastier.

One of the first such abusive groups arose against women writing about video games, claiming to be about ethics in journalism, but merged into a movement called Gamergate, a misogynistic and abusive online subculture. This was not a direct successor to Anonymous, but it drew from the same pool. In a similar way, from Gamergate sprang other extreme movements, such as 'incels' – short for 'involuntarily celibate', a movement of men unable to get girlfriends and who came to hate women – and the alt-right, the base of Trump's online far-right supporters.

Norms, narratives, tactics, even a shared language emerge from one movement to another, changing what will come next. Already QAnon has started to evolve beyond Trump, taking on the broader anti-paedophile narrative and capitalising on the backlash to anti-pandemic measures. Its private organising spaces even have new playbooks, encouraging believers to run for local office, or school boards, to spread the gospel of Q without using the word 'QAnon', which they know is toxic.[14]

A lie could always get around the world before the truth booted up, but in the internet era whole movements can arise and evolve before the mainstream even starts to understand how to counter them. The consequences of failure can be all too grave – even fatal. In August 2021 alone, there were deadly incidents on both sides of the Atlantic connected to QAnon and its adjacent movements.

On 5 August, twenty-two-year-old Jake Davison, of the UK south-western coastal city of Plymouth, killed his mother and four others, including a three-year-old girl, in a rampage with a shotgun, before turning the gun on himself. The attack was the first mass shooting in the UK in more than a decade. Davison had apparently been radicalised by multiple online movements, all originating in chan culture. Coverage at the time largely centred on Davison's public identification with the incel movement.

But Davison's online posts also reflected QAnon-like sentiments, stating his belief that 'there are many paedophiles and even reported devil worshippers.' He had posted disturbing, misogynistic videos to YouTube, which were only deleted the day after his attack.[15]

Just days later, Matthew Taylor Coleman, a surf shop owner from California, allegedly killed his three-year-old son and ten-month-old daughter in a premeditated murder on a ranch in Mexico. While Coleman has pleaded not guilty, according to a criminal complaint filed in US court, Coleman told the authorities he was 'enlightened by QAnon and Illuminati conspiracy theories' and had killed his children because they had 'serpent DNA' passed on by his wife.[16]

We should always be wary of attributing just one cause to any killing, or to any violent event. But the fact we can't definitively say QAnon is the sole cause of any given killing doesn't mean we can't say it's dangerous. It clearly is – and yet it is barely given any regard. Governments fund multi-million pound schemes against Islamist or far-right radicalisation, and yet seem to leave these more modern, hybrid phenomena to the media to tackle.

Warning after warning has been missed, and we have come closer to QAnon-connected disaster with each. In December 2022, several thousand German law enforcement agents were involved in arresting a group suspected of plotting a violent coup – based on QAnon ideology – that sought to reimpose the country's Second Reich.[17]

Simultaneously, in the US the world's second-richest man – and the owner of one of the world's key social networks, Twitter – was openly flirting with QAnon conspiracy theories, falsely suggesting that Twitter's former head of trust and safety supports the sexualisation of children, and that Anthony Fauci (the chief medical advisor of the US) should be prosecuted in connection with the Covid-19 pandemic. So overt was Musk's flirtation with the Q movement that some within it started to wonder whether Elon Musk, not Donald Trump, was the movement's promised saviour.[18]

QAnon constantly changes shape, but it just keeps coming. We can't just study each of these manifestations as some kind of independent occurrence, as if each emerged from nothing and eventually dwindled – there is a reason the internet keeps generating these movements, and until we change the internet, it will continue to do so.

In that sense, this book is both all about QAnon and not about QAnon. To the extent that it is about QAnon, it is not the movement's account of itself, but an account of its roots, its emergence, how it came to prominence and why it has turned into something new and persistently dangerous. To the extent that it is not about QAnon, it is also about how humanity needs to address the unintended consequences of the things we have collectively invented. Just as in a disaster movie something escapes a biolab and turns half of humanity into zombies, something has escaped on the internet – a disturbing, evolving, memetic virus that divides families and societies.

This book is an attempt to sound the alarm that the lab has leaked.

PART ONE

Emergence

1

Ask the Q

From the way 4chan is talked about in the media and by disinformation researchers, you'd be forgiven for imagining at some *Matrix*-movie-esque den of iniquity, the heart of darkness, a tool of the notorious dark web.

The reality of 4chan is – in some ways at least – rather more prosaic. At its core, it's a message board, just like Reddit, Quora or Mumsnet. If the site were a person, it would recently have hit adulthood, having been founded on 1 October 2003 by a fifteen-year-old who went by the online handle 'moot'.[1]

moot (the name is always lowercase) managed to keep his anonymity for five years after founding 4chan, but his real identity was eventually revealed by the *Wall Street Journal* in 2008.[2] He was in fact a New York native named Christopher Poole who had founded the board as a teenager and would continue to own and operate it until 2015 – before moving on to a five-year-long tenure as a product manager at Google.[3]

The site was founded as an English-language version of the messageboard Futuba Channel,[4] itself colloquially known as 2chan. moot's homage (or ripoff) today hosts more than sixty boards on different topics. These include anime, video games, technology, wrestling, maths, origami and LGBTQ issues. Most of 4chan is pretty innocuous, though it has multiple boards dedicated to different subgenres of pornography, some of which can be extremely graphic.

While the site itself is on the fringe, it had an outsized impact. Such was 4chan's influence on the internet culture of the 2000s and beyond that even the *Wall Street Journal*, in its 2008 article naming Poole, acknowledged it as 'one of the most talked-about sites when it comes to launching new memes'. If you've ever been rickrolled, thank 4chan. If you've ever seen a lolcat: 4chan. If you've ever used the strange online vernacular of 'o hai' or 'I herd u lik memes,' that was born on 4chan too.

Since its early days, 4chan played a unique role on the internet. It was a small core of people who spent a huge amount of time online and generated very particular memes and elements of online culture. But it also, from its earliest days, actively spread these memes out into the rest of the online world, whether for good, for lulz or for evil. It's due to this willingness to share ideas with the wider world that movements like Gamergate, the alt-right and QAnon itself started here – so it's clearly somewhere we need to understand.

4chan's influence didn't come from its boards dedicated to niche pornography or origami. Almost anything the wider world knows about 4chan came from just two of its communities – one named 'politically incorrect', known to its denizens as /pol/ (not to be confused with /po/, the origami board), and 'random', which is 4chan's infamous /b/ board.

To look at the history of these communities is to realise how they became perfect breeding grounds for movements like QAnon. In order to understand why 4chan became such an influential force in the cultural history of the internet, it's worth knowing how it works – and dispelling a few myths about its operations.

A key tenet of 4chan is the principle of anonymity: anyone can join in with any conversation on the site without creating an account or giving away any kind of identifying information. By convention, most posts are made completely anonymously, without users doing anything to make themselves identifiable to each other, even pseudonymously (that is, with an online nickname).

This affects an online community in a lot of ways. Clearly, it gives people leave to post things they might not post if they had to put their real name next to them. Online anonymity is commonly cited as a driver of abuse, though there is no shortage of racist, sexist and homophobic speech on Facebook, which has had a real-name policy since its inception. But other effects are more interesting. When you can't be identified as a longstanding member of a group by virtue of your name or online handle, the community needs to create an in-group and out-group in other ways – and one of these is to generate online slang, which becomes immediately identifiable to people in the group while being impenetrable to outsiders.

This can be totally innocuous. On several 4chan boards, users will type 'kek' instead of 'lol'. Media outlets have offered various explanations for this, but the real reason comes from the online RPG *World of Warcraft*, which launched less than a year after 4chan.[5] The game was set up so players in two warring factions, the Alliance and Horde, could not talk to one another – and represented this in the game by scrambling the chat of players from the opposing faction. If a Horde player typed 'lol', a nearby Alliance player would see 'kek'. Boards on 4chan are layered with hundreds of examples of this kind of deep internet lore.

The anonymity of 4chan is often overstated. The site doesn't run on the so-called dark web, an untraceable and encrypted version of the internet powered by special software. That means that unless users take their own security measures, their IP address will be visible to the site's administrators – who have, when asked by law enforcement, handed that information over, in line with the law. 4chan is not some pirate bay bar – it is still, by and large, bound by US law.[6]

4chan posts also disappear once they drop out of people's immediate attention. Each board holds up to fourteen pages of posts (think of clicking through fifteen pages of Google results), with posts dropping down the list once users stop engaging with them. Once a post hits where page 15 would be, it is immediately and permanently deleted from 4chan's servers – which means that if you want to be seen, you've got to be grabby.

The in-group signifiers and jokes are often not nearly so innocuous as 'kek'. Both /pol/ and /b/ – though particularly the latter – use generally shocking statements, images or more to put off casual users. This can include casual use of homophobic, sexist and racist slurs – oddly, often by users who are themselves from those groups – as well as the posting of graphic sexual or violent content, including real-world death videos and more.

One useful way to think of /pol/ and /b/ is that they are the boards where other 4chan communities directed disruptive users – those who were trolling, endlessly talking politics or shitposting (defined by 4chan itself as 'knowingly contributing low quality, off-topic or ill intentioned posts'[7]). This turned them into something of a self-selecting group of people other communities didn't particularly want.

It is worth noting that this hierarchy of the unwanted continues even between /pol/ and /b/. At the top of the /pol/ board is a warning from the admins who run it:

Off-topic and /b/-tier threads will be deleted (and possibly earn you a ban, if you persist). Unless they are quality, well thought out, well written posts, the following are some examples of off-topic and/or /b/-tier threads:

>Red pill me on X. (with no extra content or input of your own)
>Are X white?
>Is X degeneracy?
>How come X girls love Y guys so much?
>If X is true, then how come Y? Checkmate Z.[8]

That internal distinction aside, users on /pol/ or /b/ – who often refer to themselves as '/b/tards'[9] – are often teenagers, usually boys. Not to throw too many stereotypes around, but they are often people who have struggled to make many friends in the offline world. These boards can become an online home for someone like that – an anarchic, rude and often problematic one, but a home nonetheless.

At this point a confession is due: I have a very long history with 4chan, and I was for several years a fully signed-up /b/tard.[10] The early years of 4chan lined up nicely with my late teens and early twenties, and it was in all honesty just a ridiculously fun place to hang out.

For most of the time I was a regular visitor to 4chan, I was at university, from 2004 to 2008. This was a continuation of spending most of my free time as a secondary schooler on the internet, long before that was remotely normal, let alone cool. Much as I was enjoying the freedom of university, it was great to have a place that felt silly, nerdy and fun – and also often outrageously rude in a way you simply couldn't be otherwise.

The community around the boards could often be foul, but once you had adjusted you could revel in its sense of mischief. In many ways the politically incorrect and outrageous things people would post became affectionate in-jokes – you would come to believe (perhaps wrongly) that people did not mean what they were saying. Instead they used offence to scare off 'tourists' and other casual users. After a while you even started to read the board's relentless use of 'fag' as affectionate (like many others using the board and the slur at the time, I am gay).

Whatever its sins, 4chan could be *fun*. Much of what is now the bedrock of internet culture was born on 4chan's boards, and being on 4chan meant you would be several weeks ahead of most people you saw in the real world. Plus the /b/ board would regularly get involved in pranking other sites for what it would refer to as 'shits and giggles'.

Rickrolling – tricking unwitting users into watching the Rick Astley 'Never Gonna Give You Up' video – was a 4chan invention. And, as anybody who has been either victim or perpetrator knows, it remains funny when done well. Songs have charted because of 4chan and careers have been made by its users. Gate-crashing online games en masse and blocking access to key features was a good way to waste an hour or two, if not a kind one. Likewise, the thrill of undermining a thoughtful conversation online and turning it into a shouting match is certainly a dirty one, but having experienced it, it's very real. It can be *fun* to be a wind-up merchant, as almost every youngest child knows. When it was kept within decent boundaries, 4chan trolling was deeply infuriating, but a delight.

By the time I left, elements of 4chan had started to get more serious and more political – sometimes for good as well as for ill. But the reality of my stepping away had less to do with some moral stance or a change on the site than with a change in my circumstances. I was hitting my twenties, starting work and experiencing the changes in personality that come with it. Like a lot of people on /b/, as real life started to kick in, I drifted away from the board.

With hindsight, helping those who stayed on the board, which is to say those for whom life never really got started, and preventing the effect they'd have on the next generation of teens arriving, could have staved off many disasters.

In practice, I never really left 4chan for very long. My early jobs as a journalist tended to lean hard on my experience with tech and internet culture – especially hacker culture and Anonymous – not least because for a time I worked for WikiLeaks and lived with its enigmatic founder Julian Assange. As a result, not long after leaving 4chan as a regular user, I was keeping an eye on it as a journalist, and saw it change from something chaotic but fundamentally innocent into something far darker.

From mass hoaxing to mass action

Even in its early incarnation, 4chan had its dark side. One particular black spot was the practice of doxing – tracking down the name and address of an otherwise anonymous internet user, and then often doing something unsavoury with it. If doxing wasn't born on 4chan, it certainly became part of modern life through 4chan's efforts. One common prank on the site was to send dozens or hundreds of pizzas to a doxed user,[11] leaving them to handle the demands for payment.[12]

4chan was also an early proponent of what became known as 'revenge porn', and went through a phase of regularly posting celebrity nudes. When bored, 4chan users would often head to some other social network en masse and sabotage it with inappropriate content. One frequent victim was *Habbo Hotel*, a social game intended for kids that let animated avatars wander around different rooms. In 2006, 4chan users (calling themselves

'/b/lockers') cut off popular facilities – such as the swimming pool – by setting numerous avatars, all identical black men with afros and business suits, in the way, shouting 'POOL'S CLOSED' as they did so.[13] As a good indication of the site's confused politics at the time, some users believed they were flooding *Habbo Hotel* as a protest against allegedly racist moderation policies at the time. Others, meanwhile, were forming their avatars in the shape of swastikas or shouting that the pool was closed 'BECAUSE OF AIDS'.

It was in this era that 4channers learned the art of derailing conversations on other social networks, too – posing as regular users on Twitter or some other social network and trying to turn a previously sensible conversation or debate into an incoherent row, or to secure some perverse result. One particularly successful trolling effort came when 4chan decided to hijack *TIME* magazine's 2009 poll for 'person of the year' (the magazine makes its own pick, but also includes a people's choice list) – where, thanks to a series of cheats, it managed to make none other than Christopher Poole the winner. It followed this up with a win for Kim Jong-Un a few years later (*TIME* did not honour the vote).[14]

If any post shows how 4chan has both changed and yet stayed the same it is perhaps a message posted to /b/ shortly after midnight on 11 September 2007.

Hello, /b/.

On September 11, 2007, at 9:11 A.M. Central time, two pipe bombs will be remote-detonated at Pflugerville High School.

Promptly after the blast, I, along with two other Anonymous, will charge the building, armed with a Bushmaster AR-15, IMI Galil AR, a vintage, government-issue M1 .30 Carbine, and a Benelli M4 semi auto shotgun.

So, what are YOUR plans, /b/?[15]

In recent years, such posts have accompanied mass shootings, which themselves have been livestreamed online and shared widely. But the 2007 Pflugerville threat was different. After it was posted, /b/ denizens worked together and managed to find the real-world identity of the user making the threat by tracking down the metadata of an image they had posted in an earlier thread.

Authorities arrested the culprit before the school day started, and quickly determined the post had been a hoax – simply someone trolling the board (though this remained a criminal offence). The post looks like more serious ones from the present day, but /b/ worked to track them down, and the original poster did not even mean the threat.[16]

4chan could not be accused of speaking with one voice, although unwittingly, 4channers were starting to write the playbook for digital information warfare – just as a way to pass the time. A 2008 *Guardian* article best summarised the 4chan of that era: 'lunatic, juvenile … brilliant, ridiculous and alarming'.[17] It was in many ways a mob in search of a cause. They were perfectly capable of causing chaos – a group of bored, online-literate misfits, using their excess energy on whatever crossed their minds, with no particular target.

And then 4chan ran headlong into their first real adversary: the Church of Scientology.

The people of 4chan, at least in its earlier incarnations, didn't stand for much politically. As a collective, the vibe wasn't one of the left or the right, but of nihilism. Whatever the cause, 4chan would mine it for meme or trolling potential and then shrug it off – with one exception.

4chan was born in the peak era of the copyright wars, the decade or so before music and movie streaming, a time which was defined by piracy and the war against it. The teenagers and twenty-somethings who lived on 4chan and similar sites were the generation who used Napster, BitTorrent, LimeWire, Kazaa or whatever worked to get hold of music, movies and video games – and people who tried to crack down on the future made them seriously angry.[18] They certainly made me angry at the time, which is perhaps ironic given that I now make my living in the creative industries.

If 4chan were allowed to codify its own high crimes and misdemeanours, the two gravest would be taking yourself too seriously and cracking down on internet freedoms. And so it should perhaps come as no surprise that – in the public mind at least – it was the Church of Scientology that caused the transformation of small-a anonymous users of 4chan and similar boards into the movement known as Anonymous.

As a movement, Anonymous is almost deliberately poorly defined: it is described as an anarchist group, a hacker group, a political group or any number of other things. It's better thought of as an activity rather than membership of a club. When you're participating in an action under the banner of Anonymous, you're part of Anonymous.

It has no leaders or gatekeepers, and no consistent membership. Its only real calling card is the distinctive mask its members wear and use as online avatars – the Guy Fawkes mask from the 2005 movie *V for Vendetta*. It had existed, to an extent, before its clash with Scientology, but it was this that really cemented it in the public imagination. Given the collective's nebulous nature, it is obviously not synonymous with 4chan, but the board certainly played a big role in its formation.

The trouble started with Gawker, which was then a gossipy but must-read New York blog.[19] The site had in January 2008 got hold of an internal Scientology video showing Tom Cruise raving in support of the group in a manner that seemed utterly cringeworthy to those who were not already indoctrinated.[20] The whole incident might have been forgotten in days but for one mistake by the Scientologists: they sent a notice demanding Gawker take down the video.

Gawker was not some messageboard or social network but a professional media outlet, with the constitutional safeguards that provides, and with a notorious 'fuck you' attitude to boot. So they let it be known that the Church of Scientology had sent this takedown notice, and it caught fire across the internet – and became the latest target of the moment for a trolling operation that quickly escalated on a scale like nothing that had been seen before.

The operation quickly caught the eye of an academic researcher and became the start of what grew into years of anthropological study. Now a professor at the anthropology department at Harvard, Gabriella Coleman first came across my radar when I was an early-career journalist following Anonymous, 4chan and the hacktivist movements around it. Whenever you entered an Anonymous discussion thread or chat channel,[21] Biella (as she was known) would be there, tolerated as a constant presence by the Anons, like some cool aunt of the collective.

Coleman engaged in years of research into Anonymous, culminating in the book *Hacker, Hoaxer, Whistleblower, Spy: The Many Faces of Anonymous* (dedicated to 'the legions behind Anonymous'), but it was the Scientology adventure that first piqued her interest. She had been running a 'little side project' at the University of Alberta which had focused on the history of geek hackers fighting Scientology throughout the 1990s. 'And I was very secretive about it, because, you know, Scientology would go after ...' she trailed off, referencing the Church's notorious policy of retaliating against its critics in dramatic ways.[22]

When Anonymous decided to take on Scientology again in 2008, to Coleman this felt like history repeating itself – 'it's happening again' – and she was one of the few people with knowledge of the history of the two cultures. 'Scientology is just the complete polar opposite of the geek and hacker world,' she noted. That culture clash led to a dramatic series of actions, big and small, by Anonymous against Scientology, in what quickly became known as 'Operation Chanology', thanks to 4chan's endless love of portmanteau terms.

The tactics of the first early skirmishes against Scientology matched what had gone before. Anons found the fax numbers of Scientology centres around the world and sent them endless all-black pages to run out their ink, a petty but effective annoyance.[23] Others bombarded their phone lines. But the real weapon in the online arsenal was a low-level hack known as DDoSing (short for Distributed Denial of Service).

When you see the word 'hack', you probably think of someone – possibly in a cheesy movie scene – breaking into a database and stealing information. By that definition, a DDoS isn't a hack. Instead, it's a way of taking websites offline by making the site think it's getting millions of hits all at once – essentially, a higher-stakes equivalent of 4chan's *Habbo Hotel* antics. For this, Anonymous appropriated a tool known as LOIC (short for Low Orbit Ion Cannon, a joking reference to nuking a site from orbit), used to test whether sites can hold up under high demand, to take down and keep down Scientology sites.

The status of DDoSing is disputed among different authorities and different countries. In Germany, for example, a DDoS with no financial motivation is regarded by the law in the same way as a protest outside a building.[24] Other countries, however, treat DDoS attacks as more intrusive and deliberate forms of hacking, as crimes subject to punishment, potentially even with jail. Unfortunately for them, some less experienced Anons didn't realise that using LOIC in this way is illegal in some jurisdictions, or that the tool did nothing to hide their identities – and some ended up being prosecuted and convicted for their actions against the church.[25] At least one participant was sentenced to a year in US jail.[26]

In a break from their past form, Anonymous – or one member of Anonymous – even produced a video, narrated by what became their trademark synthesised voice and pompous tone.

'We recognize you as serious opponents, and do not expect our campaign to be completed in a short time frame. However, you will not prevail forever against the angry masses of the body politic,' the narrator warned, shortly before ending in the group's well-known sign off. 'You have nowhere to hide because we are everywhere … We are Anonymous. We are Legion. We do not forgive. We do not forget. Expect us.'

The video became known as 'the video that made Anonymous'.[27] It had more than 2 million views within a week of publication, and at the time of writing has had more than 5.4 million.[28] But it was what the actions and the video sparked in the real world that really changed things.

In a break from previous tactics, Anonymous tried to organise protests in the real world – with no idea if anyone would really turn up. Alien as it sounds today, the internet was not really used by groups who didn't know each other to coordinate real-world actions at that time. This group was defined by its members' ability to stay anonymous, even to each other, and to stay behind their keyboards. No one knew if it would be ten people or a few hundred who appeared when 10 February 2008, the chosen day, came around.

When the day came, people showed up. In fact, thousands of people arrived outside Scientology centres – many of them with placards bearing Anonymous slogans, or wearing Guy Fawkes masks – in at least 100 cities.[29] The centre in London alone hosted a protest of more than 200 people. The online world had successfully merged with the offline world, and things would never be quite the same again.[30]

The immediate consequences were not so dramatic. Despite a Scientology spokeswoman referring to the group as 'little terrorists',[31] Anonymous eventually lost interest in Scientology and fragmented once more. Some went back to the messageboards and random trolling. Some looked for new causes. Some took exception to the new, worthy, political version of Anonymous, condemning users as 'moralfags',[32] and trying once again to ruin the reputation of 4chan, even releasing videos intending to cause photo-epileptic seizures onto support forums for people with epilepsy.[33]

Anonymous, rather than becoming a consistent movement, would rise and fall from the headlines – popping up to support WikiLeaks, or the Arab Spring, or to release details from a hack of Sony Pictures carried out by North Korea in protest of the movie *The Interview*.[34] The seeds Operation Chanology planted for the longer term are much easier to see with hindsight, as Coleman notes.

'On the one hand Anonymous did convert people into social justice movements,' she says, before adding that because Anonymous was never a movement united behind a particular ideology, such as anti-capitalism, it never coalesced into something solid. Some people wanted to promote free speech causes, others the Arab Spring, and so Anonymous proved prone to fragmenting and dissipating.

Anonymous showed internet users they could have huge effects in the real world, even if only temporarily. They could take down the sites of multinational corporations,[35] or feel as though they were helping topple corrupt governments in the Middle East.[36] They could even see clips of pundits on TV news talk cluelessly about the threat Anonymous posed to society.

The people who 'led' Anonymous – though Anonymous would always deny having leaders – largely did not go on to lead the movements it spawned, such as Gamergate, the alt-right or QAnon. Instead, they demonstrated what could be done and what tactics worked in the online era – and as they moved off boards like 4chan, the people who stayed behind took note.

'It was huge, because people met in person – in Paris, in Dublin, in New York and Boston. So that was brewing … they broke away and formed their own networks,' Coleman concludes. By 2011, her research shows, the so-called 'hacktivists' who had birthed Anonymous out of chan culture had moved beyond boards like 4chan and existed in their own online spaces.

The question then becomes: what's left behind on 4chan now that crowd has left?

'There's still all the trolling motherfuckery,' she says. 'There's more reactionary stuff. And then there's also people who were part of Stormfront and other Nazi parties – who very explicitly hit the boards for recruitment. So I see it as a bifurcation at that point.'

The dangers of 'survivorship'

There is a (true) story told as a cautionary tale to prospective statisticians, and it goes roughly like this: during World War II, the US military was looking to improve the survival rates of its bombers, and had found it could add a certain weight of extra armour to its fleet without hampering the planes' ability to fly.

The question was: where was the best place to add that extra plating? Given the life-or-death stakes, the military decided to be rigorous in its analysis, and surveyed the bullet holes on returning planes to see which areas were most in need of the plating. The pattern of the evidence was clear: there were far, far more bullet holes in the wings and tail fins of planes than in the engines or cockpits.

The military's preliminary conclusion was that this made the case for adding the extra plating to the wings and tail fins – but for a second opinion, they consulted with an expert panel of statisticians they had convened to help the war effort. One of them, Abraham Wald, had a startling conclusion: the military was completely wrong, and the armour needed to go where the bullet holes weren't.

What Wald had spotted and the US military had missed is that the planes which returned weren't a full sample of planes that had gone out on bombing runs. The ones that were hit on the wings and tails returned to base, and lived to tell the tale. The ones that were hit in the engines, though, never made it home – and so the armour needed to go where the surviving planes hadn't been hit.

The above is perhaps the most famous case of *survivorship bias* – the idea that the group that returns from some endeavour, or stays in some place, is not necessarily representative of the population that was there at the beginning.

With 4chan, the people whose teenage angst and loneliness passed – as thankfully for most of us it does – and turned into a new and different set of adult problems moved on. But that means that not everyone did – and so when a new generation of teenagers discovered the forum, it wasn't something new. It had long-time residents already, and they were not necessarily happy.

The survivorship problem is compounded by the problem of attenuation. Humans are incredibly adaptable creatures. Fairly quickly, anything can seem normal. This can be a physical effect, as any heroin addict chasing that first perfect high can attest. But we can also experience this in our everyday lives: after long enough on a luxury holiday, we find ourselves getting bored and thinking of home.

With communities out to shock and to troll, that kind of attenuation can lead to content becoming ever more extreme. What was shocking three months ago is passé today. To carry on getting a reaction, behaviour has to become more sexist, more racist or more dangerous.

This manifested in thousands of ways. One of the more low-key is the evolution of 'kek', 4chan's version of 'lol', once a simple internet lore joke (which to many is still all it is). Several years after the first evolution of 'kek', users noticed there was a frog-headed ancient Egyptian god named Kek. As this coincided with the adoption of a cartoon frog named Pepe by the alt-right, this led to the rise of the 'ironically' misogynistic cult of Kek across 4chan's boards.

A more alarming manifestation was the escalation of the 'pranks' carried out to victims of doxing: from sending pizzas, through threats of violence and rape, to 'SWATting' – tricking a police SWAT squad into storming a target's home, a 'prank' that has led to multiple fatalities at the hands of heavily armed police.[37]

Today's /b/ and /pol/ boards lean further to the right than before, are more viciously misogynistic than ever and are altogether darker in tone, but have still not lost their sense of chaos or playfulness. This combination can have dramatic results. In 2017, one of the more popular games on 4chan – carried across from other social networks – was to pose as a whistleblower from inside the Trump administration, in some department or other, with secrets to spill.

Faking leaked secrets had a long history on the board, but posting supposed secrets on 4chan was more like a game than a troll. Generally, a poster would assume that other 4channers (at least experienced ones) would be in on the joke. One of the most famous early cases of creating a puzzle or game with apparent real-world elements (known as LARPing, or live-action role-playing) was posted to 4chan in 2012, and became known as Cicada3301.

The post said it was looking for 'highly intelligent individuals'. 'To find them, we have devised a test.' The post, signed off with '3301', included a black-and-white image of a cicada in which a secret message was supposedly encoded. Attempts to solve it were frenetic, as were efforts to guess who was behind it – with the NSA, GCHQ or CIA being common guesses.[38]

This idea of live-action role play proved a persistent one. The term itself is a broad one – strictly defined, it would include people who engage in historical re-enactment of famous battles, or who play sci-fi or fantasy role-playing games, or even escape rooms. But it also includes online games and mysteries, often with a real-world element. One of the first, *Perplex City*, merged a fictional alternative universe with card-based puzzles and a broad mystery through which players could find a hidden cube in the real world and win £100,000.[39]

The Cicada group continued to iterate their puzzles, even posting one using the phrase 'FOLLOW THE WHITE RABBIT' just weeks before Q's first post.

Play-acting mysteries and posing as secretive sources was common practice on 4chan that autumn. While supposed 'resistance' accounts on other social networks might be made in the hope that other users – or even the mainstream media – would take them seriously, 4chan generally knew better.[40]

And so it was that in the autumn of 2017, 4chan was full of accounts like 'WhiteHouseAnon', 'CIA Anon' or 'FBI Anon' – to the point that anyone looking to try to set up some new and intriguing source of leaks would have to start getting creative.[41]

Eventually, someone hit upon the idea of 'QAnon', based on 'Q clearance' – in reality a clearance used by the US Department of Energy, which handles the USA's nuclear arsenal, as well as decommissioning of old stockpiles.[42]

The clearance is often mistakenly believed by online users to be some form of secret 'above top secret' level, but in practice is just the result of a department-specific classification system. One theory as to why 4chan hit upon 'Q clearance' is that an episode of the adult spy cartoon *Archer*, first aired a year or two earlier, features the titular character shouting 'I have Q clearance' to gain access to a CIA base.[43]

This, then, is the context of Q's emergence – one supposed insider among many, dropping cryptic hints to a small but extremely online audience largely in on the joke. But something about Q's enigmatic posting style and cryptic hints proved much more compelling than the other accounts, which rarely lasted more than a few days and didn't escape 4chan's orbit. Reading QAnon posts felt different:

> Mockingbird
> HRC detained, not arrested (yet).
Where is Huma? Follow Huma.
This has nothing to do w/ Russia (yet).
Why does Potus surround himself w/ generals?
What is military intelligence?
Why go around the 3 letter agencies?[44]

It would take a will of steel not to be intrigued, especially as just days before Q's first posts, Donald Trump had enigmatically referred to a meeting with his generals as 'the calm before the storm' to the media and refused to elaborate on what he meant – the subject line Q then chose for his first posts.[45] To the casual observer not paying too much attention to dates, the accordances felt like proof of insider knowledge.

This is where the weird world of 4chan lands us – never quite sure what's a joke and what's serious, when someone is spewing hate when they say 'fag' or when they're just using it to be part of the club, almost as a term of affection. When does someone genuinely believe they're getting a real intelligence leak, and when are they just playing along? When does the distinction stop mattering?

It is hard not to feel from our modern vantage point that the chaos and nihilism of 4chan has, over the site's twenty-something-year lifespan, seeped out into the wider world. And while Coleman rightly thinks it is unfair to draw a straight line between Anonymous and QAnon, it is clear that they grew out of the same place, and that QAnon learned much from its forebear.

But Anonymous and QAnon are very different. Anonymous was born at least in part as a social justice movement, and clearly has very different DNA to QAnon. There are other movements born from 4chan that have more claim to serve as direct forebears to QAnon: Gamergate and the alt-right. This is a story of the ripple effect, and how one man's bitter vendetta against his ex, fuelled by our bizarre online ecosystem, arguably gave rise to much of Trumpism. It's this we turn to next.

2

Comet Ping Pong

'It is early on a Monday morning. You are a mid-twenties human being.'[1]

It all started with a video game about depression. To those who haven't played video games from independent studios, the game – called *Depression Quest*, and released in 2013 – might not even seem like a game at all. *Depression Quest* takes place entirely inside a normal web browser window, and is text-based. The player is presented with information about their current status as a twenty-something with clinical depression, and given multiple options for what to do next.

It is, to be honest, not all that much fun to play, but it does serve as an effective, if somewhat earnest, interactive explainer of what it is like to live with depression, for someone who has never experienced the condition. It is hard to think of an indie side-project that could be more innocuous and well-meaning than this one – and yet it inadvertently set into motion a chain of events that birthed some of the most toxic political movements of the last few decades.

The backlash against this game evolved into a backlash against modern, liberal games coverage more broadly. This energised and newly connected group, unified by challenging a politically correct 'feminist' establishment, fed into a nascent right-wing movement – the alt-right – which in turn fed into QAnon. None of them is the successor of the other, strictly speaking. But it is hard to see how any of them could have emerged in the forms that they did without the others. QAnon itself is hardly the final stage of a process – a movement that began with specific predictions about Donald Trump and Hillary Clinton has evolved into a loose coalition protesting lockdowns, vaccines, Bill Gates, the World Economic Forum and elites in general.

It is said that dislodging a few loose rocks at the wrong time in the wrong place can set off a landslide. With that in mind, here's how one well-meaning game changed the world – for the worse.

It began with a blogpost by the ex-boyfriend of one of the game's developers, Zoë Quinn. (Quinn at the time went by 'she/her' pronouns, but now uses 'they/them'. We will use the latter here.) Quinn's ex lay out a lengthy charge sheet against them, including the suggestion they had slept with at least one gaming journalist in exchange for favourable coverage on major gaming sites.[2]

Quinn had been in a relationship with the writer in question, Nathan Grayson, who was employed by the gaming site Kotaku. But Kotaku had only mentioned *Depression Quest* once, in a round-up of similar games written by a different author entirely, and the piece was at best mildly positive about the game.[3] Grayson, meanwhile, had written about Quinn briefly on another site, but not as a game review, and before any relationship had started. Suffice it to say, the allegation Quinn had slept with journalists for good reviews was totally and utterly unfounded.[4]

Despite the apparent lack of truth to the accusations against Quinn, they nonetheless tapped into something on 4chan and related online chat forums. Posters circulated naked photos of Quinn, speculated on their sexual history and even discussed what they could do collectively to drive them to suicide.[5]

The specific grievance soon spiralled into something broader. Another early target was media critic Anita Sarkeesian, who had been publishing a popular series of YouTube videos titled *Damsel in Distress*. Part 1 was called 'Tropes Against Women in Video Games'.[6] The putative mob harassed Sarkeesian to the point where she was forced to flee her home and file complaints with the police. As the invective against her mounted, she was eventually forced to cancel public talks after facing death threats against her person and terror threats against venues at which she was slated to speak.[7]

What had started as an abusive campaign against one individual had evolved into a broader protest against video games and the coverage of them. It had picked up a name (and hashtag) in the process: Gamergate. Opponents of the movement categorised it as an abusive and misogynistic campaign centred around young men who were throwing their toys out of the pram at the inclusion of women, people of colour and LGBT people within gaming and its coverage.

Gamergaters, meanwhile, said it was nothing of the sort – despite the swathes of threats and harassment suggesting otherwise – but was instead about too-cosy relationships between developers and journalists. The group's unofficial public-facing slogan became 'actually, it's about ethics in gaming journalism'.[8]

It was perhaps no coincidence that the movement arose just as games writing was having something of a renaissance. As the medium was finally coming to be given more notice by mainstream publications (the games industry is larger than the music and movie industries combined),[9] it was starting to be treated seriously as a cultural product. This meant analysis of its tropes, prejudices and more. It also meant that games journalism was being written for groups outside the stereotypical gamer (generally a young straight man). It seemed to many of these new games writers that Gamergate was a group that wanted gaming journalism to speak solely to them – and to leave the social issues that brought in a wider audience at the door.

The fans quickly found a new tactic, writing to the companies that produced games and consoles, upon whose advertising money every specialist games journalism site relied. This was 2014, long before companies were used to dealing with these kinds of angry and coordinated online mobs – meaning that companies had no kind of playbook as to what to do about it.

Mobilised via 4chan and IRC, the movement started email-bombing advertisers on sites that had hosted content critical of Gamergate. When Leigh Alexander, then an editor-at-large at GamaSutra, wrote an op-ed critical of Gamergate on the site, saying the world had moved on and they could be left behind,[10] they came for GamaSutra. The email campaign told advertisers that the article was insulting to gamers and to the site's audience – advertisers' core customers. The campaign quickly secured a victory: Intel, the world's largest chip manufacturer, pulled all of its advertising from the site.[11]

Inevitably, this caused a large public backlash from the larger crowd of people who consume gaming journalism but aren't reactionary idiots. While Intel apologised for wading into the row, it did not reverse its decision to pull the adverts. The message to Gamergate was clear: they had the power.

This struggle between a new and unprecedentedly aggressive online grouping on one side and mainstream tech, gaming journalists and games developers on the other often took a turn for the surreal – as I was to learn. At one point, Gamergate adoped a tactic of threatening to boycott sites that posted coverage critical of their movement that they didn't deem to be fair. As a journalist working at the *Guardian* at the time, I tweeted something along the lines of saying I would be *thrilled* if no one in the Gamergate movement ever read the *Guardian* again, thank you very much. As a white man, I was spared the worst of the death and rape threats – but Gamergaters quickly started trying to find connections between me and the targets already on their radar. Did I know Quinn or Sarkeesian, perhaps? What could they find?

Having failed to find any obvious dirt,[12] Gamergate instead went through the *Guardian*'s editorial code, trying to find some rule I had broken.[13] As a reputable outlet, the *Guardian* had rules against conflict of interests for reporters – rules meaning they can't, for example, cover a company in which they hold shares, just as they can't accept any gift worth over £25.[14]

Gamergate's innovative interpretation of these rules was to suggest that by saying no one from the movement should read the *Guardian*, I was depriving the newspaper of the advertising revenue that would come with those page views. As a result, my conduct was in conflict with the *Guardian*'s interests, and so I was in breach of its ethics rules.

My bemused editor at the time received several dozen 'formal' complaints on exactly those lines, calling for me to be dismissed or disciplined. Instead, nonplussed, they asked me what the bizarre complaints were all about, followed by a lengthy eyeroll at their expense.

Others had it far worse, especially as the movement gained momentum and attracted more followers, not least thanks to mainstream coverage of its activities. 4chan was and is a niche site, but its influence became broad thanks to the media and to memes that started there permeating across the wider internet.

At least one other developer, Brianna Wu, was forced to flee her home and go to the police following a hail of death and rape threats that included specific details about her life and movements.[15] Sometimes the tactics became flat-out deadly: in early 2015 Gamergate advocates attempted to get a SWAT team sent to the home of Israel Galvez, a vocal critic of the group.

'SWATting', as mentioned, has resulted in fatalities on multiple occasions. It's hardly a surprise given that police are told someone in the house is trapped and being held by an armed invader. Luckily for Galvez, he had warned police this tactic might be used against him, but armed officers nonetheless visited his home.[16]

The utopian ideal of the internet had been that it would mobilise people into leaderless movements,[17] with usually left-ish dreamers imagining groups in their image taking on corporate and governmental power. But as academic Angela Nagle noted in her book *Kill All Normies*, they were only half right:

> Instead, this leaderless anonymous online culture ended up becoming characterized by a particularly dark preoccupation with thwarted or failed white Western masculinity as a grand metaphor ... this leaderless formation can express just about any ideology, even, strange as it may seem, that of the far right.[18]

Opportunists started to see possibilities in the Gamergate movement. They were a motivated, extremely online crowd looking for champions, and with money and time to spare. This could provide an income, a fanbase and a platform all at once. One such figure was Milo Yiannopoulos, then best known as a failed UK tech journalist who had parted acrimoniously from the *Telegraph* and seen his own start-up flop among a flurry of unpaid wages and bitter wars of words.

Yiannopoulos was a moderately well-known conservative blogger and tech writer in the UK, but his focus had never been gaming. Having previously said that games 'attract damaged people', in a 2013 post for his now-defunct tech site The Kernel, Yiannopoulos called adult gamers 'an awful lot of unemployed saddos living in their parents' basements'. In the same post he went still further: 'there's something a bit tragic, isn't there, about men in their thirties hunched over a controller whacking a helmeted extraterrestrial? I'm in my late twenties, and even I find it sad.'[19]

Nonetheless, as Gamergate picked up momentum, Yianno-poulos became its most prominent cheerleader, pushing it in front of new audiences and serving to legitimise some of its baser elements. Gamergate couldn't be homophobic, he argued by example, as here he was, a flamboyantly gay man serving as one of its key spokespeople.

4chan had sparked plenty of flare-ups against different sites and online communities before, but Gamergate was different. For one, it was sustained – people's attention didn't wander after a few days or even a few weeks. It was also more politically cohesive than movements that went before it. Gone was the political confusion of the occupation of *Habbo Hotel*, replaced with a single-minded focus on the idea that women and political correctness were ruining gaming, encroaching on territory where they were not welcome.

More than any of these dynamics, though, was the fact that, to its participants, Gamergate itself was like playing a game on an epic scale. Who is connected to whom? What are they hiding? What should we do about it? What will the results be? The ability to solve these mysteries in real time and to collectively decide what action to take are the exact same reward feedback loops of which great games are made.

Without any one person creating it, a real-world and months-long game (known as a 'metagame') was born. The LARPing that had previously been confined to intriguing and ultra-difficult puzzles like Cicada3301 was now playing out – but with no one directing it. Instead, it operated in an unfocused way against a perceived elite that was shutting gamers out of gaming.

This was reinforced by Yiannopoulos and the right-wing media ecosystem that he plugged Gamergate into, most notably Breitbart, a far-right website launched by right-wing firebrand Andrew Breitbart, and which was helmed at the time by Steve Bannon, the man who went on to be Trump's chief strategist and later convicted of various money laundering, fraud and conspiracy offences. Yiannopoulos's Gamergate revelations told followers what they already believed: the gaming establishment was secretly coordinating against them. One headline read: 'Exposed: The Secret Mailing List of the Gaming Journalism Elite'. The article revealed 'a secret mailing list on which they discuss what to cover [and] what to ignore'. Seeing journalists 'engaging in activism' on the topics they covered would, he wrote, 'be disturbing to many in the industry'.[20]

With one simple article, a fairly mundane group email between writers in a small corner of a profession – who naturally tend to know one another – was elevated to a secret that had just been uncovered. That fed a powerful narrative which kept its participants engaged.

Reflecting on this element of Gamergate years later, *Atlantic* staff writer, cultural critic and occasional gamer Helen Lewis noted that it was this behind-the-scenes element that made the movement so compelling to its adherents. 'There's a whole narrative that you're not going to hear from the press – about the fact that running game is corrupt, they're all sleeping with each other … you're invited to find out all of these things for yourself.'[21]

The mask becomes the face

I wrote in the previous chapter that when 4chan joked about 'fags' – its favourite epithet of that era, though foul racial slurs were also common – I had been fairly sure most people were joking. But the tone became more and more confusing as 4chan got older, and as groups such as Gamergate emerged out of it.

Gamergate threads were full of rape 'jokes' and increasingly graphic descriptions of rape, often of particular named individuals. Challenges to such behaviour became fewer and further between, but if they did come, they would be defended with the old argument that it was all still just a joke, just a more intense form of trolling. This started to build layer upon layer of meaning, with logos, colours and references tipping those in the know to rape 'jokes', while looking innocent to an audience unaware of their history.

Thanks to 4chan's deep history in arcane and obscure memes, unpicking these layers of meaning took expertise. The group, for example, produced an innocent-enough looking mascot for Gamergate named 'Vivian James' (a play on 'video games'). James was a thin, pasty-looking woman wearing a headband with 4chan's logo and a green and purple sweater – all unobjectionable enough, unless you know that on 4chan that combination of colours has another meaning. The colours were a reference to an extremely graphic gif which had portrayed one anime character sodomising another (the posting of which would get a user an instant ban from 4chan's video games board).[22]

Such endless series of coded references meant that those who knew the code knew when they were being threatened or insulted, but any attempt to point this out to the general public would look borderline insane. But it also had the effect of trapping people in so many layers of meaning that no one could quite tell what was a joke and what was serious. The mask was becoming the face.

Gamergate, then, became a group with a defining set of traits: intrinsically of the internet, rooted in misogyny or frustration with women, feeling defeated by some elite, socially liberal group, and looking for a mission. These are forces that were never going to stay confined to the gaming world. It was in 2015 when these festering traits hit the world stage – as a parallel right-wing movement and elements of the Gamergate phenomenon met and fused into something more.

Five years earlier, American white supremacist and neo-Nazi Richard Spencer had founded his own online outlet,

AlternativeRight.com,[23] a supremacist site aimed at defining itself against the traditional far right and building up a new and younger support base. That 'alternative right' soon picked up the moniker Alt-Right and found a natural membership base among the 4channers of this era, particularly among the followers of Gamergate.

Soon, previously vastly different online groups started to merge, seeing a common enemy in 'the elite' or 'the establishment' – code for some, but not all, of those using the terms for Jews – in whatever form they took. Once again, the ambiguity of the terms and the layers of meaning therein became a strength of the putative movement. Hardened neo-Nazis could say 'the elite' or 'globalists' and know for a fact they meant Jews. Others might be aware that the terms could serve as a code, but be unsure as to when they were actually being used as such. Many, if not most, would be completely unaware of that second level of meaning – which made it all the easier to hold a coalition together, and perhaps also for subtle in-group dynamics to slowly radicalise those who had previously not been in on the joke.

Gamergate and its fervent base found a broader cause, subsumed into broader online wars aimed at 'owning the libs'. Where 4chan had once stood for equal-opportunities trolling – taking on anyone just for the kicks – it now targeted its focus on the elites, whether in gaming, politics or elsewhere. After all, who is more fun to wind up than people who take themselves seriously? And who takes themselves more seriously than the liberal elite?

Deliberately or otherwise, the group found ways to slowly radicalise those who were pulled into its orbit. The tone of alt-right online communications was always laden with innuendo – anything could be dismissed as a joke, or a bid at trolling, and if you took it too seriously, the joke was on you. Any comment could be dismissed as something said merely to shock or to scandalise. And there was much old-school 4chan fun to be had by causing trouble in more mainstream corners of the internet.

Those like Milo Yiannopoulos, leveraging Gamergate into the bigger media platform of the alt-right, made the jump without hesitation – despite being gay (though as of 2022, currently identifying as 'ex-gay') and Jewish (although not being raised in the faith). Yiannopoulos spotted a commercial opportunity in the alt-right and became one of its cheerleaders, touring from rally to rally and cashing in all the while, boasting frequently of his financial takings from fans.[24]

Soon, the bizarre would mix with the deadly serious. One of the absurd fights of the era was over Pepe the Frog, an initially harmless comic frog character created by artist Matt Furie. Pepe first appeared in the 2005 comic strip *Boy's Club*. His most famous appearance for many years centred on a joke about peeing with your trousers around your ankles – on being caught doing so, the frog commented: 'feels good man'.[25]

Pepe somehow became the mascot of the alt-right, and was photoshopped into numerous racist or homophobic reaction gifs, adopted by Donald Trump in one famous tweet,[26] and eventually recognised as a hate symbol by none other than the Anti-Defamation League.[27]

Furie, who had nothing to do with the alt-right, desperately tried to reclaim his creation's image, urging fans to create positive Pepe memes – provoking a huge flurry of even darker memes than had existed before. Taking on 4chan in a meme contest is never wise. Despairing, Furie even killed off his creation, still to no avail.[28]

However, the frenetic but often silly online battles of the alt-right were just froth compared to the mobilisation going on alongside it, especially in the US. By 2015, the alt-right had a presidential candidate who talked like they did and railed against everything they hated: the establishment, the elite and women who didn't know their place. From the moment he emerged as a real candidate in the Republican primary, Donald Trump became the alt-right's dream candidate – and then their dream president.

The alt-right became his foot soldiers, creating pro-Trump memes, boosting his online image and increasingly staffing his campaign – which was run by none other than Breitbart's former executive chair Steve Bannon. Breitbart had once sat on the fringes of US politics, providing a home for Gamergate and the alt-right while the establishment ignored it. Now its boss was running a presidential campaign and staffing it with his site's former fanbase.

In its early days, the rise of the online far right was largely ignored by mainstream observers, but there were some exceptions. Among those was Julia Ebner, a senior research fellow at the Institute of Strategic Dialogue, a counter-extremism think tank, who spends much of her time undercover in extremist online communities.[29]

By 2017, when Ebner was on the forum threads, chat channels and Discords (private voice chat channels widely used by online communities, including some extremist communities) of the alt-right, Trump was president and the alt-right was a powerful but uneasy online coalition of far-right groups with very different beliefs. That group was getting ready for a rally at Charlottesville.

'White shirt, khaki pants. Clear shields, black gloves, black helmets,' Ebner recalls the group agreeing as a dress code for those attending the rally. No swastikas were to be brought, and guns were discouraged. It was too early, they argued, for violent insurrection – that could come later. For now, they wanted to look mainstream to attract new recruits.

Ebner noticed another common factor unifying those involved, beyond their being overwhelmingly male – a sense of isolation from either or both of society or the opposite sex. 'Five years no friends. Then four years no dates,' one noted in her presence.

On the day of the Charlottesville rally, though, loneliness was the last thing on the group's minds. The 500 or so people who turned up to the rally were met by a large Antifa (anti-fascist) counter-protest, some of whom were happy to match aggression with aggression and violence with violence. Those watching remotely via online live streaming wanted escalation, Ebner reveals:

hang em again
THIS IS WAR
DEATH TO ANTIFA
SMASH ENEMY TRANSPoRT[30]

Mere minutes after these exchanges, James Alex Fields ploughed his car into a large group of counter-protestors, killing Heather Heyer and injuring nineteen others in the most severe of multiple outbreaks of violence as the result of the alt-right's first major rally. Harassment, doxing (tracking down people's addresses, phone numbers and relatives) and swatting were already high-stakes tactics, but now the new wave of online radicalisation could be tied directly to real-world deaths and injuries. The stakes were rising ever higher. The amalgamation of the online nihilism of the chan sites, the alienation and resentment of Gamergate and the extreme ideology of the neo-Nazi and extreme right groups that formed the alt-right had created something new and especially toxic.

To look at the 2012 and the 2016 election campaigns is to feel as though you have either travelled to a different country, or travelled in time by decades. One of the dominant debates of the 2012 election was what Mitt Romney meant when he said 'I like being able to fire people',[31] or that he had 'binders full of women'.[32] By 2016, there was a fervent debate on whether or not it was morally permissible to punch a Nazi (the jury was and still is out).[33]

For the *Atlantic*'s Helen Lewis, there is an explicit connecting factor between Gamergate, the alt-right, QAnon and even many other more benign online movements: everyone thinks that there's some elite, or some group in charge – and everyone thinks they're not in it. 'It's that idea of the elite, right, and that does come up in Gamergate, and in the alt right, more generally – the idea that someone else is making the decisions and the normal people are completely shut out of that process,' she muses. 'The fascinating thing about all modern conspiracy theories is how much they do invoke the idea that someone's controlling everything, whether it's the deep state or the Jews, or you know, Russian troll farms or whatever it might be … it's all these fantasies that someone's actually in charge.'[34]

This is a common thread between populism and conspiracy theories. The two of them tend to run together. Populism (whether of the left or the right) suggests that entrenched elites are the blockage preventing easy solutions to the problems facing us as a society, and are generally why problems can't be fixed using existing political structures.

Conspiracy theories take that a step further. They suggest that the elite is either supported by some nefarious means or coordinating among itself to commit criminal acts of some sort or another. The disempowering aspect of this idea is countered by the idea that you and your fellow believers are wise to what's happening, and might play a part in bringing it down. When it's coupled with the LARPing elements born on 4chan, it turns global politics into a game with you as its hero.

In a sense the idea that there's an elite running the show is something almost of us believe to some extent – not least because it's at least partly true. In the UK, for example, only 7 per cent of people are privately educated, but 59 per cent of Liz Truss's first cabinet were. Top journalists and top politicians are often married to one another. The ultra-rich know and socialise with each other – PayPal founder and billionaire Peter Thiel knows billionaire and former PayPal CEO Elon Musk, who socialises with Google founder Larry Page, and so on.

But the reality of it being a small world at the top is transformed into a conspiracy theory that they are actively conniving and running the show as a cabal of some sort. It's a theory that is perhaps oddly more reassuring than the idea that everything is just random, and everyone is fumbling their way through life. When it mixed with the other characteristics that had emerged through the years in these particular online subcultures, this idea of a hidden elite was about to take on a deadly new edge.

4chan meets the Clinton emails

By the 2016 US presidential election, chan culture had evolved into something toxic and dangerous, but its offshoots had still not lost touch with reality in the way that the QAnon movement would. It was a move by two other entities who wanted Donald J. Trump to win the 2016 election that would – entirely inadvertently – send elements of 4chan and the alt-right down that path.

The Russian state had, according to Western intelligence assessments,[35] decided to put what effort it could into helping Trump win. This does not in itself mean that there was any knowing cooperation or collusion between the campaign and Russia, merely that the Russian state had made the decision to interfere in the election in Trump's favour.

One possible outcome for Russia was to succeed in getting Trump rather than Hillary Clinton into the White House – someone perhaps more easily controllable and by nature more warmly disposed to Putin's Russia. But even if pro-Trump efforts failed to secure victory, they could help entrench divisions in the US and so destabilise its politics – itself a win in Putin's zero-sum view of foreign affairs.[36]

There were several operations to this end, but the one that interests us involves the activities of a supposed lone hacker named 'Guccifer 2.0' – believed by US law enforcement to be in reality a group of hackers working for the GRU, Russia's military intelligence unit.[37] By sending so-called phishing emails – emails impersonating customer services or some other service – to key personnel, Guccifer managed to access email archives belonging to the Democratic National Committee (DNC) and to John Podesta, a key Hillary Clinton aide.

The trick now was to get those documents somewhere they would attract maximal US media and public attention. The whistleblowing website WikiLeaks was perfect for the task. First, it had a mission of disclosing confidential documents. Second, its founder, Julian Assange, bore a personal grudge against Clinton, who had been in charge of the US response to the State Department cables the site had released in 2010. Finally, though it's not clear whether the Russian hackers were aware of this, Assange had an interest in Trump winning the election, believing he would be much likelier to drop any possible prosecution or extradition bid over WikiLeaks' activities. Later in the race, it emerged that WikiLeaks had been communicating with Donald Trump Jr over its handling of the leaks, even proposing that Trump should suggest Assange for an ambassadorial post.[38]

No one knows if Assange was aware that the documents he was receiving were the result of Russian state hacking (he has denied that they were), but he was certainly not about to spend too much time asking inconvenient questions of his anonymous source. Over the course of the US presidential election, WikiLeaks timed releases of emails from its new cache for maximum impact.

For outlets like Fox News, the ability to spend a summer saying 'Hillary Clinton' in proximity to the word 'emails' was enough – it could imply a connection to Clinton operating her own email server, even though that was nothing to do with this hack.[39] The fact of the emails made news again in the race when the FBI declared it would check disgraced congressman Anthony Weiner's laptop for classified emails[40] – again creating a false connection in people's mind with Clinton's leaked emails.[41]

The very fact of the email leaks was significantly damaging to the Clinton campaign, and so hugely helpful to Trump. The trouble was that once you looked closely, there wasn't really anything all that interesting in their contents. The DNC emails raised questions for Bernie Sanders supporters as to whether they'd shown bias in favour of Clinton in the primaries, but didn't reveal any secret crimes.[42] The Podesta emails revealed even less of interest. Other people's emails – even when they work for presidential candidates – are nearly as boring as our own, it turns out.

Yet this was a huge cache of online documents, published by a reputable but thoroughly anti-establishment outlet, about perhaps the ultimate US establishment insider, Hillary Clinton. Could any target be more compelling for the 4chan denizens of 2016?

Whether as a joke, a troll or some sort of political act, a few 4chan users jumped on the Podesta emails and decided to try to stoke up some interest in them. One technique worked beyond the wildest imaginings of anyone involved. A group of users decided that the seemingly innocuous emails were in fact a code.

'Hotdog', they decided, meant 'boy'. 'Pizza' meant 'girl'. 'Cheese' meant 'little girl', while 'ice cream' meant 'male prostitute'.[43] The seemingly innocuous Podesta email cache in reality contained proof of a highly sophisticated child abuse ring operated by key aides of Hillary Clinton – and they had cracked the code used to discuss their crimes.

The regulars of 4chan would absolutely know this was not true, and that they had made this up. But it would make excellent bait for the rest of the internet. 4channers started seeding the idea on mainstream social networks and with fringe news outlets. Alt-right social media accounts – many of which by now had huge followings – promoted the theory,[44] prompting mainstream outlets to tackle it, if only to debunk it, bringing the idea to whole new audiences.

People with no idea of the conspiracy's origins began investigating – just as the Gamergaters had investigated their own marks – but this time with a code to unravel and much higher stakes. This was LARPing on a whole new scale, with the people playing having no idea they were playing a game and instead believing they were solving real crimes. The Pizzagate conspiracy was born.[45]

People had been motivated to make death threats and even launch potentially deadly SWAT raids simply because they didn't like people's views on video games, or disliked their opposition to a group they were part of. What might people do if they became convinced that murderous paedophiles were operating in their midst, close to the centre of power, and with no chance of being convicted through the criminal justice system?

The world did not have to wait long to find out. The internet's unique style of investigation lends itself to joining the dots, putting two and two together to make 20. At some point, possibly due to nothing more than simple confusion, 4chan's code – using 'pizza' to mean 'girl' – was connected to the idea of using actual pizza places as a cover for child abuse. People started looking for pizza parlours with connections to the Clintons or the Washington elite.

For those searching for such a venue, there could be few more perfect than Comet Ping Pong, a pizza parlour located in Northwest DC, where many of the Beltway elite reside, just a few doors down from Politics and Prose, a bookshop and DC fixture. Comet (as it is known to locals) was co-founded by James Alefantis, a connected member of DC's elite once named on *GQ*'s list of the fifty most powerful people in Washington,[46] who had dated senior figures in the not-for-profit world (including the CEO of left-wing media watchdog Media Matters for America).[47]

The dark corner of the internet that was Pizzagate had now convinced itself not only that there was a child abuse conspiracy underway, but that they knew where it was happening – in the basement of Comet Ping Pong. Inevitably, someone took things into their own hands. In the middle of the afternoon on 4 December 2016, Edgar Maddison Welch walked into Comet Ping Pong with an AR-15 rifle (the civilian version of the US military's M16 automatic rifle) and a Colt .38 pistol, and fired three shots into the air, demanding to be allowed to investigate the pizzeria's basement and the crimes within.[48] By some miracle no one was injured, and before he was detained – alive – by law enforcement, Welch was shown a simple fact about Comet Ping Pong he could probably have discovered without heavy weaponry: the restaurant did not have a basement. Welch was eventually sentenced to four years in prison.[49]

On this occasion, no one was hurt. But by this point at the end of 2016, the breeding ground that was 4chan had over the previous decade evolved a number of traits that would soon come together to form QAnon, and would continue to evolve. Movements spawned from this environment had shown the ability to extend to more 'normal' parts of the internet; to radicalise their own members; to connect with offline extremist groups; to mobilise their members in the real world; to launch game-style investigations into real-world issues; to tap into loneliness and isolation; to believe in a morally bankrupt elite 'other'; to believe that the elite were engaged in child abuse; and finally, to radicalise a small fraction of their number into violent direct action.

This was the ultimate digital tinderbox – something was always going to ignite it. That something happened to be a 4chan poster who came to be known as Q. The spark became a flame that spread across the world faster than anyone could have imagined.

3

Breadcrumbs

It's August of 2021, and Nicky Woolf is sitting alone in the dimly lit back room of a North London pub.[1] In his mid-to-late thirties, markedly dishevelled and with his arm in a sling – he'd dislocated it a day or two before – Woolf is agitatedly waiting for the first guests to arrive for the launch party of his new podcast.[2]

Producing it has taken Woolf across continents, trying to crash the party of winning Congressional candidates, staking out ranches and speaking to both current and former followers of the QAnon movement along the way. That's all because Woolf has just spent eighteen months trying to find the person behind Q – the controller of the account that lit the spark which went on to set the world on fire. It was posts from that account that captured the imaginations of hardened conspiracy theorists and fringe teenage extremists alike, going on to provoke protests, riots and criminal acts across the world.

Many people have searched for Q. The reason we're in this pub back room with Woolf is that he can claim something most of the rest cannot. Woolf almost certainly actually found him, met him in the flesh and even, after a fashion, spoke with him.

Most cults are centred around a charismatic leader and collapse in their absence. If QAnon were just a digital version of a cult, the identity of Q (just like the ideology of Q) would be central to it. How would Q direct his followers? What would happen in his absence? Looking at who might be behind the Q account – and, spoiler alert, what happened when the account disappeared – is essential to seeing how QAnon is something different altogether.

Dropping crumbs

Before we meet the man, though, we should see more of the persona, and how it caught on when dozens of similar conspiratorial accounts did not. In the introduction to this book we referred to Q's infamous first post on 28 October 2017, dropped onto 4chan's /pol/ board:

> HRC extradition already in motion effective yesterday with several countries in case of cross border run. Passport approved to be flagged effective 10/30 @ 12:01am. Expect massive riots organized in defiance and others fleeing the US to occur. US M's will conduct the operation while NG activated. Proof check: Locate a NG member and ask if activated for duty 10/30 across most major cities.[3]

It is hard not to find the post compelling – it is very specific, has an almost omniscient tone and assumes a good level of knowledge on the part of the reader. What really pulled people in, though, was that the account kept posting further snippets over the following few days.

It's fair to wonder at this point how anyone would know further posts came from the same account. The answer is that while every post on 4chan is completely anonymous – no one can make an account or register a name – different anonymous users can prove they're the same person who made a previous post via what's called a 'trip code', an optional addition to a post which is unique to each user.[4] This means people could establish that posts from the account now known as Q were from the same individual.

Q quickly established a particular voice that couldn't have worked better for the 4chan audience of 2017 if it had been scientifically engineered to do so. It was pro-Trump, anti-establishment and littered with mysteries and questions, urging people to work out the answers for themselves. Q's second post, less than two hours after the first, followed just that pattern, as this extract shows:

Mockingbird

HRC detained, not arrested (yet).

Where is Huma? Follow Huma.

This has nothing to do w/ Russia (yet).

Why does Potus surround himself w/ generals?

What is military intelligence?

Why go around the 3 letter agencies?

What Supreme Court case allows for the use of MI v Congressional assembled and approved agencies?

Who has ultimate authority over our branches of military wo approval conditions unless 90+ in wartime conditions?

What is the military code?[5]

One could reasonably wonder why Q would have to dance around the point, if they were trying to share urgent, sensitive and classified information at such high risk – but Q had an answer to hand for that, too, suggesting that they were only able to give elliptical clues so as to avoid automatic internet-scanning software deployed by the deep state, leading to several posts a day of this sort:

Some of us come here to drop crumbs, just crumbs.

POTUS is 100% insulated - any discussion suggesting he's even a target is false.

POTUS will not be addressing nation on any of these issues as people begin to be indicted and must remain neutral for pure optical reasons. To suggest this is the plan is false and should be common sense.

Focus on Military Intelligence/ State Secrets and why might that be used vs any three letter agency

What SC decision opened the door for a sitting President to activate - what must be showed?

Why is POTUS surrounded by generals ^^

…

Operation Mockingbird

Patriots are in control. Sit back and enjoy the show.[6]

The concept of 'crumbs' or 'breadcrumbs' became a central one to QAnon.[7] It was taken from the fable of Hansel and Gretel, who left a trail of breadcrumbs showing their path. Those who could learn how to follow the crumbs, who could do their own research, could get to the truth that the establishment was trying to hide. But those breadcrumbs led to some deeply strange and unsavoury places.

We'll leave Q's individual posts behind soon – unpicking them all would be a very different and much longer book – but it's useful to know one more thing about the context in which Q's first post (which came to be known as 'drops') appeared. Q was not the only account posting – playfully, in line with 4chan's LARPing (live-action roleplaying game) tradition, or otherwise – about the imminent arrest of Hillary Clinton.[8]

Around 90 minutes before Q's first drop, a different account made a drop of its own:

Hillary Clinton will be arrested between 7:45 AM - 8:30 AM EST on Monday – the morning on Oct 30, 2017.

No one remembers this post now, not least because the board's response was to be underwhelmed, with more than one poster flat-out accusing it of LARPing. For both 4chan and the alt-right, always treading the line between joking and not joking, trolling or sincere, this kind of intelligence play was the trend of the moment. Q could easily have been just one LARP among many, albeit one which caught on in a way others didn't.

One thing Q secured that others didn't was backers: people who either earnestly believed what Q was saying, or were willing to put their real names and identities behind it and who stand by – at least in part – everything Q has said even years after many of its promises failed to materialise. One of Q's earliest and most enthusiastic public backers was Paul Furber, a South African tech journalist and web programmer in his early fifties, who doubled as a volunteer moderator on 4chan's /pol/ board, on which the Q account made its drops.

Apparently motivated by a desire to see Q's important message reach a wider audience – he had been an ardent believer in Pizzagate and was a lifelong conspiracy theorist[9] – Furber was one of the people who in early November 2017 started seeding Q's information across the internet. 'A bunch of us decided that the message needed to go wider so we contacted YouTubers who had been commenting on the Q drops,' Furber told NBC News in 2018.[10]

One Q post from early that November helped popularise a phrase – 'the calm before the storm', echoing cryptic remarks made by Donald Trump at a public address a few weeks before[11] – that soon became a mantra of Q's followers:

> What is Q Clearance?
> What hint does that explicitly refer to?
> DOE?
> Who would have the goods on U1?
> Does stating 'Q' refer that person works in DOE?
> No.
> Does it refer that someone dropping such information has the highest level of security within all departments?
> Why is this relevant?
> …
> The calm before the storm.[12]

QAnon was, for now, confined to the fringes of a single board on 4chan. That would not last. As Q had suggested, the storm was indeed coming.

***

Before we talk about how Q escaped the confines of 4chan, we should try to pin down the core tenets of QAnon. The problem is that doing so is like trying to nail jelly to the wall. Q constantly turns and shifts, responding to current events or adjusting to accommodate predictions that have failed to materialise and thus need to be explained away. Compounding this is the mantra of following the breadcrumbs, or doing your own research. This cleverly allows people to follow the aspects of a conspiracy that speak to them while downplaying the bits they do not believe. This means that there's no fixed set of beliefs that make up QAnon.

It has also been more than five years since the first Q post, and much has changed since then – not least Donald Trump being voted out of office in 2020. If QAnon was not capable of shifting its theology over time, it would have died long ago.

With all of those caveats aside, here is my interpretation of what the core components of the QAnon conspiracy were in the closing months of 2017:

> Donald Trump, on becoming president – or possibly as part of a plan hatched before his run – was working with a small group of trusted generals to overthrow a corrupt Deep State that had been running the US and the world for many years prior. Trump was having to act cautiously and carefully because he could not trust the Secret Service, CIA, FBI or NSA, but had military intelligence on his side.
>
> Usually, elections are carefully stage-managed, but a small group of 'patriots' had helped Trump win by preventing the vote rigging that usually occurs. As a result, there was a high chance of assassination or some other means (such as impeachment) to remove Trump. Both Obama and Hillary Clinton were high-ranking members of the cabal, which was able to stage false flag operations, mobilise protestors and more – but Trump would soon secure their arrest, likely causing widespread unrest and violence orchestrated by that cabal.
>
> Not quite core to the conspiracy, but widely believed, was that the cabal was heavily involved in large-scale child abuse, quite probably for satanic or other ritual purposes, with many people following Q also believing that either the cabal or Trump's forces were making use of a huge network of secret tunnels under the USA.
>
> Finally, a sizeable minority of those involved in QAnon believed in secret technology used by both the cabal and Trump's resistance to it – up to and including a small group that believed in Project Looking Glass, a secret project that literally allowed people to see into the future, which some came to believe informed Q's drops.[13]

Hopefully, this all comes across as nonsense. Elaborate claims such as these are largely immune to fact-checking due to the impossibility of proving a negative, and the fact that if someone accepts the possibility of such things being true, that requires mistrusting any mainstream source. This means that debunking would require 100 per cent primary sources, which would likely be a lifetime's work.

There is also the challenging truth that elite rings centred around the worst of crimes, such as child abuse, do exist: Jeffrey Epstein died in jail while awaiting trial for running just such a ring,[14] while his consort Ghislaine Maxwell was convicted on five counts for serving as his facilitator in a sex trafficking conspiracy.[15]

In other words, conspiracies do exist and happen every day. If a group of three people plan to defraud a fourth, that's a conspiracy. If presented with a group of possible conspiracies – 9/11 was an inside job, JFK was not assassinated by Lee Harvey Oswald, the government has covered up alien landings or the government drugs the public via chemtrails (a theory that the trails of water vapour left behind planes are laced with mind-controlling chemicals) – around half of US adults will believe at least one.[16]

What stops a 'conspiracy theory' just being a dismissive term for a conspiracy we don't personally believe in? A good general rule of thumb is to think along two lines: if the conspiracy theory were true, how many people would be required to be sworn to secrecy, and how easy would the behaviour be to rationalise as a good thing?

The bigger the group required to keep the secret, and the worse the behaviour, the quicker the conspiracy would fail. Anything requiring thousands of people to hide something monstrous crosses into conspiracy theory. As Michael Butter, professor of American Studies at the University of Tübingen and author of *The Nature of Conspiracy Theories*, puts it:

[C]onspiracy theories usually imagine far more comprehensive and ambitious – and hence impracticable – plots than actual conspiracies, which are very limited in terms of their scopes and objectives. Above all, conspiracy theories assume a false view of people and history in claiming that history can be planned and controlled over any length of time.[17]

If anything ever claimed history could be 'planned and controlled' more than is remotely possible, it is QAnon, which not only imagined a supremely organised evil cabal but also made Donald Trump the genius mastermind orchestrating an equally complicated counter-movement.

QAnon would – as we'll see – perpetually evolve and shift as it spread to new communities, but this was its core as it started to hit the mainstream. And hit it, it would.

Breaking out beyond 4chan

While your message is only on 4chan, it isn't going to go very far. At the time of writing, 4chan claims only 225,951 active users.[18] To get something to a mass audience, you need the message to be where they are, among the 1.5 billion users of Instagram, 2.5 billion users of YouTube or 2.9 billion users of Facebook.[19]

That's exactly where QAnon was heading. By November 2017, a group of volunteer moderators of 4chan's /pol/ board – coordinated by Paul Furber – had been getting in touch with YouTube influencers, and some of them were listening.

One of the very first was Tracy Diaz, known online as Tracy Beanz, who was the target of Paul Furber's early messaging as he tried to spread the gospel of QAnon. Diaz was a fringe YouTube figure who, according to NBC – all her online content has subsequently been removed from the internet – had previously posted videos analysing the Pizzagate conspiracy from a sympathetic viewpoint, alongside other WikiLeaks email releases.

Diaz's first video – posted on 3 November, less than a week after Q's first drop – analysed Q posts and what the cryptic clues might actually mean. It reached 250,000 views, starting a trend of YouTube influencers bringing Q posts to people who would never try to navigate the niche and technically complex world of 4chan.[20]

These kind of analysis posts are the bread-and-butter of YouTube fandoms, though are often applied to far more innocuous subjects. Taylor Swift, for example, notoriously loads her social media posts, music videos and more with layers of hidden meanings and references, often clues about forthcoming albums. Her August 2017 video for 'Look What You Made Me Do' was so laden with these so-called 'Easter eggs' that even *Elle* magazine noted, 'Everything is Deliberate'.[21]

Deconstructing Marvel movies to speculate about future plotlines or characters, or potential future plot twists, was similarly popular, becoming a huge generator of attention for new Marvel movies, as well as a path to fame for influencers.[22] The game of over-analysis and speculation was not a new one to the YouTube audience.

And so when Diaz started breaking down the oh-so-tempting and oh-so-elliptic QAnon drops for her already conspiratorial YouTube audience, it's no surprise that they took off, or that those high engagement numbers then meant that Diaz's content was pushed to new audiences via YouTube's algorithm. QAnon was taking off outside of 4chan.

Having seen Q was where the conspiracy numbers were at, others followed to be on to the hot new thing. But the new context tore away any remaining joking-not-joking doubt – YouTube is not 4chan, steeped in endless layers of irony. When people watch conspiratorial material here, it's because they're genuinely interested in it. Any chance that Q would be seen in the context of LARPing, of a particular subculture playing, was dashed within a week of Q's very first post – something not seen with similar role-playing accounts, but distinctive to Q.

Diaz, once again working with the still-enthusiastic Furber and other 4chan moderators, helped set up a community for 4chan on Reddit, a much more mainstream text-driven message board, which doesn't rely on anonymity. QAnon similarly spread to the news-driven social network Twitter.

Soon, Q would not post onto 4chan at all. One of Q's earliest posts – on 2 November 2017 – had dropped a hint about content being deleted or disappeared:

Please refer back and collect my crumbs.
As discussed, we've anticipated the Twitter and other social media blackouts.
Rogue agents/programmers.
Per sealed Federal orders, we quickly tracked and reinstated.
Expect outages periodically (infiltrated).
If this doesn't signal what I've been saying I don't know what will.
Q[23]

This came to pass less than a month later. On 27 November, a new Q post appeared – but not on 4chan. Instead, the post appeared on a rival site – 8chan. It had a stark warning about Q's old home:

Test
Test
4Chan infiltrated.
Future posts will be relayed here.
Q[24]

8chan is essentially 4chan, but worse. There are, perhaps unbelievably, some limits to what 4chan will host, and some content is deleted. This was simultaneously seen as unacceptable – but also as an opportunity – by one 4chan user in 2013.

American Frederick Brennan, who lives with brittle bone disease and uses a wheelchair, founded 8chan as a more extreme spin-off of 4chan on which anyone would be able to say anything, with absolutely no limits. Multiple reports have documented how, as early as 2014, 8chan was routinely used to share images of child sex abuse, with no effort made to delete or moderate that content.[25] If 4chan had become something of a cesspit, 8chan was the cesspit's cesspit.

The board originally struggled to attract users, but finally found a ready-made userbase in late 2014,[26] when Gamergate fell foul of one of 4chan's few sacrosanct rules at the time: don't cross the founder. 4chan was at the time still administered by its founder, Christopher Poole, better known as moot.

One Reddit user characterised 4chan's core rule at the time as: 'No doxxing, no raids, no things that will cause moot shit because he's tired of going to court.'[27] moot and his admins deleted threads in which Gamergate users doxed women in their sights, and in retaliation the Gamergaters posted abuse all over 4chan. The result was a ban from every major 4chan board.

Gamergate found a new home on 8chan, and the site had a smaller but even more on-side user base for Q, for whatever reason the person behind the enigmatic account had made the switch. For so long as Q would continue to post – and Q kept posting until December 2020,[28] shortly after Trump lost the US election – they post exclusively on 8chan, initially on /pol/ and eventually in their own community, /qresearch/.

QAnon's move to 8chan raised some eyebrows, given it had previously only really been known for hosting content after it had been banned by 4chan – which Q had not been. Frederick Brennan was no longer the owner and operator of 8chan, since he had sold the site in 2014 to a father-and-son team, Jim and Ron Watkins.[29] Jim was a former US army helicopter pilot who at the time operated a strange and sprawling set of businesses out of the Philippines. His son Ron helped him in the operation of his online empire.

Jim Watkins' business experience perhaps made him well suited to be the owner of a site like 8chan. For a start, he was a longstanding admirer of Barry Goldwater, credited as the father of the USA's conservative resurgence and a leading figure in the libertarian movement. For another, Watkins had made his money online through pornography – predominantly Japanese – which he then expanded into an online sales and advertising venture. The magazine *Mother Jones* traced several domains controlled by Watkins' NT Technology company as hosting material relating to child sexual abuse, aside from the material hosted on 8chan itself.[30] Watkins extensively denied the allegations, accused *Mother Jones* of attempting to smear his reputation, and denied having a 'direct link' to the companies concerned. He also argued he had no direct link to any of the domains and that any child abuse material that appeared on 8chan was removed and that it was "one of the strictest websites on the internet". He added that any domain names suggestive of child abuse were held for "domain squatting" – the practice of buying a domain in the hope of selling it on at a profit – and hosted no content. He said his companies would always delete offending material if they were aware of any issues.

Just as Gamergate had provided a sizeable active audience to 8chan when it had previously had almost none, securing Q was a coup for the site. It is also one that has posed many questions since – how was Q convinced that 8chan would be a safer place to post than 4chan?

Forensic analysis carried out on behalf of the *New York Times* in 2022 sheds some light on the mystery by using linguistic analysis to try to determine who was behind the different posts made by Q. Looking at the early posts of QAnon across 4chan and 8chan, the researchers came to a conclusion with 98 per cent certainty: the author of the early Q posts was none other than Paul Furber himself.[31]

This would, of course, help explain Furber's enthusiasm for spreading Q's message more widely – perhaps because he believed the fundamental truth of his posts, even if he knew he didn't have 'Q level clearance', or perhaps just to see how far he could push a joke – but he has always denied ever posting as Q. Instead, Furber has argued that the similarity is because Q's messages 'took over our lives' and so everyone started talking like him.

That would soon change. Early in 2018, mere weeks after Q had been tempted to jump across to 8chan, the forensic analysis suggested something dramatic: someone new was now posting as Q, and their writing didn't resemble Furber's at all.

Three mass shootings

During that time (and long beyond), QAnon would wreak havoc across the world – but we'll follow that in other chapters. For now, we'll keep our focus on the tiny core Q community, the die-hards who would spend their time on 8chan – and follow a conspiracy obsessed with uncovering mass child abuse while spending their time on a forum that hosted it, seeing no contradiction between those two things.

A seismic break in the 8chan QAnon world occurred in August 2019 following three separate mass shootings with ties to 8chan, and possibly to Q. The shooter in the horrifying mosque attack in March 2019 in Christchurch, New Zealand, had been an 8chan regular.[32] The killer behind the Poway synagogue shooting in California in April 2019 posted a manifesto on 8chan.[33] And when a man killed 23 people in a Walmart in El Paso, Texas, police soon found a manifesto on 8chan.[34]

This wave of violence would prove too much even for Frederick Brennan, who would soon launch a frenetic media war against the site he had created. 'Whenever I hear about a mass shooting, I say, "All right, we have to research if there's an 8chan connection,"' he told the *New York Times*, before adding that all too often such a connection was easy to find. 'Shut the site down.'[35]

The 2019 backlash brought a whole new level of attention to the site's new owners, the Watkins duo, both of whom had become public QAnon backers and boosters. They claimed to believe and follow Q themselves, although others suspected their public avowal of Q was intended to encourage all the traffic it brought to their site. When Brennan broke with the Watkinses and spoke out against the site, he called for the sites working with it to pull their support and take it offline.

Cloudflare, a huge online service provider which protects sites from attacks taking them off the internet, was forced to pull its support.[36] The companies providing the services to make 8chan's web address work pulled their services soon after.[37] 8chan was left effectively offline for two months, eventually resurfacing under a new (and somewhat offensive) name.[38]

All of that, though, was but a sideshow to the main event of the conflict between Brennan and the Watkinses, because Brennan was alleging, very publicly, that he knew the new identity of Q.[39]

Finding Q

This was the mystery that Nicky Woolf had been hired to solve on behalf of Tortoise Media for the podcast that became *Finding*

Q.[40] The problem, he explained, over a double vodka and Coke – which he'd persuaded the bar staff to pour a little before the pub officially opened, let alone the start of his event – was that he hadn't been all that sure at first whether the identity of Q was even important.

'My original thought was that it's still going to be some LARPer,' he explained. 'And therefore lost to the mists of time, so it could be anyone. At the very beginning it almost didn't really matter.'

Luckily, even the early research for the podcast backed up what Brennan and others had suggested, and which the later forensic analysis corroborated: someone had taken over the account early in 2018. Where once Q posed questions, it increasingly spoke in grabby statements. The tone shifted, as the account's thousands of eagle-eyed followers could notice.

One of the people Woolf spoke to for the podcast was Paul Furber, whom Woolf took to be something of a naïf who had been drawn into the movement. Furber advanced the theory to Woolf that after joining 8chan Q had their identifying trip code stolen.

Given that Q had said they wouldn't post to 4chan again, and that the trip code was *the* identifying mark, that would leave the original poster with few options. Should it be the case that the forensic analysis was correct and Furber was the poster who lost the trip code, of course he would have plenty of insight into that process.

'The more I looked into it, the more it became clear that at some point someone had taken it over – and was using it … if not for financial gain necessarily, certainly something like their own gain, or their ego, or for political ends,' Woolf concluded.

For Woolf, Furber's earnest explanation of his theory that the account had been stolen served also as proof that he was an early believer in the conspiracy who would like to see the 'real' Q found. 'If he *was* the original author, and it is right about [the trip code] being taken away from him, which we believe he is, then why is it worth it for him to still be committed to the bit at this point? But who knows?'

At this point in our meandering conversation, I was getting anxious that the party might start before we got to the main point – so I very subtly tried to get Woolf to it:

Me: 'So ... who's Q?'
Woolf: 'It's Ron Watkins.'

If guilt requires means, motive and opportunity, Watkins Junior meets two of the three criteria almost by default. Ron Watkins had been working as the administrator of 8chan and his father's other sites since Brennan parted ways with their company. This gave him the access to the trip codes of any user of 8chan, suggesting that if they had managed to lure the original Q to 8chan, and have him discredit 4chan in the process, the account could be there for either taking or handing over. Ron was also by far the more tech-savvy of the Watkinses, placing him in a position where he could become Q and control the narrative. The *New York Times*'s forensic analysis corroborated the other evidence, this time with 99 per cent certainty that Watkins was the author of the posts from 2018 onwards.

Given that Watkins has always denied being Q, it has not been possible to look into what most motivated him to post – attention for 8chan, control over the world news agenda or the strange thrill that comes from leading a movement. But it was enough to keep him – if it was him – posting for three years, until Woolf and his crew got a little too close.

Woolf was not the only person to come to the conclusion that Ron Watkins was behind Q, by far,[41] but he has a stronger claim than most to be the reason that Q stopped posting for good – which is perhaps best told in his own words.

'We circled Jim [Watkins] and eventually we tracked him down,' Woolf recounts.

Everyone thought he was in the Philippines. We tracked him down to Northern California. We staked out his house – he threatened to have his friends hit me. He then said he'd turn up for an interview, which we didn't think he would but we were there anyway.

And on his live stream that morning, he talked about like having a hatchet, which was kind of weird. Then he actually turns up and ends up sitting down and it became clear that … he's just some kind of clueless Boomer type.

Very shortly into the interview, Woolf was convinced that Jim Watkins, at least, had not been all that involved in the ruse of being Q – leaving his son squarely in the frame for the whole thing.

'I think he didn't know about it at first. Exactly when he knew about it, we're not sure. But Q also stopped very soon after we turned up at Jim's house. We are kind of operating with the theory that he called up Ron and was like, "Cut that shit out." '

It didn't take long for things to start moving.

'After we doorstepped his dad Jim posts this weird video – we're on our way driving back – saying after all these tumultuous times, I'm resigning as 8chan administrator. "Today I bring the ship to dock." '

When it comes to why Ron Watkins might have wanted to spend several years of his life as Q, though, Woolf draws a blank, saying that he 'grew up sort of like a vaguely normal kid with his mom in Seattle, Washington. We talked to his best friend growing up, he used to sing barbershop … he's just some dude.'

If Ron Watkins was indeed Q, and most people who have looked into the mystery believes he was, then there is little to go on as to why. Perhaps it was a ruse to keep people on 8chan and keep the site in the public eye. Perhaps it was just a game. But the man himself is giving nothing away. When Woolf's production company sent a detailed letter to Ron Watkins asking for comment, they didn't receive the written response they expected.

They got a video.

'It is the most profoundly haunted piece of media I've ever seen,' Woolf recalls. 'He's speaking in front of a babbling brook, and he's wearing a cowboy hat, a black cowboy hat. At some point, he looks straight into the camera, and it's weird, kind of like uncanny valley, because the audio doesn't quite match the video. He goes, "I'm not – nor have even never been – Q." And then he stops and pulls the hat over his eyes.'

What little doubt remained over who had taken over the Q accounts was dispelled still further in the summer of 2022 when, after a silence of fifteen months or so, Q suddenly woke up and started posting on 8chan again – lighting up the old core accounts and Telegram groups that had religiously followed the posts.

The posts came as Jim Watkins was mounting an unsuccessful primary run for a Republican Congressional seat in Arizona, with the first post – sent using Q's unique trip code – asking: 'Shall we play a game once more?'[42] Unfortunately for Watkins, he was soon duped into believing someone had hacked the Q trip code, causing him to panic and take the whole site offline after posting a series of messages to social media – sparking speculation that this time, it had been the father rather than the son who was posing as Q.[43]

What was also apparent, though, was that no amount of revelations as to who was behind Q or just how little access they had to any of the secrets of the supposed US deep state would stall the chain of events Q had set in motion. By this stage, the reality is that the person behind Q is almost just a curiosity when it comes to analysing why it rose to prominence and why it caused such havoc. None of the men believed to be behind the account has ever worked for an intelligence agency, let alone been a senior and well-placed insider within one. Neither seems to be particularly motivated by a particular agenda. Q never sought to direct his followers to any particular action or cause, or even to give money to any particular place.

All of this supports the idea that Q was a prank that got out of control. It understood its audience and their drivers almost too well, creating something that had just the right blend of ingredients to encourage some people to play along and others to buy into it wholeheartedly. While only a tiny percentage of Q's followers would ever have first encountered him on 4chan or 8chan, these were the breeding grounds that let a meme, or a series of memes, become perfectly engineered to the public mood.

Once it had left 4chan and hit the mainstream outlets – which it did in less than a week after the first post – any hope of stopping it was dashed. Once outside that digital viral reservoir, QAnon would spread and mutate further, with huge consequences in the real world. Perhaps the most telling change, though, took a few years to happen. So embedded are QAnon's ideas in the conspiratorial corners of the internet that there are now hundreds of thousands of people who subscribe, at least in part, to QAnon – without ever having heard of Q or QAnon itself.

4chan and 8chan had always been incubators for fringe and extreme ideas. These could burst onto the wider internet and information ecosystem – as Gamergate and others did – but then tended to eventually wither away. QAnon, though, proved able to spread and mutate in a whole new way – as we'll now explore.

PART TWO

Infection

4

Patriot Research

Tracy 'Beanz' Diaz was the first QAnon influencer on YouTube,[1] but she was by no means the last. Her original videos have since been swept down the memory hole, a result of long-overdue action. Google, which owns YouTube, finally announced a ban on QAnon-related content in October 2020, almost three years after Diaz started boosting the conspiracy.

That ban may have come far too late – QAnons in their hundreds of thousands had plenty of alternative ways to communicate by then, as we will see later in this chapter – but it was also woefully incomplete. To this day, the videos of many early acolytes of Q remain live on YouTube.[2]

One such video, catchily titled 'Cabal Lies, Cabal Dies', comes from Roy Potter, who styles himself as a former US lieutenant colonel, and his video series *The Potter Expositor*. Posted in December 2017, and with more than 68,000 views to date, it is hardly on the fence in its analysis of QAnon.

After a series of opening stills and messages – including 'let's end child trafficking' and 'No pedophile is safe' – the video features a suited Potter standing awkwardly in front of a world map. Potter expresses concerns about the QAnon movement being infiltrated: 'it moved from 4chan to 8chan … which certainly helped,' he opens – somewhat ironically given that it was the shift to 8chan which seemed to facilitate the theft of Q's account.

Potter goes on to express concern that Q's drops won't lead to enough action. 'Where are the indictments?' he asks rhetorically, before noting that Trump can't go through the regular channels because of the 'leftist Marxist' courts. 'How many people have been duped by the cabal? How many people think that the truth is what the MSM [mainstream media] says it is?'[3]

The video continues in that vein – adopting the idea of a cabal covering up mass child abuse, encouraging radical action from veterans and others to help Trump tackle it, accusing every mainstream institution of collusion – for almost 31 minutes. At the time of writing, Potter is still regularly posting new videos to YouTube, with a total of more than 1,700 videos and 17.7 million views.[4]

Potter and posters like him are able to jump into a language that their audience will just automatically accept – a sort of extreme version of tropes and language that has grown up from Fox News and its surrounding ecosystem. 'Leftist' is a handy shorthand for anything conservatives dislike, while 'Marxist' bears no relation to Karl Marx or anything he wrote. For this particular crowd, socialism, communism, Marxism and leftism are all interchangeable terms for what's bad.[5] A Republican judge appointed by George W. Bush could just as easily qualify as a socialist as a Black Lives Matter activist.[6]

The genre of Q influencer and explainer videos became a whole micro-industry of its own, capitalising on the speculation format familiar to conspiracy theorists and mainstream YouTube fans alike. Few took their efforts nearly so far, though, as Dutch filmmaker Janet Ossebaard, who – inspired by Q – created a ten-part online documentary entitled *Fall of the Cabal*. Ossebaard, who had spent much of the previous two decades researching crop circles,[7] styled herself as an independent researcher looking into the claims of QAnon, and styled her documentary in a similar way to Q posts.

One of the most notable similarities was the video's opening few seconds. Just as Q urged readers to follow his 'crumbs' – with 'do your own research' becoming a mantra of the movement – so does *Fall of the Cabal* open with a prominent disclaimer.[8]

[This documentary] contains thousands of hours of research.
I urge you to accept nothing as the truth. Please do your own

research and double-check everything I present to you. That is the only way to wake up and become a truly independent thinker.

Disclaimers like this are a fantastic way to build trust, and often persuade people that they don't need to check something, as why would someone encourage them to do their own fact-checking if they weren't confident? David Icke, widely perceived as an antisemitic conspiracist – who has long advanced the theory that lizards have secretly taken over the world[9] – does much the same thing in his own interviews.

What follows the disclaimers in Ossebaard's ten-part, three-hour video presentation is a series of falsehoods so ludicrous that to dismiss them all would be the work of a PhD thesis. The lengthy series of videos builds to an hours-long documentary that – if watched for any length of time – gives an unnerving sense that you are being indoctrinated into a cult. Continuing to watch feels like a tacit endorsement of the claims made so far, just as you keep watching even more fantastical claims building upon them.

From the framework Q had provided, Ossebaard built a much more elaborate narrative, drawing in material from numerous, older conspiracy theories. Allegations made during the course of the video include:

- Diseases such as Ebola, SARS and HIV are all patented (they're not), which serves as proof that they were deliberately bio-engineered (they weren't)
- The Vatican owns a satellite telescope named Lucifer (nope)
- Children's cartoons contain hidden, subliminal sexual and violent images, aimed at priming their brains to suit the cabal. (Subliminal messages were long ago debunked.)[10]
- Abraham Lincoln and JFK were both assassinated because they tried to take on the cabal (as opposed to the Confederacy, in the former's case?)
- Every nation's central bank, along with the IMF, is actually privately owned, mostly by the Rothschilds, whose actual net worth is in excess of $500 billion (where to begin with this)

- James Alefantis (of Comet Ping Pong) is related to the Rothschilds, and was indeed running a child sex ring out of his restaurant (which is, of course, untrue)

'Worldwide, children are stolen and sold to elite paedophile rings. They are tortured, raped, and murdered as part of satanic ritual ceremonies ... Whether or not you believe in the existence of Satan is not relevant. They do. And according to each and every eyewitness who has the guts to step forward, Pizzagate is real.'

You get the gist. By the time someone had watched this video, they would have been presented with a narrative weaving together the core elements of QAnon with alternative medicine, old-school banking and finance conspiracies, with the final one being one of the oldest of all: blood libel itself.

Ossebaard concludes by pulling in much of the standard QAnon narrative. France's *gilets jaunes* protests (in actuality a populist protest that grew out of a backlash to a fuel tax)[11] was in reality an anti-cabal movement. QAnon was on the verge of taking down the cabal. Every tiny movement made by Donald Trump in public – up to and including his weird way of drinking water[12] – was a subtle signal to the resistance.

QAnon was rapidly becoming something of a choose-your-own adventure. By encouraging people to come to their own conclusions and to do their own research, Q was already suggesting that people picked the parts of the conspiracy that most appealed to their initial beliefs.

With boosters like Potter and Ossebaard further honing that – adding on theories of their own, or trimming bits off – QAnon was rapidly becoming a one-size-fits-all conspiracy, with the added bonus of a community and a call to action. Its incoherence became its strength.

One conspiracy to rule them all

This ability to take in existing conspiracy theories and to evolve rapidly is not unique to QAnon – once someone has accepted thousands of people will collude for one shady act, it is not a big leap to believe they'll do the same for another – but it does help to explain how a conspiracy that emerged in a niche as specific as 4chan broke out of it.

On the face of it, it's almost incomprehensible that a fringe far-right conspiracy caught the imagination of millions of Americans, but the spread of QAnon (or variants of it) globally is even harder to understand, given the central role the conspiracy gives to Donald Trump, a figure with a minimal international fan base. For all that his celebrity was global, in 2018, 91 per cent of Mexicans, 93 per cent of Spaniards and 90 per cent of Germans and French citizens had no confidence in Trump.[13]

This ability of QAnon to feed off existing beliefs and conspiracies is key. For the US audience, Q was tapping into a much more widely held belief than most people might realise. In April 2013 – more than four years before Q's first drop – the polling company PPP asked Americans this question: 'Do you believe that a secretive power elite with a globalist agenda is conspiring to eventually rule the world through an authoritarian world government, or New World Order, or not?'[14]

More than one in four Americans – 28 per cent of respondents – said they believed the new world order conspiracy. That varied across the political divide, but was by no means restricted to Republicans: 15 per cent of Democrats agreed with the statement, alongside 34 per cent of Republicans and 35 per cent of registered independent voters.

That idea of a shady cabal – often tied to ritual child abuse – managing world events behind the scenes is a very old one that has been accommodated into many conspiracy theories, and helps explain why this apparently American conspiracy theory took root in Europe too. Peter Knight, professor of American Studies at the University of Manchester, specialises in researching conspiracy theories, their emergence and their development – and says many of them have their roots in historical antisemitism, and have evolved over the ages.

'It's the idea that there is some kind of shadowy group behind the scenes – puppet masters pulling the strings. In a sense, QAnon is a new version of the Illuminati, which is a new version of antisemitism, which has its roots in Europe,' he explains. 'The underlying ideas are there from at least the 18th century.'

Knight notes that there is a long history of conspiracy theories merging into 'mega umbrella conspiracy theories', just as QAnon was doing by this stage – but 'obviously QAnon can then build on previous mega conspiracy theories to weave everything together.'

Within this framework of QAnon, there is one core conspiracy theory that merely changes with the times – whether it's the Knights Templar, the Illuminati, the Masons, the pope or the World Economic Forum and Hillary Clinton. It's about a secretive, evil cabal controlling the world, usually from behind the scenes.

Thinking of this as the core of QAnon perhaps explains how easily it survives annoying details that seem to contradict it, just as it also explains how other, smaller conspiracies (such as those concerning vaccines, chemtrails or fluoridisation) could be absorbed into it. At its core, QAnon's beliefs are tried and tested – they have the DNA of a conspiracy theory that has lasted for a millennium.

QAnon also had something to offer that other conspiracy theories in history did not. Throughout history, visibly believing in or promoting a conspiracy theory has been something that would isolate you from your community. If you live in a small village there is a limit to the amount of conspiratorial gossip you can spread (perhaps depending on how charming you are). Speculating wildly in the local pub about what different residents of the village are up to might be welcome gossip. Stray too far and too frequently into suggestions that the government is covering up alien abductions and you'll pay a social price for that, as you're unlikely to find many people who share your view.

But on the internet, where the entire world is just a click away, you'll find no shortage of people amenable to almost any idea, however niche. There are 5 billion people globally with internet access.[15] If you've got an ultra-fringe theory that only one in a million people believe, that's 5,000 people online sharing it. All you have to do is find each other.

'QAnon is not just a bunch of crazy people. We need to ask: "What are they getting out of this?" Given that, if QAnon is true, then it's incredibly depressing,' says Knight, with no small degree of understatement.

This is worth unpicking somewhat, as it's easy to gloss over conspiracies without thinking what it means to fervently believe in one. The people following QAnon closely and in detail believe that hundreds of thousands of children are being abused and murdered on an industrial scale in horrendous ways. They believe that it's being done by the people in power, that tens or hundreds or thousands of people know about it, and that all are happy to either tolerate or participate in it.

That is not a belief you can hold lightly. For most of us, if we sincerely believe this, it would come to dominate our thinking and our lives. What could be more urgent than this? What would be a more clear-cut case of good versus evil?

As Knight suggested, it is also a particularly dark vision of the world – as if reality isn't bleak enough – and one that suggests that democratic power is fake. Given all of that, why don't people turn away from QAnon, as people often turn away from the news headlines in dark times? Knight's answer is that people gain something else from being part of the group that knows the 'truth'.

'So what's the psychological payoff? If they're being pushed down the rabbit hole by both, individual trauma and collective ennui … what's the payoff?' he asks.

> A large part of it is community. And I think this is what's been so successful about Q, is that collective meaning-making. That has really struck a chord with a lot of people. Doing your own research is both individual, as it's putting the onus on you, but it's also collective. It's that sense that 'we', collectively, have seen through the lies of those so-called experts, and 'we' together are piecing together the truth that is being denied to us by the government, the media, academics, and scientists.[16]

The seemingly disempowering and depressing message of QAnon comes with hope, a community of fellow believers and a job to be done: to get to the truth and to help to take down the cabal. In a sense, QAnon believers were LARPing just as much as the people on the boards of 4chan ever were – it's just that this much larger latter group weren't even aware they were doing it.

Bringing the far-right and wellness gurus together

QAnon and its various offshoots built what at first glance looks like an incredibly unlikely coalition, bringing together extremely online teenagers, old school far-righters and also suburban mums and their health and wellness gurus.

QAnon managed the kind of coalition-building that most politicians can only dream of – but crucially, absolutely none of it was led by, orchestrated by or even really guided by the man behind the Q account. Once the ideas got into the informational bloodstream of the internet, they spread like wildfire.

Conspiracy theories tend to create the kinds of unlikely coalitions that surpass traditional politics. For different reasons, the far left and the far right were both likelier than those with mainstream politics to believe 9/11 was an inside job, for example.[17] A sizeable minority of people of all politics believe JFK wasn't killed by a lone wolf shooter. In a strange way, conspiracies can bring people together just as easily as they can pull them apart. QAnon brought together some incredibly disparate online communities. To see how it spread beyond the boundaries of 4chan, it's worth looking at these in turn.

One of the most obvious communities for the nascent QAnon movement was the existing US conspiracy community, a group very visibly led by Alex Jones of Infowars. Jones, who founded Infowars in 1999, is notorious for hosting a daily 'alternative news' show in which he often descends into furious tirades, his face turning beet-red as he screams into the audience's face.

On any given day, Infowars' home page may feature headlines like 'Global Bombshell! Eugenics Op Exposed: Hospitals Caught Mass Murdering Covid Patients with Lethal Injections', alongside a poll asking 'What False Flag Are the Globalists Most Likely to Unleash to Escalate War?'.[18]

Outside of the conspiratorial fringe, Jones is best known for accusing the parents of the twenty six- and seven-year-old children killed in the Sandy Hook Massacre of being agents of the deep state acting in a false flag operation, for which they (understandably) have taken him to court. The first of ten families secured damages of almost $50 million in a July 2022 ruling.[19] Later rulings brought the total payout due from Jones to the victims of his disinformation to $1.4 billion.

Lest anyone think that Jones is some small-time operator, financial documents released as part of that case and reported by the Huffington Post reveal that in the three years from 2015 to 2018, Infowars made more than $165 million in sales.[20] Jones' operation is particularly resilient as his money doesn't come from advertising. Instead he aggressively markets vitamin and other supplements at huge markups, including products such as iodine (useful against radiation exposure) to apocalyptic preppers.

Jones needs hours' worth of material every day to fill his show, and so generally hops on any conspiracy theory that moves, from chemtrails, to water fluoridisation, to the Catholic Church. He is not known for being discerning.

Naturally, QAnon was for Jones the gift that kept on giving. He could invite on QAnon influencers and supporters, sometimes keeping a little apparent distance from them and asking a seemingly sceptical question or two, but often not even bothering with that. Thanks to Jones, Q could break through to a very receptive audience. He gave it respectability in the conspiratorial world. Jones continued to give Q supporters a (relatively) friendly welcome until at least 2021.[21]

The connection between health and wellness and QAnon is perhaps a less obvious one than the road from being an Alex Jones viewer to a member of Q's resistance – but this was another well-trodden path.

On the surface, CrossFit – a branded high-intensity fitness programme that costs around $279 a month[22] – would sound like a practice for the elite or the establishment (and it generally is). But one of QAnon's most visible – and most obviously antisemitic – influencers was identified by VICE as a CrossFit trainer who also worked as a chiropractor in Denver.

The principles of chiropractic medicine are as hippie as they come.[23] It is based on the idea of a universal energy in all matter, which can allow the body to heal itself of many maladies. Though it is often confused with sports massage or physiotherapy, it is based firmly in spiritualism, and its effectiveness as a treatment for any condition, even back pain, is unproven.[24] This kind of spiritualism and universalism is not usually connected to far-right conspiracy theories, but according to VICE, Craig Longley of Denver was pushing just this sort of material.

Within weeks of the first Q drop, Longley was trying to recruit patients in his chiropractic clinic to the cause, with one saying Longley tried to 'redpill' her (a term from *The Matrix*, now used to mean waking people up to the supposed truth of QAnon and related conspiracies) after one session in November 2017, talking about Epstein, Obama and the Clintons as he did.

His online material was more extreme, including messages where he said he was looking forward to the USA having no Jews left by the time Trump left office, and referred to the 'Rothschild dynasty' as the 'synagogue of Satan'. He also filmed himself taking what had become the QAnon oath – the Congressional oath of office, followed by the trademark Q slogan 'Where we go one, we go all!'

Longley might be dismissed as an isolated case if there weren't numerous others. Modern wellness and alternative medicine is often predicated on the idea that Big Pharma – in cahoots with millions of doctors and medical professionals across the world – is deliberately conspiring to keep people sick, and to suppress cheap, effective therapies in the name of profits.

This creates a much larger overlap between the beliefs of movements like QAnon and the baseline of those deeply into wellness than might first appear. Both groups have a deep mistrust of 5G and the motivations of those rolling it out; they are likely to be suspicious of fluoride, might believe in chemtrails and more.[25]

Plus, there is the fundamental rule of conspiracy theories: once you believe thousands of people – in this case doctors – will conspire against the public on one thing, it's much, much easier to believe they will do so on another. If you believe the medical establishment is against you, why not the political establishment too? This pulls people into groups where the infamous 'globalist' and 'elite' dogwhistles are common – and may not be heard as such at first. While wellness fanatics and the far-right might not seem like natural bedfellows, it turned out to be eminently compatible.

Other eventual QAnon boosters came further from leftfield. Prior to 2016, Mike Lindell was pretty much the image of a self-made Bible Belt evangelical businessman. He had been addicted to gambling and drugs as a younger man, causing the collapse of his first marriage. He found God, was born again and founded MyPillow – a company selling, predictably enough, pillows.

The company grew from four employees to 1,500, making donations to Republican politicians and causes, as well as to Christian charities. It wasn't beyond reproach – like many companies that sell primarily through TV infomercials, it faced lawsuits over questionable buy-one-get-one-free promotions, and more seriously over spurious medical claims that the pillows could help prevent severe conditions such as multiple sclerosis and fibromyalgia.[26] These were later settled without any admission of liability on the part of MyPillow.

In 2016, though, Lindell became one of the early enthusiastic backers of Donald Trump for president – a double endorsement for Trump from a fellow businessman, but also from a prominent evangelical.

'Things started happening that never happen, and I knew they had to be God,' Lindell told students at the religious Liberty University, at a 1,200-person event at which he was presented an honorary doctorate. (In return he gifted every attendee a free pillow.)[27]

Trump, who used to operate the Miss World franchise, has had three wives and infamously boasted he could 'grab them [women] by the pussy',[28] was always an odd fit for the USA's evangelical movement – and so, in a strange way, the rise of QAnon and the acceptance of at least some of its ideas made him a better fit. If Christianity is full of anything, it's unlikely saviours standing for righteousness against apparently superior odds, and against established worldly interests.

Lindell – by now a regular fixture on Fox News and other Trump-boosting media – never became a particular follower of Q himself, but instead became one of the heroes of the movement, as one of the most fervent believers that Trump had been robbed of the 2020 election by a conspiracy – putting millions of dollars of his own money behind trying to prove this was the case.

His fervour for the cause would see him be sued by voting technology company Dominion for $1.3 billion,[29] and got MyPillow delisted from major stores around America.[30] Over that time, Lindell clearly became energised by ideas shared by the QAnon movement and its allies on how Trump might somehow be reinstated as president (despite there being no constitutional function to allow this), and was lionised by the movement at the time.

The affair culminated in an event hosted by Lindell where none other than Ron Watkins himself presented electoral records he claimed had been hacked from Mesa County, Colorado – a key district watched by followers.[31] Unsurprisingly, the records turned out to be nothing of the sort and Donald Trump was not returned as president.

Almost no group was entirely resistant to the lures of QAnon. Business execs, wellness gurus and devotees of traditional religion alike could find something to draw them into the ever-evolving movement. The algorithms that power the mainstream social networks on which QAnon was in this era flourishing only helped that motion. Once someone had watched one conspiratorial video, it would helpfully recommend more and more to them. Those doing their own research would find the algorithm serving as their frenetic research assistant, pushing material right in front of their faces.[32]

There is a bit of nuance needed here. Too often when the media talks about how YouTube can aid in radicalising people – whether towards Islamist extremism, the far right or conspiracy theories – it implies that one moment you can be watching videos of kittens falling off walls, and the next you're watching a video explaining the world is run by lizards.

A systemic piece of research carried out by academics at Dartmouth College suggests that this is hardly ever the case, representing fewer than 0.02 per cent of autoplay recommendations in their sample. What did happen, though, was that once someone watched a conspiratorial video – following a web link, an email or a recommendation from a friend – it would recommend them much more conspiracy content.

The researchers found that 80 per cent of all conspiratorial content seen during the study was watched by 0.6 per cent of participants. On one level, the algorithm in this instance is working well – once people get into conspiracies, they tend to get into them hard. On another, the algorithm is doing exactly what was feared: taking people likely to get sucked into QAnon and similar movements, and showing them lots of content that would do just that.[33]

When we think of QAnon as a grab-bag of some of history's most successful conspiracy theories, it becomes a lot easier to understand why it eventually caught on across the world – though as we'll come to see, the Covid-19 pandemic amped this up by orders of magnitude – and why its early boosters came to see it.

In the UK, one of the most visible backers of QAnon was John Mappin, who owns a hotel in Cornwall within Camelot Castle, which was built in the nineteenth century. (He claims it overlooks the original site of King Arthur's (mythical) home.) Mappin had been a prominent UK follower of Scientology for many years, but became a figurehead for the UK wing of QAnon after quite literally flying the QAnon flag over his castle hotel.[34]

Mappin also reportedly routinely left pro-Q material in hotel rooms for his guests – a bit of a change from the usual Gideons Bibles – as well as leaflets claiming he had invented a technology that could prevent war. Having avoided the Twitter ban which hit most QAnon accounts, Mappin continues to post pro-Trump, pro-Russia and Covid conspiracy content.

In that he is joined by the former LBC radio host Maajid Nawaz, who rejects the term 'conspiracy theorist' as applied to anyone. Nawaz is a self-admitted former Islamic extremist who went on to found Quilliam, a think tank focused on anti-extremism and deradicalisation – which for the first few years of its existence was funded by the UK government.[35]

As that think tank wound down, Nawaz pursued a career as a talk radio presenter for the UK's national station LBC, but raised alarms as he started to promote a series of seemingly separate but linked conspiracy theories. Nawaz would via social media push posts suggesting that Trump had been the victim of election fraud (while claiming to take no view on the issue), that Anthony Fauci was an investor in a biolab in Wuhan connected to Covid-19, and even that the Capitol riots of 6 January had been a false flag operation by Antifa.[36]

Not only could Nawaz serve as a respectable voice for such theories in the UK – thanks to his mainstream show on strictly regulated UK radio – but he was also something of an establishment figure, having set up a publicly funded think tank.

One final international example for the moment comes in the form of Attila Hildmann, a vegan chef in Germany who became the de facto leader of the QAnon movement in that country – another example of the wellness-to-conspiracy pipeline. In time Hildmann would come to describe himself as an 'ultra-right-winger' and say that the genocides of Adolf Hitler were a 'blessing' compared to those he believed Angela Merkel was planning.[37]

Patchily, and in fits and starts, QAnon was demonstrating that it could be just as virulent internationally as it had proven to be in the USA.

Social media – inaction, then bad action

With little more than the occasional exception, between 2017 and mid-2020, QAnon had free rein across all of the major social networks to spread its gospel, with very little in the way of pushback from either Big Tech or the mainstream media. With hindsight, this was a monumental mistake by the supposedly all-powerful and cabal-controlled media – but aside from a few dissenting voices, most people at the time thought this was the correct response. Without social media and mainstream outlets both failing to act, though, it's possible QAnon could never have taken off in the way that it did.

A large part of the dangerously misguided – but all too logical – reasoning for inaction among fact-checkers and journalists that cover fringe movements was based on the fact that it takes far less effort to make an outrageous false claim than it does to disprove it. As an example, it takes seconds for me to say that the pope secretly owns 70 per cent of McDonald's through secret intermediaries,[38] but someone looking to disprove the claim has to not just look up McDonald's shareholders, but also who in turn owns each of those shareholders, which could easily add up to several days of work.

Only large newsrooms have even one or two reporters assigned to tackling misinformation, and so they have to pick their targets very carefully. Anyone trying to fact-check the entire internet will find themselves quickly exhausted,[39] even leaving aside the question of whether providing accurate information debunking conspiracies stops anyone being drawn in.[40]

The other reason the mainstream kept away is that there is a significant backlash effect associated with major outlets covering niche conspiracy theories. This is best thought of by analogy with, for example, a TV show with 10 million viewers. If that show covers and debunks a conspiracy theory that 99 per cent of the audience has never heard of, and does it so well that 99 per cent of people fully accept the show's version of events, it still risks persuading 1 per cent of the audience to check that conspiracy out. In the case of that show, that would be around 99,000 potential new recruits.

As such, outlets wait until they are sure a conspiracy theory has a real hold on the popular imagination before covering it – but in the case of QAnon, because the theory sounded so outlandish, reporters and producers were caught off-guard by how widely it had spread, beginning to cover the phenomenon seriously only far too late (with some honourable exceptions).[41]

The reasons for social media's inaction over QAnon are a little more mercenary and politically complex. Social networks are competing for users and for attention. The longer someone is using a social network, the more advertising they can be shown, and the better the active user metrics look in quarterly reports to investors.[42] QAnon users might be questionable, and potentially a reputational risk, but they could also be extremely active and engaged. Of particular concern to any network that might act unilaterally would be those users migrating en masse to a rival, hampering its relative position.

But this was only one part of the calculus. As significant as the economic factors behind QAnon users were, they were vastly overshadowed by the politics. Every major global social network is based in the USA,[43] and so all are very sensitive to US laws, regulations and executive orders.

QAnon was hardly an apolitical movement: the overlap between QAnon believers and Trump supporters is huge, and the social ties between the two groups were significant – even before over the years the boundaries between Q and mainstream Republican thinking blurred almost to nothing.

To move against a large cohort of Trump supporters would be taken by the president as a deliberate political act – one to which he would certainly retaliate. Just as the networks were paralysed by indecision on whether or not to ban Trump himself,[44] they were facing this dilemma over banning his supporters, especially as Trump never disavowed the QAnon conspiracy theory (and later all but openly endorsed it).[45]

This years-long delay by the mainstream in facing up to QAnon had two effects. One was to let it spread unabated for three years, but another was to make sure that the hardcore followers of Q were well prepared when social networks finally took action and banned Q-related accounts – which the major networks did in succession in 2020. Twitter banned Q-related accounts in July, with Facebook and YouTube finally following suit in October.[46]

Because of the long run-up to action, QAnon supporters had mobilised and created a number of private groups, mostly on the social networking app Telegram. This had the effect of hiding much of the conversation on QAnon from view. The sense of being in a private community – and having faced censorship from the supposedly cabal-controlled internet companies – may have intensified the fervour with which the members of the Telegram group believed in the gospel of QAnon.

The shift to private groups also made measuring the size of QAnon's core support much harder. Gauging whether kicking the movement off major networks had been effective would rely on an almost impossible calculation. Was reducing the risk of new users encountering Q-related breadcrumbs worth the risk of radicalising those already down the rabbit hole?

Jordan Wildon, journalist and open-source intelligence (OSINT) researcher, made one of the first comprehensive efforts to actually judge the size of the core QAnon movement when it moved to Telegram in 2020.

'It was just like a big exodus where everyone then moved to Telegram … it picked up really quickly,' he says. 'QAnon, at least on Twitter, still exists if you know how to find it, but if it gets any real traction, it gets nuked pretty quickly.'

Wildon, working alongside his colleague Marc-André Argentino, wanted to create a number that was a conservative estimate of the lowest bound of QAnon accounts in Telegram groups. They started by culling down a list of possible groups to only include those which were definitely primarily or predominantly focused on QAnon, and found plenty across the world.

'We had the US. We had groups across Europe, including a number in the UK, and we had broader international groups,' Wildon recalled. 'Israel has a QAnon movement – that surprised me.'[47]

The figures produced by Wildon and Argentino are cautious: they found a total of around 2,000 groups with some reference to QAnon, but used only a core few dozen for their calculations. They found in July 2021 that across the groups there were at least

639,909 accounts that had posted at least once – ignoring those who might just be present reading but not posting – and that 227,797 of those were still active in the groups.[48]

This number might not sound large, but it should be taken to represent the absolute inner core of QAnon supporters – people who would spend often hours a day in private groups dissecting world events through the Q lens. To join a private messaging app and participate in it is a much more active thing than to occasionally watch a YouTube video or follow a Twitter account – and even months after Trump had left the White House, that core QAnon following numbered in the hundreds of thousands on Telegram alone.

Q's influence would be felt much more widely thanks to a new wave of adherents who had typically not even heard of QAnon, but the shift to Telegram also had human effects, especially for the families of those who were starting to follow Q. For many, the shift to Telegram marked the moment Q stopped being a sideshow causing some arguments and started to take over their loved ones' lives.

For this chapter, we've focused on the spread and scale of QAnon. Next, we'll look at what it's done to the people dragged into the movement, willing or otherwise.

5

Follow The White Rabbit

One typical feature of traditional cults is the requirement to cut off people who might pull you out of its grasp. Scientology does this with the concept of a 'suppressive person', a term coined by founder L. Ron Hubbard and defined as someone whose antisocial nature suppresses those around them and so must be avoided.[1]

Hubbard estimated that such people made up around 2.5 per cent of the population, but conveniently the church defines anyone who tries to talk a relative or loved one out of Scientology (or a former Scientologist who does the same) as suppressive, requiring the adherent to cut them out of their life entirely.

NXIVM – a sex cult which masqueraded as a multi-level marketing company – had a very similar system, leading to a prominent member cutting off her actress mother, only for the latter to wage a very public (and eventually successful) campaign to get her daughter back.[2]

Both of those movements have (or, in NXIVM's case, had) charismatic leaders who were making these demands, but QAnon soon developed much the same behaviour without anyone giving the orders. When people post about family, partners or housemates trying to make them leave the movement, the suggestion is inevitably raised – often kindly – that maybe they should stop talking to them, at least until they wake up to the truth.

Just as common, though, is loved ones outside of Q watching their relationships disintegrate, and becoming increasingly alarmed by the beliefs and even actions of their families. It is sufficiently common that in the course of my investigation I even started finding people whose family life was being threatened by QAnon almost entirely by accident. In the early stages of researching this chapter, I had mentioned to a couple of friends and acquaintances that I was looking for such families. To my surprise, someone I had mentioned it to delicately approached me away from others to say something unexpected: his mum was an increasingly obsessive QAnon devotee – and he didn't know what to do about it.

With his permission, I've put some of our conversation below, but he's asked not to be named so as not to risk further damaging his family relationship. I'm going to call him Mike – but that's not his real name.

Mike, his mum and her then-partner had been interested in alternative views – perhaps even conspiracies – for some time, almost as something of an idle pursuit. 'I remember we were watching this film in 2012,[3] my mum wanted to watch it and I had been at university, I'd been smoking a lot of weed and we sort of entertained more alternative views,' Mike recalls. 'I was starting to challenge and question things that I always took to be true, so I watched that film with them. And for a while, I definitely took on board quite a lot of the conspiracy theories in it – which I now look back on and think: you're a clown.'

In the years following that, Mike slowly drifted away from conspiracy theories as his mum got ever more into them, but without ever becoming all that political, he says, or it intruding all that much on their life – until the Covid-19 lockdowns began.

'I think it's been accelerated by lockdown. Mum has, for a few years now, been quite religiously following these really alternative blogs … a lot of it is sort of really abstract, about awakening, and pseudo-spiritual and pseudo-scientific stuff. I didn't realise she was in on all the Q stuff until this year, when I suddenly overheard Trump's voice coming from her room!'

Mike – who lives with his mum in the south of the UK – found she was spending almost all day following a Telegram group 'called Trump Patriots Group, or something like that'.

'She basically has totally disengaged from any mainstream news whatsoever,' he continues. 'She's so disengaged from mainstream media that in her mind, all of the information that's being shared there [on Telegram], regardless of how well known it is, is all really secretive and she's in on some sort of detective bureau of information that the rest of us aren't engaged with, which is obviously so dangerous.'

Demonstrating QAnon doesn't only divide families, but sometimes brings them together. Mike's mum had been estranged from her sister, who lives overseas, but they had been bonding again through a shared belief in QAnon through lockdown, sharing insights they had spotted or new mysteries on a daily basis. But the constant investigation of QAnon was coming to fill their days, aside from perhaps an hour or two watching television.

For Mike, a turning point – for the worse – with his mum came when QAnon was kicked off mainstream social networks.

'I think all of the efforts that have been done by big tech and by governments to try and tackle this basically poured more petrol on the fire,' he says. 'Mum's completely disengaged, and I don't think she will ever come back – the censorship's completely backfired, well intentioned though it was.'

Mike's mum had previously accessed QAnon mainly through Facebook and the open internet, until the ban. When that was introduced, she shifted to Telegram, which served to radicalise her and dramatically increase her engagement with QAnon, a phenomenon Mike fears could be widespread.

'It's like they are actually in a cult now,' he says. 'Before they had some cultish tendencies, but once you've been forced into these sort of little bubbles [on Telegram], there's kind of a quasi-cult there.'

What was worse was that the group treated almost anyone who didn't accept QAnon in the same way, whether it was someone they knew or a total stranger. 'If you denounce some of the things they say, they all say "They've been got to by the cabal." They treat people the same way that most cults do. It's a mess. I don't know how we fix this as a society. I think we're in a really potentially dangerous place if we don't get it right soon.'

Mike is left sharing a house with someone he loves, but can't hold down a simple conversation with. 'We can't even watch the news together,' he says. 'I mean, to her, it's like a triggering event. She just goes on a rant every time about you know, whatever, just connecting it as part of the global conspiracy … It's sad, because I feel like I don't see any way out. In the same way that I don't see a solution for the world, I don't see any way of getting my mother [out of this]. I've tried so many different things. I'm at the place now where I'm just realising there is nothing I can do.'

QAnon meets the elite

Mike's story is one that is repeated across hundreds of thousands – if not millions – of families around the world. QAnon has ended marriages, stopped parents seeing young children and had siblings (even twins) cut one another off.[4]

When families don't live together, separation is much easier. As we'll see later, though, an end of friendly relations is by no means the worst thing that can happen to those who are around people who fall into QAnon or a related movement.

The pace of growth of a Reddit community set up for relatives of QAnon followers to support one another, /r/QAnonCasualties, says something about the scale of the problem. The subreddit was set up in July 2019, and by June 2020 had 3,500 members. By October 2020, that had ballooned to 28,000.[5] By March 2022, it was 234,000.[6]

Posts on the forum – styled as a place to 'heal, deal and deprogram' – illuminate the daily lives of people whose lives have come to revolve around Q, often without them ever having believed in him. 'Qmom might lose medical license,' reads one.[7] Others include 'QAnon in Japan! I don't even know what to do here',[8] 'Cutting off without leaving',[9] and 'What does it feel like to have lost someone you care about to Q?' – posted by a former Q follower of eighteen months.[10]

With so many QAnon followers, and so many QAnon families across the world, it was all but inevitable that eventually the movement would come to claim some families with additional stresses and responsibilities.

Perhaps the most common reaction of relatives of Q followers who have tried to 'save' their loved one is a feeling of helplessness – a trait common across almost any interview with such relatives. But what happens to this feeling when the loved one in question is in a position of power or influence?

Families of QAnon followers in the military or police have good cause to worry on this front, as too have families of medical staff, as QAnon increasingly merged with the globalantivaxx and anti-Covid lockdown movements. Some families have had a level of concern even beyond that – what do you do if the conspiracist you love, or the conspiracist you're related to, has political power or connections?

Politically connected QAnon supporters are an obvious problem in the USA: President Trump, his advisor Mike Flynn and at least one sitting member of Congress have at least flirted with support for QAnon – but, despite what people might believe, it doesn't stop in America. This was the problem Karen Stewart, an accountant living near Canberra, New South Wales, unexpectedly found on her plate – what do you do when you discover your brother is the face of QAnon in Australia?[11]

Stewart had been seemingly happily living as a self-described 'boring accountant',[12] sitting on an industry body for the trade and volunteering on the board of a local charity supporting homeless people and survivors of domestic violence.[13] The story of how her Twitter biography also came to include 'Apparent enemy of the QAnon movement' begins a decade ago, long before the first Q drop.

Stewart says she had enjoyed a 'reasonably close' relationship with her brother Tim through childhood and early adulthood, saying he hadn't to her recollection been all that into conspiracy theories in that time. But in 2012, Tim went into bankruptcy, and as a qualified accountant, Karen took over his financial affairs.

'As part of that I realised the people that he'd been investing with were very, very odd,' she recalls, saying Tim had invested much of his money with one man who claimed to be an entrepreneur in numerous fields – but had no online presence she could find whatsoever.

'Then I found another guy that I thought was a con artist as well, and chased him up a little bit,' she says. 'So again, I began to realise that Tim believes some pretty weird things.'

'There was one about a secret banking system that only the Rothschilds had access to. So, if you give me $100,000, I'll give you back $100 million in two weeks – he almost got money out of my parents on that one. I had to step in. I caught that just the day before.'

From that point, in Karen's words, she and Tim 'began to clash a little bit'. Karen persuaded her parents to remove Tim as an executor (though not a beneficiary) of their will, because 'he's a crazy person,' while Tim continued down a conspiratorial rabbit hole – 'following the white rabbit', as QAnon fans (borrowing an idea from *The Matrix*, which in turn had borrowed it from *Alice in Wonderland*)[14] like to say.

Tim became a believer in the 'birther' conspiracy – the idea that Obama was secretly born in Kenya, rather than Hawaii, and so was ineligible to be president, a conspiracy heavily boosted by Donald Trump throughout Obama's presidency. As the 2016 election approached, Karen thought her brother would get behind Bernie Sanders as an anti-establishment candidate, only to find him supporting Trump.

Soon, he was volunteering strange ideas such as that Australia had, years before, been 'sold' to the USA – a trope quite common in QAnon circles and affecting multiple different countries.[15] Tim even, according to Karen, came to believe the David Icke theory that the Queen of England was secretly an alien lizard – and that there were pictures to prove it.

'He was in that really weird space. But believed he was capable of things that were ridiculous. He wanted to start a bank – and he was a bankrupt,' she said. 'And that was so frustrating, him just everyday ringing up wanting something. You know, "I want to do this", "I want to do that". And you just try to say to him: 'You can't do anything, you're bankrupt!" But even if someone was really giving you a gift of $250,000 – it wouldn't be a gift. No one does that …'

'He always had something weird enough going on that I had to say to him, "That's rubbish." And I think that's when he started to get annoyed. And now he's *so* annoyed. He doesn't talk to me any more, but that's fair enough.'

By 2017, Karen was worried enough about Tim's mental health that she had shared concerns with their parents, but things continued in a form of uneasy truce until around the middle of 2018, when Tim started to spout what Karen now knows to be QAnon theories – though she says 'It wasn't called QAnon then, there was just some Q guy.'

Things came to a head at her son's eighteenth birthday party. 'He was yelling at me saying, "You, you're so judgmental, you should love Trump and he's a good guy," she recalls. 'I represented, I guess, the left wing to him … he got really drunk and was screaming and carrying on, it was quite sad.'

At that same party, Karen realised Tim's son Jesse had also been deeply indoctrinated into QAnon and believed that there was a global satanic cabal. She also discovered Tim had been phoning their parents three to four times a week, each call lasting up to three hours, talking about Q and the cabal.

These clashes and Tim's descent down the Q rabbit hole came to alarm Karen and stir childhood fears that she had never previously discussed – making her worry that her brother might have a violent streak.

'I tell people he was a lovely brother,' she says. 'But when we were kids, he was not a lovely brother. Not all the time. Sometimes he was, but … he shot me with slug guns and hung Cabbage Patch dolls from nooses, you know, things that had a reasonably violent connotation, things that I would never tell mum because I was a bit scared of him.'

By the end of 2018, it was apparent to Karen that QAnon had claimed her brother entirely – he could talk about absolutely nothing else. 'I'd set my husband up [with him] but every time we tried to talk about movies or music he'd go, "No, no, Bruce Willis is a paedophile." "Tom Hanks is a paedophile." "I can't watch those movies." You know – "Green Day, paedophiles." '[16] Everyone was a paedophile so you couldn't have any conversation. And eventually my husband was just going, "SHUT UP!" And so, it didn't end pleasantly.'

Eventually, both Tim and Jesse told Karen's parents she had become an enemy.

'In the end, he goes, "Well, she's stopping my destiny. She's trying to stop me achieving my destiny." And so that was pretty hard. And his son also said a similar thing: "She's taking action against our movement, and so the gloves are off. She's become an enemy of QAnon." And I figured that was not a good position to be in.'

By this stage, though, Karen's concerns were not restricted to herself. She was particularly worried that Tim might exert an influence on some of his close friends. One friend in particular, in fact. Because in August 2018, Scott Morrison – the man Karen describes as Tim's best friend – had just become prime minister of Australia.

Karen's concerns continued to mount as she saw photos of Morrison and Tim together that appeared to be taken from official government buildings, and witnessed Tim start to build up a bigger online following of his own, hitting around 30,000 on Twitter. 'There are standards that we have to have in Australia,' she noted. 'We are a bit Hicksville, but still, it's really getting to a point where QAnon have a lot of power, via Tim.'

If you're a signed-up conspiracy theorist and you're good friends with the prime minister, this raises the question of why you would not simply ask them to launch an investigation into the abuse you believe is going on – or at least ask them if it is true. This is especially pronounced for QAnon, whose core belief was that the US president was on their side and ready to fight the cabal.

This resulted in lots of elaborate theories: Trump did not yet know who he could trust, and knew that the official channels (such as the FBI and the judiciary) could not be trusted to handle the situation. Scott Morrison might be too new in government to really know what was going on, or who could be trusted.

Part of conspiratorial reasoning is working to come up with alternatives to the obvious explanations. None of that, of course, addresses what goes on in Donald Trump's head – he must surely know he isn't leading a crusade against a satanic ring, but he has always seemed happy to exploit the fact the people believe that if it benefits him. He also seems to think there's a deep state acting against him – when he complains about FBI raids and his 2020 defeat,[17] he seems to believe his own spin. But who can ever know?

Jumping back to Karen Stewart in Australia, though, her brother's new close connections to the prime minister had persuaded her to go public. She started by connecting with journalists (first *Guardian Australia*, then Crikey) and politicians to get questions asked about Morrison's connection with the Stewarts.

One glaring thing that stood out for Karen was that early in Morrison's premiership, a long-running royal commission on child sexual abuse had recently reported after nearly five years,[18] and the prime minister had agreed to give an apology on behalf of the Australian authorities for years of failings in the area. But Morrison's apology included an odd phrase. Among the other things he mentioned, the prime minister referenced 'ritual child abuse', a core piece of QAnon phrasing not used in the royal commission review.

'I sort of thought, that's pretty weird,' Karen says. 'And then on my mobile phone was my nephew, Jesse, saying, "Did you hear that? Did you hear that? That's the first time an Australian prime minister has used the phrase 'ritual sexual abuse'." '

'I realised that that was QAnon – they got that in there. Mum had known for two weeks before that, that was the term Tim was trying to get into the speech. And he did. That's when I just went, "This is too much now." '

Morrison later denied backing QAnon in any way, but also criticised those trying to 'cancel' Tim. Morrison also denied his phrasing had the meaning suggested by the Stewarts. After this moment, Karen stepped up her campaign with Australian journalists and politicians, but Tim and especially Jesse retaliated, primarily with online abuse, harassment and threats, in an escalating, running conflict. Eventually it hit what must once have seemed like an unimaginable point: Karen's family reported their own relatives to the authorities.

Karen's other brother reported Jesse – largely because of his erratic Twitter presence and threats – to national security and New South Wales Police. But Karen felt that concerns about Tim needed to be raised at a higher level, so got in touch with Malcolm Turnbull, Scott Morrison's predecessor as prime minister.

'He said: "Okay –you need to get some media focus on this." And then he said, "I'm going to forward on these details to the director general of ASIO [Australian Security and Intelligence Operations]," which is our spy agency.'

The Stewart family's concerns were eventually turned into an hour-long documentary on ABC,[19] Australia's national broadcaster. It was roundly rubbished ahead of broadcast by Scott Morrison,[20] thanks to what Karen believes was a planted question at a press conference. Morrison dismissed the documentary as "pretty ordinary" and denied any association with or support for QAnon, though he did resist a Freedom of Information request from the *Guardian* to release his correspondence with the Stewarts.

Tim's wife left the employ of Morrison in late 2020, though Karen believes the families are still close friends.

'I was terrified the day it was due to go to air,' Karen says, daunted by going against a sitting prime minister. 'I actually phoned Malcolm Turnbull, and I said … can he hurt me? What powers does he have?

'He said: "Karen, we live in a country where someone like you can speak truth to power. Whatever happens, he can't undo the past. Clearly, he has a relationship with your brother. He can't change that. And that's what you're coming out to say." '

The ordeal has taken its toll on the family, especially on Karen's parents. But she still believes it was her duty to warn the authorities and the public about the danger posed by her brother and her nephew.

'It was so hard on Dad. He wept on several occasions,' she says. 'He's really, really found this hard. He just said: "Look, this is this boy that made me a father. He was my firstborn." He really struggled with it a lot, probably more so than my mum, who was a bit stoic.'

It was ultimately a conversation with her husband Shannon that convinced Karen and her family to take the drastic action that they did, although Tim Stewart told Four Corners he did not promote or support any form of violence.

'Let's say that there was an attack, a terrorist attack,' they had mused together. 'And Tim and Jesse were part of that. I imagined I was answering questions from a journalist or something, and they were asking, "Were there any signs of this?" I would have to say yes – I would have to answer yes, there were millions of signs ...'

'It was then that we had to ask ... where does our civic duty lie?'

The QAnon ascendency

There is little evidence of Tim Stewart having altered Scott Morrison's views or actions to a great extent, but when we look at the US under Donald J. Trump, it is a very different story. Not only did multiple key political figures either sincerely believe in Q, or else happily appear as if they did, but their involvement in QAnon appeared to influence their actions.

It had appeared to infiltrate members of the elite Republican establishment as well as new insurrectionist candidates. Perhaps the most visible political face of QAnon is Marjorie Taylor Greene, who became a Congressional candidate and eventually representative for the fourteenth district of Georgia while running on a QAnon ticket. Greene, generally referred to by the initialism MTG, occasionally disavows elements of the conspiracy, but her litany of public comments and writings speaks otherwise.

MTG in 2018 wrote that Californian wildfires had been deliberately started by a 'Jewish space laser'.[21] She rejected evidence that the email leaks that helped Trump win the 2016 election were the result of Russian hacking, instead claiming they had come from a Democratic whistleblower, Seth Rich – a man who was murdered in DC in 2016 – claiming Obama had been behind the killing.[22] Greene also pushed the Pizzagate conspiracy, shared Q posts and videos on social media, and called Q a 'patriot'.[23]

MTG was not alone in running for office while at least flirting with QAnon. Lauren Boebert, now the Representative for Colorado's third district, hasn't publicly gone so far down the rabbit hole as her Republican colleague, but has appeared on Q-supporting channels, said she is 'very aware' of the movement, and suggested she ascribes to at least some of its beliefs.[24]

Candidates are, if anything, getting more obvious. In 2020, most QAnon-linked candidates would hedge their bets when asked if they believed in the movement, cautious not to lose votes. For the 2022 elections, one candidate for Iowa's House of Representatives filed his election paperwork to the state's Secretary of State wearing a QAnon t-shirt. The Secretary went on to post the photo to his official page.[25]

In reality, though, when it comes to DC politics, most members of the House of Representatives are pretty low down the food chain. Unless they sit on particularly influential committees – and MTG was stripped of all of her committee assignments in a rare moment of bipartisan action[26] – then a congress member is just one voice among 435.

Presidential advisors are a different matter. They can take action in their own right, and they can influence the holder of what is still the world's most powerful political office (for now). And Trump was surrounded by people willing to at least flirt with QAnon or related ideas. Sometimes this could be subtle – such as when then-counsellor to the president Kellyanne Conway invented 'alternative facts'[27] – but often it was blatant.

Mike Flynn, for example, spent 33 years serving in the US military, retiring in 2014 at the rank of lieutenant-general (better known as a three-star general, the second-highest rank commonly awarded in the US military). In his last years of service, Flynn acted as director of the Defense Intelligence Agency.

In the first days of the Trump administration, Flynn was appointed to one of the most sensitive intelligence roles in the USA: National Security Advisor – a role in which he lasted only 22 days, after it emerged he had been engaged in backchannel communications with Russia during the presidential transition, and then misled the vice president and others about it.[28] Despite these apparently impeccable military and intelligence credentials, Flynn was filmed on 4 July 2020 reciting the QAnon oath of allegiance, alongside adding the #TakeTheOath hashtag to his (subsequently banned) Twitter account.[29]

The move was not so much a dogwhistle as an airhorn. Flynn had told the QAnon movement he was on their side. Flynn, alongside Trump lawyer and fellow QAnon supporter Sidney Powell, would later become an instrumental figure in Trump's effort to overturn the legitimate results of the 2020 election.[30]

Powell claimed on television in November 2020 that she and the president had a 'kraken' – a huge dossier of evidence that would prove widespread voter fraud and that Trump had won the election. This claim was in line with a QAnon theory that Trump had set up a sting operation with watermarked ballots in a dozen or more states.[31]

#ReleaseTheKraken became a common QAnon-linked conspiracy hashtag. Needless to say, no actual evidence of voter fraud ever materialised,[32] even in the few recounts that were conducted.[33]

Despite that, Flynn and Powell were willing to drive US democracy to the very brink to defend their claims. In what began as an impromptu Oval Office meeting, according to media reports, but quickly descended into a series of shouting matches, the pair suggested the president could invoke martial law as part of his efforts to resist being removed from office – an idea the Commander in Chief's White House Counsel and Chief of Staff had to go all out to oppose.[34]

Trump himself has, of course, occasionally seemed to flirt with QAnon-related ideas in his public speeches, though it is rarely clear how much the famously technophobic president actually understands about the group,[35] and how much is just an aide or one of his sons suggesting a key phrase or two.

Perhaps more alarming for the long term is a series of text messages from Ginni Thomas, the wife of Supreme Court Justice Clarence Thomas, published in March 2022 – which seem to show that Thomas not only believes the QAnon lines on the election, but used them to try to encourage the White House Chief of

Staff to overturn its result. Clarence Thomas declined to recuse himself from cases relating to the 2020 election, despite his wife's activities.[36]

Supporters of QAnon – especially those in America – could see visible public figures, whether celebrities, generals or politicians, all appearing to endorse one of the most sweeping and dangerous conspiracy theories in history. QAnon suggests that not only are our elections rigged, our central banks a con and a secretive world order in charge of it all, but that this world order is satanic and involved in child rape and murder.

Inevitably, that could only roll over into violence, whether on an individual scale, through riots and direct action, or on a scale far larger than that. Our next chapter examines the real-world dangers posed by a digital virus that no one noticed until people started dying.

6

The Storm

It was clear that extreme online movements could mobilise people into committing real-world acts of violence long before the emergence of QAnon. Cyber stalkers have tracked down their victims offline and killed them,[1] while arguments in online games have provoked people to murder – in one case, taking a 3,000-mile round trip to murder a teenage Twitch streamer.[2]

The spawning grounds of the QAnon movement – the 4chan and 8chan boards – had been tied to grave violence before, too. One notorious case in 2014 saw thirty-three-year-old David Kalac murder his thirty-year-old live-in girlfriend. Before the murder was discovered, Kalac had posted pictures of his victim's corpse to 4chan with the caption: 'Turns out it's way harder to strangle someone to death than it looks on the movies.'

Kalac appeared to reply in the same thread to commentators who suggested the photo had been faked. 'Check the news for Port Orchard, Washington, in a few hours,' he wrote. 'Her son will be home from school soon. He'll find her, then call the cops. I just wanted to share the pics before they find me.'[3]

As the Pizzagate-connected raid on Washington's Comet Ping Pong showed, QAnon's direct antecedents had an ability to mobilise and radicalise people into real-world violence. But as QAnon stepped up both in scale and ferocity, the drip-drip of incidents soon became a trickle, and in time a storm – a fitting enough term for the escalation, given QAnon as a movement would often refer to 'the coming storm' as a shorthand for the rebellion against the supposed cabal.

The first major QAnon-related incident would come long before most people had heard of the movement – and before most of the media was paying it any attention. On 15 June 2018, thirty-year-old Matthew Wright drove an armoured truck onto the Mike O'Callaghan–Pat Tillman Memorial Bridge,[4] which connects Nevada to neighbouring Arizona.[5]

The bridge also happens to be one of the most tightly secured publicly accessible areas in America, heavily patrolled by US Federal Agents and with strict access controls nearby. That's because it passes incredibly near to, and overlooks, the 726-foot Hoover Dam – America's largest – a curved wall of concrete embedded into the canyon's granite walls.[6]

The dam has topped America's security concerns since at least World War II. Taking it out would not just risk dumping four years' worth of water all at once onto the people downstream, but would also take out a significant chunk of power for multiple states, including California.[7] As a result, any incident near the Hoover Dam is automatically considered serious.

Wright used his armoured vehicle to block the middle of the bridge, leading to a ninety-minute standoff with federal authorities and the closure of multiple roads for a significant area around him. In the window of the truck, Wright placed a crudely handwritten note: 'RELEASE The OIG Report'.[8] OIG stands for Office of the Inspector General, a name used for multiple units within different federal agencies responsible for investigating internal waste, mismanagement, fraud or other issues. As there isn't just one OIG and each investigates multiple issues at a time, the request might initially seem a vague one.

But in QAnon circles at the time, *the* OIG report was a report by the Justice Department's OIG, which had been investigating the FBI's conduct in relation to the 2016 presidential election. This had been published that month – June 2018.[9]

QAnon, though, still guided by the actual Q account itself at that time, was convinced there was a second, secret report that contained all of the dirt on the FBI, the Clintons, the Obamas and others that they had been promised. Wright's armed stand-off – he had two rifles, two handguns and 900 rounds of ammo in his vehicle – was directed at Donald Trump.

A video apparently recorded in the truck's cab and posted by the far-right influencer (and two-time failed Republican congressional candidate) Laura Loomer included his demand:

> 'No more lies. No more bullshit. We the people demand full disclosure. We elected you to do a duty,' the man continues, apparently addressing President Trump. 'You said you were going to lock certain people up when you were elected. You have yet to do that.'[10]

Wright closed his video address with QAnon's most famous slogan: 'Where We Go One, We Go All'.[11]

Like the Comet Ping Pong incident, Wright's intervention served more as a warning than as the start of deadly action. After a stand-off of around ninety minutes, Wright attempted to escape the area, and was eventually apprehended by police. In February 2020, Wright pleaded guilty to terrorism-related charges,[12] and was sentenced in January 2021 to seven years and nine months in prison.[13] Worse was to come.

***

In the years between the genesis of QAnon and Q's eventual disappearance a few days after the 6 January attack on the US Capitol Building there were essentially two tracks of QAnon. The first was a broad movement, a mix of all ages and likely majority women,[14] who accessed QAnon influencers through major mainstream social networks like YouTube, Facebook and QAnon. Only a hardened and much smaller cadre actually hung out on 4chan and 8chan, the boards where Q actually posted. This group was younger, overwhelmingly male and far more influenced by the traditional tropes of the online far right.

These movements, as previous chapters discussed, were often also fuelled by isolation and loneliness – which often manifested itself as a violent hatred towards women who were rejecting these men. This was inherent to Gamergate, often manifested within QAnon and was the core focus of a different but overlapping movement also born on those boards – the incel community. The term 'incel', short for 'involuntarily celibate', originated on a website in the 1990s run by a student known only as Alana, who was coming to terms with her bisexuality and lack of a partner.[15]

That supportive online community was eventually supplanted by an increasingly bitter and ideological anti-woman movement which used chan sites as a home. Though this wasn't intrinsically a part of QAnon, it was one of many adjuncts which had a considerable overlap in membership and often in ideology – and in its members' propensity to violence. Between 2018 and 2020, this web of related movements – Gamergate, the alt-right, QAnon and the incel movement – spawned an increasing number of violent attacks, primarily in the US but then across the world.

The threat this book is warning about is one of social contagion – of corners of the internet turning into spawning grounds for dangerous ideas, which then intermingle, merge and spread into the wider world. As such, looking at any one incident and trying to tie it to solely the incel movement, the online far right or the core of QAnon is to misunderstand the nature of the threat each poses.

Individuals are often members of multiple groupings, while the ideologies of each of the movements overlap. As they mix – particularly on Telegram and the chan sites – they pick up elements of each others' characteristics, such as the propensity for violence. Where once posting a threat to 4chan would likely be a hoax and end with no one getting hurt, they had become all too real.

That interlaced threat, and how the different movements seem to have radicalised people to action, became undeniable in this period – an intensifying drumbeat of violence that we are yet to find a way to silence.

Nine months after the Hoover Dam siege, twenty-four-year-old Staten Island resident Anthony Comello came to believe a local crime boss was an agent of the cabal and believed his arrest or execution would be sanctioned by President Trump, who would ensure he would not be punished for the crime. Comello said he had intended to arrest his victim, but instead fatally shot him in the street. Comello had, a month before, tried to similarly arrest prominent democrats – including House Justice committee chair Adam Schiff.[16] In 2020, Comello was found to be mentally unfit to stand trial.

In 2019, thirty-seven-year-old Jessica Prim started live-streaming a journey from Illinois to New York, telling those watching that she had brought along one dozen knives and intended to 'take out' Joe Biden. During her livestream, Prim referenced a notorious rumoured video supposedly showing Hillary Clinton and her close aide Huma Abedin ritually murdering a child, wearing its face as a mask and drinking its blood (the original blood libel once again).[17]

The video does not exist and has never existed – it is not a deepfake or some other bit of trickery. Instead, it is something that QAnon followers believe was found when FBI agents raided the home of Anthony Weiner (who was then Abedin's husband) in 2020. They insist this video was found by FBI agents and saved under the codename 'Frazzledrip'. No amount of fact-checking or official denials has persuaded conspirators that it doesn't exist.[18]

Alongside this, Prim had posted a semi-coherent message as she drove: 'Hillary Clinton and her assistant, Joe Biden and Tony Podesta need to be taken out in the name of Babylon [generally a reference akin to invoking Christ]! I can't be set free without them gone. Wake me up!!!!!'

Prim was eventually detained by police and taken to Mount Sinai West for treatment, and was later charged with eighteen counts of criminal possession of a weapon.

Another QAnon believer, Floridian Neely Petrie-Blanchard, was arrested on the accusation she had shot dead her own lawyer, fifty-year-old Christopher Hallett (himself a conspiracy theorist), in November 2020, after becoming convinced he was involved in the deep state's conspiracy to separate her from her two children, who had been placed in their grandmother's custody (Petrie-Blanchard was facing kidnapping charges after trying to take them from her home).[19]

Perhaps the most dramatic, though not the most deadly, US incident in this era came in the early morning of Christmas Day 2020. An RV (a motorhome to Brits) had been parked outside an AT&T building since shortly after midnight. At 5:30 a.m., there was a loud sound of gunfire (actually played through live speakers in the van) followed by loud warnings to evacuate the area.

One hour later, as a police bomb squad was on the way and officers were helping clear the area, the van – after playing the 1964 classic song 'Downtown' – detonated in a huge explosion, injuring eight people.

The only fatality was the occupant of the van, sixty-three-year-old Anthony Quinn Warner. Warner was a lifelong conspiracy theorist with many QAnon-related beliefs – an undercover cabal running the world, using 5G as a tool (hence AT&T), and more,[20] though it is disputed how much he followed that particular movement.[21]

A 2021 study by the US National Consortium for the Study of Terrorism and Responses to Terrorism (START) found at least seventy-nine QAnon-related offenders – and discovered that they did not resemble the perpetrators of more 'traditional' forms of terror. The average age of the offenders was forty-three, while more than a quarter were women. Thirty-two of the seventy-nine were married, and forty-two were parents.[22] This is a stark contrast from more 'traditional' terror arrests. In the UK in 2021, 94 per cent of arrests were of men, and more than half under thirty. Actual perpetrators of major attacks trended even younger, and exclusively male.[23]

A further START study that same year found more than 100 QAnon-related offenders,[24] and warned that traditional counter-terror approaches would be unlikely to work for this issue, especially as it was believers' loved ones who were most at risk.

While QAnon presents a danger, it is not a traditional terrorist threat. QAnon offenders have not displayed the motivation or capabilities required to successfully carry out terrorist attacks. Rather, QAnon adherents have been primarily motivated to commit acts of interpersonal violence, often targeting those around them, including their own children …

QAnon crimes have been committed by a significant number of women, as well as individuals struggling with mental health concerns, substance use disorders, and family disruptions. Traditional counterterrorism strategies are not designed to mitigate threats of violence that are primarily found in the household. We argue that a public health response based on violence prevention and support services would be a more effective strategy for countering the conspiracy theory.

Violence relating to these movements did not remain confined to the borders of the US. The perpetrator of the 2019 Christchurch mosque shootings in New Zealand (which killed fifty-one people attending two different mosques) was an 8chan regular, though regarded YouTube as a bigger 'inspiration' for his actions.[25] But while Christchurch is the most deadly and traumatic of the international incidents connected to the movements to date, it was far from the only one.

In February 2020, a seventeen-year-old armed with a machete entered a massage parlour in Toronto, Canada.[26] After a frenzied few minutes, twenty-four-year-old Ashley Noell Arzaga – described as an 'outgoing, positive ... genuinely good young woman' and the 'loving mother' of a five-year-old daughter – was dead inside the building, with two more people injured outside, lying near the dropped machete.[27]

Three months later, Canadian authorities added terror charges to the murder and attempted murder charges already laid against the seventeen-year-old, citing that it was a terrorist act connected to the 'movement commonly known as INCEL', making it the first such attack to be formally connected to the movement.[28]

It was not to be the last. In the UK, twenty-two-year-old Jake Davison shot and killed his fifty-one-year-old mother in her home before then killing four others – including a three-year-old girl – and injuring two more, finally turning the gun on himself. The attack was the first mass shooting in the UK – where firearms are very strictly controlled – in more than a decade, and used a gun for which Davison had a legal licence, despite his having a history of mental health problems and having been previously stripped of his gun licence after assault allegations.[29]

UK police initially treated the attack as a 'domestic incident' that had spilled into the streets, but evidence soon emerged revealing Davison was an active member of the incel community, posting videos to YouTube full of misogynistic and homophobic content. Posts also surfaced on Reddit showing Davison making numerous derogatory comments about his mother,[30] eventually leading to calls for the incident to be treated as a terrorist attack.[31]

In different ways, the core QAnon ideology was spreading and spawning extreme action in countries across the world. Lola Montemaggi was found hiding in an abandoned music-box factory in a small Swiss town. She had become convinced that France's child social services were part of an international child abuse plot and that she should be given custody of her eight-year-old daughter, who lived with her grandparents. With help from multiple QAnon supporters – some of whom travelled across the border from France with her – she sparked an international kidnapping hunt before she and her child were found safe.[32]

Other cases ended tragically. Matthew Taylor Coleman, a forty-year-old father of two, crossed the US border to Mexico with his children before allegedly killing them with a spear-fishing gun. While Coleman has pleaded not guilty, according to a criminal complaint filed in US court, he had come to believe the QAnon movement needed him to do that, as his wife was using them for satanic purposes – and this was the only way to 'save the world'.[33]

In Germany, QAnon has manifested a huge following in the hundreds of thousands of people pulled largely from the ranks of its existing far-right and neo-Nazi movements, already known for their propensity for violent gatherings.[34] In a moment with chilling historic echoes, a gathering of 38,000 people in Berlin, led by some prominent German QAnon influencers, attempted to storm the parliamentary building,[35] a disconcerting echo of the 1933 burning of the Reichstag.

None of these incidents can be laid solely at the door of 4chan, 8chan or any of the movements they spawned. Each is tied to the individual circumstances of the perpetrator's lives, their mental health, their ability to access healthcare and their underlying propensity for violence and extremism. Yet these movements have undoubtedly served as a catalyst, unleashing demons on a global scale. And they all pale into significance compared to some of what was to come – not least the infamous assault on the US Capitol.

Believing in the (impossibly) bleak

Before we get to the actual events of 6/1 – and the weeks leading up to it – we should take a brief step back to look at two contributing factors to why and how QAnon and its related movements were so able to mobilise people.

The first of these is psychological. It is a thesis presented by *Atlantic* writer and US Naval War College professor Tom Nichols, who set out to answer the question of why people would find themselves drawn to something like QAnon given the absolutely awful implications for society if it were true.[36] After all, if QAnon as a movement is even half right, the world is run – and always has been – by a collective of thousands of people who are willingly sacrificing and/or raping children, and who are engaged in malign population control in order to continue their rule. Whether it is murder, nuclear weapons, natural disasters or more, most of it comes from this elite, who have virtually no opposition.

Nichols has a different answer to those offered by others to the perennial question raised by QAnon: why would people want to believe something so horrifying? For him, the answer comes from looking at Cold War-era cults, which anticipated imminent nuclear war and centred around making plans for what would happen afterwards. These obviously involved immense suffering – the deaths of much (if not most) of society during the initial attacks, hardships from fallout and nuclear winter, and so on.

But people also imagined different societies afterwards: such as a romanticised return to their vision of hunter-gathering, with everyone knowing their place. Or they could picture a world in which alpha males (like them?) could have easy access to women – it being everyone's duty to repopulate humanity. Once the suffering was past, people could be heroes of their own story. Plus, they could be the ones in charge, instead of the current idiots, who were going to lead us into nuclear war.

QAnon in this framing becomes essentially a post-watershed version of *Star Wars* – a small resistance fighting against a much more powerful force, potentially with a tiny number of allies on the inside giving them the information they need to resist. The only problem is that if you keep expecting the results of that resistance to materialise and it does not, then you need to do something. It is hard to be a hero, even in your own mind, if all you do is sit at home and wait for something good to happen.

The second issue is quite how easy it was to access QAnon information before 6 January 2021 – and how slight the transition was between so-called mainstream Republican opinion and talking points and outright conspiracy. Joe Biden had won the popular vote in the 2020 election and had comfortably won the electoral college.[37] Despite this, the president, many of his advisors and many Republican politicians were happy to suggest there had been widespread and major voter fraud on a scale which would have involved thousands of conspirators – and thousands more to cover up the huge amounts of evidence. And it is a golden rule of conspiracy theories that once you firmly believe in one, you are far more open to others.

Facebook and other sites for years made no major effort to ban either QAnon or election fraud claims from its network, though it and Twitter made some efforts to work with fact-checkers to restrict circulation of the latter.[38] QAnon had (with some inadvertent help from the mainstream) evolved to make itself irresistible to all sorts of different groups through the US and world population. Facebook and co. had helped make sure people would keep getting exposed to it.

What's more, Facebook knew that its own algorithms contributed to people's radicalisation – and then took barely any action until after the insurrection. As the *Wall Street Journal* reported in 2021, based on documents from Facebook whistleblower Frances Haugen, a Facebook staffer created a profile for 'Carol Smith', purportedly 'a politically conservative mother from Wilmington, North Carolina'.[39] Smith's account, set up as part of an internal research project, followed Donald Trump and Fox News, as well as highlighting interests in 'politics, parenting and Christianity'.

Within two days, Facebook's algorithm was suggesting 'Carol' join multiple Facebook groups connected to the QAnon conspiracy. Even though the account did not join those groups, content from them kept being pushed its way. The *Wall Street Journal* concluded: 'Within one week, Smith's feed was full of groups and pages that had violated Facebook's own rules, including those against hate speech and disinformation.'

By January 2021, a conspiracy theory born in 2017 and allowed to grow through the neglect of social media giants and the inattention of the political and media mainstreams, suddenly aligned with a president's desperate bit to stay in office. This is what happened next.

Making an insurrection

The sixth of January 2021 should have been a boring day in US politics.[40] It is two weeks before the inauguration, the peaceful and seamless transition of power between one elected president and the next. Around this time, the Twelfth Amendment of the US constitution requires the vice president, in his[41] role as president of the Senate, which goes with the job, to preside over the certification of the election results by Congress.[42] This is a ceremonial role and is granted no actual powers to scrutinise the results, which have already been ratified by electoral officials.

But backed by some of his advisors, the most fanatical members of his base and a large quorum of QAnon supporters, President Donald Trump had come to focus on 6 January as his best chance to stay in power – having scrambled through various options, including legal challenges, all of which had amounted to nothing.

As Pence was overseeing the count, he argued, it was well within his power – in fact it was his job – to refuse to confirm the count, because of all of the supposed fraud. In some versions of events, this lack of certification would merely delay the inauguration until a fresh count was done. In others, Republicans would simply declare Trump the winner by fiat and have him serve another term.

Trump therefore started a consistent campaign – via social media, TV interviews and rallies – to whip up crowds to a frenzy in a bid to force Mike Pence to do the 'right' thing. Trump's eventual last roll of the dice was a lunchtime rally by the White House for some 30,000 or so hardcore supporters. For many days ahead of time, extreme groups of the alt-right and QAnon had planned to turn it into something bigger.

Trump spoke for around an hour, condemning his vice president repeatedly, including by name, and urging the crowd to march on the Capitol Building – even claiming that he would be walking with them. Testimony to Congress later revealed that Trump had tried to arrange to join the march on the Capitol in the days leading up to the event. He was even alleged to have grabbed the steering wheel of his presidential car in an attempt to drive himself there.[43]

It is worth taking a moment to reflect here: it is only thanks to the security concerns of the Secret Service that when a violent mob invaded the US Capitol the president wasn't on site at the time. It is just one of hundreds of ways that 6 January, awful as it was, came within inches of disaster on a much larger scale.

Capitol security was hopelessly outmatched, with no National Guard or similar support called up as support ahead of the riot – again, a result of the president's open support for the crowd at his own rally.[44] Given their huge advantage in numbers, and the obvious presence of weaponry among the throng, the crowd quickly busted through three separate layers of security barriers and raided the building.

Once inside, many of the people in the Capitol seemed bemused and surprised by their success – merely aimlessly wandering around the building, perhaps wondering how, if the US was run by such an all-encompassing conspiracy they had got to the seat of power so easily. Some eventually burst into the Senate Chamber, but police had succeeded in delaying them until it had been evacuated. The vice president was moved to a secure panic room, while Congressional staffers hid in locked offices.

Some rioters went looking for key hate figures, such as Nancy Pelosi. Some of them were well prepared with weapons and cable ties to serve as handcuffs. Pipe bombs were found at both the Democratic and Republican National Committee headquarters, the DNC device located just metres from where vice president-elect Kamala Harris had passed hours before.[45]

As the dust settled on the day, five people were dead and at least 138 police officers were injured, while dozens more officers appear to have caught Covid-19 as a result of the day's activities.[46] In the weeks and months following the carnage, more than 800 people were charged with offences in connection to the insurrection.[47] The political shock to the USA's system was more seismic still, with subsequent inquiries revealing just how close some key figures came to peril,[48] and just how grave a threat to functional US democracy the day had been.[49]

A demonstration held by a sitting president against his own vice president had ended with a violent assault on the Capitol Building and multiple people dead. The president appeared to have used followers of what elite opinion had dismissed as a niche conspiracy theory in a bid to, in effect, overthrow his own government.

The relationship between Trump and QAnon had become symbiotic, with the president seemingly influenced by QAnon beliefs on one hand, but on the other also able to use the followers and their alienation to his own advantage. Lauren Boebert, the occasionally Q-supporting Republican congresswoman for Colorado, seemed a big fan of the insurrection on the day, tweeting first that 'today is 1776' (the year the American Revolution began) before giving live updates on the location of Nancy Pelosi – one of the armed mob's top targets.[50]

More than a year after the insurrection proper, Trump's own conduct on 6 January faced renewed scrutiny after investigators found a mysterious seven-hour gap in his phone records on the day, leading some to conclude the president was using a 'burner phone', a term for a throwaway temporary mobile phone used to avoid scrutiny and tracing.[51]

Trump came out soon afterwards claiming he'd never even heard the term 'burner phone', despite his having used it three times in a recent lawsuit against his niece, and despite the FBI finding sixteen phones when they searched Trump's personal lawyer Michael Cohen's properties, and a further eighteen when they did the same to former New York City mayor and Trump legal advisor Rudy Giuliani.[52]

The idea put forth by the Trump team – that he had intended a peaceful protest with non-violent supporters, which was then, without any foreknowledge from him, hijacked by extremists – becomes even harder to buy in these circumstances. But there is more that makes it still more difficult to believe.

In July 2021, Democrats on the Oversight Committee released handwritten notes taken by senior Department of Justice officials who met with Trump on 27 December 2020, shortly before the Capitol riots. The note showed Trump was clearly trying to push the DoJ into action – but also revealed where he was getting his information.

'Just say the election was corrupt and leave the rest to me and the R, Congressmen,' the notes record the president as saying. 'You guys may not be following the internet the way I do.'[53]

That combination of extreme insiders and extreme outsiders came to a head in more dramatic ways on the day of the insurrection. Charging documents for one of the alleged rioters – Thomas Caldwell – showed a series of texts through the day from an unnamed sender who appears to have close inside knowledge of people's whereabouts.

Caldwell, who has pleaded not guilty to all criminal charges, allegedly received detailed descriptions of where to go – and disturbing suggestions as to what to do. 'Tom all legislators are down in the Tunnels 3floors down ... Go through back house chamber doors facing N left down hallway down steps ... All members are in the tunnels under capital seal them in. Turn on gas.'[54]

The events of 6 January couldn't have happened without *both* the spark lit by QAnon and its ready-made core of adherents, and the (often cynical) manipulations of Trump and his inner circle.

The combination of a deluded president determined to cling on to power at any cost and the mounting and violent conspiracism of a subset of his followers had brought the US to the brink.

Through December, QAnon had been further radicalised by Trump's rhetoric about a 'stolen' election – and then in turn appears to have helped radicalise his key advisors and in turn the president himself. Through December, key QAnon influencers quickly started endorsing 'military' options to prevent Trump losing power, and then started considering civil war and direct action.[55] A deadly feedback loop had been created.

For a time, the backlash to the Capitol riots – and the fact they had revealed nothing and accomplished nothing – led people away from QAnon, and saw some of its more 'respectable' boosters turn on the movement. In the short term, QAnon-related accounts (Q himself had fallen silent a month before) suggested something big would happen on inauguration day.

That day came and went without incident, leading many journalists to suggest QAnon would now wither away. It did not. Marjorie Taylor Greene filed impeachment documents against President Joe Biden on 21 January – less than twenty-four hours into the job – and the beat went on.[56]

But it's at this point that QAnon began to change into something new once again. Some people remained knowing, signed-up members to something called QAnon. But by transforming in different ways for different audiences, something with its core principles started grabbing followers in ever-larger numbers – most of whom had never heard of Q, 4chan or 8chan at all.

The splintering groups took quite different paths. One was the core QAnon followers, whose belief system often became even more profoundly strange. Another formed the global #SaveTheChildren movement – perhaps the most well-meaning and yet malign global trend of the internet era.

But it was the third that propelled ideas QAnon had taken on into the stratosphere – a global pandemic, begun in China, which damaged Donald Trump's electability and saw Joe Biden enter the White House was just the breakthrough any conspiracy theory needed.

We might hear the name 'QAnon' less than we used to. But that's just in the same way that it's easier to see a smaller mountain than a larger one, or to see more of an iceberg that's far away. The amorphous digital virus that we call QAnon had already escaped its breeding grounds of 4chan and gone international. Now it was about to become a pandemic.

PART THREE

Transmission

7

#SaveTheChildren

How does a conspiracy theory as lurid as QAnon pull in a well-meaning group of people who spend far less time online than the average young man? In QAnon's case, it was by stripping down to its very core. The central moral mission that came to power the broader QAnon movement was essentially a decent and understandable one – the desire to protect children from danger, specifically in this case from sexual abuse and murder, which the elite was supposedly either turning a blind eye to, or actively facilitating.

Beginning in 2019 and rising through 2020, a global movement arose across Instagram and Facebook groups – its core message being 'save the children'. Gone were the memes and layers of irony of 4chan and 8chan, replaced with clear and earnest messaging on the all-too-familiar theme of child abuse on a massive scale. If anything could demonstrate the ability of QAnon to shift across communities, audiences, influencers and the type of site it called home, it was this movement.

It is not a ridiculous idea that people in power might engage in rape, sexual assault or harassment, or that perpetrators might use their power and connections to escape the consequences of their actions. Harvey Weinstein stayed at the top of Hollywood for many years despite widespread rumours of sexual abuse dating back for decades, only finally being brought down and eventually convicted of rape and sexual assault as a result of the #MeToo movement.[1] Jeffrey Epstein, as mentioned earlier, ran an international sex trafficking network that enabled both him and his wealthy friends to sleep with minors – typically teenage girls – for decades, all the while mixing in the public eye with celebrities and top politicians, including both Bill and Hillary Clinton and Donald Trump.

In the UK, broadcasting icon and friend of the establishment Jimmy Savile, who in his lifetime was awarded both an OBE and a knighthood, was followed by dark rumours for decades of his life. But the full horrors of his conduct emerged only after his death, with hundreds of his victims over multiple decades coming forward with horrifying stories of child sexual abuse.[2] Getting those stories out turned into a nightmare, as the BBC – which had put Savile on air for years and given him the opportunity to interact with many children unsupervised – repeatedly killed stories on his conduct, leading journalists involved in trying to report the story to quit the institution.[3]

These make up just a handful of real cases, but serve at least to stress that people should not be dismissed for listening to those who claim there is an epidemic of elite child abuse that the mainstream isn't covering. That has been true in all of these cases, and more.

The real numbers, though, are nothing on the false numbers that get thrown around by groups semi-affiliated to Q. The statistic bandied about by QAnon and QAnon-adjacent influencers is that '365,348 children went missing in 2020', as QAnon congresswoman Lauren Boebert once tweeted, citing the stat to the FBI. 'You haven't heard a word from the media about it. There enlies [sic] the problem.'[4]

Variations of this statistic pull in concerned parents in their millions – especially as a quick glance at the FBI figures suggest it's accurate. In reality, it relates to the number of missing persons reports put in for children across the entire year, not the number who are currently missing.

Most missing child reports are resolved in less than twenty-four hours, and only a small fraction involve abduction. The vast majority of those abductions are from parents or loved ones and are related to care or custody disputes. The seemingly high figure (actually down 60,000 or so on a year earlier) isn't widely reported because most of the missing child cases are actually very mundane.

In general, considerably more than 99 per cent of missing children in the US are found alive, and even in the most high-risk category – abduction by strangers or by a family member with an outstanding felony arrest warrant – 97 per cent of children are found and recovered alive.[5]

That initially alarming figure in the hundreds of thousands might not actually be quite so disturbing when analysed, but it can just as easily be turned into something more disturbing. Though Boebert's phrasing was at least slightly careful – she said 'went missing' – other QAnon influencers use the statistic as a figure representing how many children have actually been abducted, a very different thing entirely.

The bid to cite the FBI is itself interesting: the core belief of the Q-adjacent movement that became #SaveTheChildren throughout 2020 is that authorities across the world are ignoring the epidemic of missing children, and yet those involved will cite statistics from the FBI – a federal US agency – as evidence of the problem. Belief can be a very malleable thing in the conspiracy world. When the FBI's statistics support the conspiracy theory, they are sacrosanct. When they challenge it, they are fabrications and can be dismissed out of hand.

'Save The Children' and its accompanying hashtag was in part a deliberate effort from some sincere QAnon believers to bring new people into the movement, and then an organic response from people seeing the posts and hashtags and being animated to action. The framing proved particularly effective with women, especially mothers.[6]

In particular, the #SaveTheChildren movement appealed to conservative religious mothers, who in the evangelical tradition are well primed to believe in satanic influences and conspiracies. There is a darkly ironic overtone to this because of the church's own largely undiscussed problems around child abuse. One researcher found that in 2016 and 2017 alone, there were '192 instances of a leader from an influential church or evangelical institution being publicly charged with sexual crimes involving a minor, including rape, molestation, battery and child pornography'. As a grim footnote, that research was only concerned with church leaders (not more junior clergy), and only with crimes against children.[7]

The framing was also a useful one to capture a wider set of the New Age and wellness communities, which were frequented by much of the same demographic. #SaveTheChildren memes were often widely shared among these kinds of Instagram hashtags and communities. Organisers of what became regular #SaveTheChildren street protests would often insist their protest was unconnected to QAnon, often while standing next to people wearing QAnon apparel or banners.[8]

Like almost every component of the evolved QAnon ideology, the idea of ritual or satanic child abuse conducted by secretive and powerful cabals was hardly a new one – even when divorced from the millennium-old concept of blood libel. The 'satanic panics' of the 1970s and 1980s leapt in part from a then-fashionable psychological idea of repressed memories, a doctrine which held that adulthood mental health problems typically stemmed from suppressed childhood memories. Patients would be hypnotised and asked to recall their traumas – and if those traumas were felt to be minor or insufficient by the therapist, they would be pushed to reveal more, to 'explain' their adult issues. Over multiple sessions, patients would 'recall' ever more lurid instances of abuse, escalating to large-scale ritual murder. These were then held up by therapists as proof the technique worked, when in reality study after study has shown that traumatic memories are rarely suppressed, but that this technique does strongly encourage patients to fabricate traumatic memories that they then come to believe are real.[9]

These techniques were eventually extended to be used on children, sparking an infamous spate of nursery and day care criminal trials and convictions in the US, UK, Canada and beyond through the 1980s – ruining the lives of the innocent nursery workers involved.[10]

Such is the widespread belief in them among some psychologists and law enforcement staff to this day that even in the 2010s the Metropolitan Police spent months investigating claims from an anonymous supposed whistleblower codenamed 'Nick', who alleged senior politicians had subjected him to ritual child abuse and murdered other children while he watched. Nick, whose real name is Carl Beech, was found to have fabricated the lurid accusations, and was eventually himself convicted for possession of images of child abuse.[11]

People tend to remember the lurid and grim details of the accusations and trials more than they remember the debunking, if they notice them at all – meaning that #SaveTheChildren had no difficulty spreading well beyond America, thanks to a decades-long wellspring of similar allegations.

Marching 'for the children'

In August of 2020 – with Covid-19 restrictions temporarily relaxed but large gatherings still firmly banned – Laura Ward and Lucy Davis led a group of 500 or more protestors in central London on a campaign to 'Save The Children'. The protest, unrelated to the UK charity of the same name, was mirrored in a dozen cities across the UK and more than 200 across the world. And it had grown directly out of QAnon.

Though like their US counterparts they denied a direct QAnon connection, protestors at the London gathering were pictured wearing shirts with hand-penned slogans. '#PizzagateIsReal' read one. 'It can't be a conspiracy theory if it's true,' another read.

Ward was the co-founder of Freedom For The Children UK,[12] one of the UK's first QAnon-connected Facebook groups, which at the time had 13,000 members. Over the course of 2020, UK followers of QAnon-related groups rose from under 20,000 in March to more than 130,000 by September – more people than follow the Conservative Party on Facebook.[13]

There were numerous famous or semi-famous boosters of QAnon's child abuse thesis and #SaveTheChildren – including one somewhat bizarre Pizzagate rant by none other than the pop star Robbie Williams, in an interview clip posted onto YouTube and Twitter in 2020.[14]

'Look, there might be a personally reasonable explanation for that language, who knows. The fact that we don't know means that nothing has been debunked. Yes, there was no basement in the particular pizza place,' says Williams.[15]

> Nobody's been asked, nobody's said and there's been no answers. But the overarching reporting on this story is debunked fake news. It's not. The right questions haven't been asked to the right people in the right places.
>
> Just as I take my popstar hat off, my celebrity hat off, and just talk as Robert from Stoke-on-Trent, ST6 7HA, opposite the Ancient Briton, big up Stoke-on-Trent – just as that guy for a moment, that's watching from the terraces, why aren't those questions being asked?

Williams appears to have been drawn into the conspiracy after having received similar baseless accusations from those within it as many other onetime A-listers – but rather than dismissing it due to its claims against himself, instead did his own research, in Q's parlance.

One man, though, did far more – Native American rapper and model Scotty 'the Kid' Rojas, who helped propel #SaveTheChildren into the Instagram mainstream.[16] From June 2020 onwards, Rojas revealed he had been following QAnon and said the claims it was a conspiracy were from those 'too lazy to do their own research'. Rojas went on to wonder whether the summer's Black Lives Matter protests and accompanying movement had been orchestrated as a distraction to the 'real' issue of mass child abuse.

Soon afterwards, Rojas announced on Instagram that he would hold a march on Hollywood in late July to 'save the children' – believed to be the beginning of that movement. Posters for the event included a 'WWG1WGA' logo – an initialism of QAnon's 'Where We Go One, We Go All' mantra. Research by the Media Manipulation Casebook, a team within Harvard researching misinformation and disinformation,[17] found tweets relating to the protest and hashtag were retweeted 66,000 times in the week following the march.

Rojas then announced plans to hold #SaveTheChildren rallies in 100 cities worldwide in August 2020 – and encouraged his Instagram followers to each try to lead one. However much organisers might try to deny (often believing their denial to be true) the movement's QAnon origins, they were undeniable to anyone who had followed QAnon even casually.

Of course, as with anything on the internet, Rojas was hardly a controlling mastermind: several people spontaneously organised their own rallies and protests connected to #SaveTheChildren, having seen the movement begin. As ever, QAnon is not a movement that needs or wants leaders.

The eventual count of August 2020 #SaveTheChildren rallies was around 250 cities – mostly in the US, Canada and the UK, but also several other countries. #SaveTheChildren was now firmly established around the world. It was the same as QAnon, but its members had many of the same beliefs, and it had a wider and perhaps more respectable member base. Over that summer, it did however show the same love of frenetic online research that came to characterise QAnon. In the summer of 2020, thousands of people online thought they had finally cracked the cabal's code.

What's in the box?

Many people discovered the online furniture retailer Wayfair during the pandemic. With hundreds of millions – perhaps billions? – of office workers suddenly working from home, trying to secure some home office furniture became something of a priority. For those in countries (like the UK) which enjoyed unusually great weather during early lockdowns, garden furniture became almost impossible to acquire – and so everyone was on the hunt.

But in the summer of 2020, people connected to either or both of QAnon and #SaveTheChildren started to notice Wayfair, too – and what they saw alarmed them greatly.

To be fair to those concerned, what they found did look legitimately weird. In early July 2020, Twitter and Instagram users started finding products on Wayfair – pillows and shower curtains – that looked identical to products costing $100 or less, but which were priced at $9,990 or even $12,999.

Wayfair products are often given human names, and so the huge price points prompted people to – you've guessed it – do their own research. That research quickly revealed that several of the names tallied with missing person reports.

In July 2020, one user posted:

'Y'all this Wayfair Human trafficking thing is crazy. Look at this, there are two pillows/shower curtains that are the exact same, but one is $100 and the other is $10K. The $10K one is named the same thing as a Black girl missing in Michigan ...'[18]

A flurry of similar posts and outrage followed. 'Anons may have busted a human trafficking ring from a seller on WayFair. Selling $10K cabinets that are worth $200 with names of missing children,' one post read.[19]

Others called – eventually with some success – for the FBI or Homeland Security to investigate the mystery. Of particular interest was a series of very normal-looking cabinets that were inexplicably priced at $12,699 to $14,999, all with female names, several of which corresponded to missing person reports.[20]

One such cabinet was the Samiyah, a '5-shelf Storage cabinet by WFX Utility™',[21] retailing for $12,899. This was in July 2020 connected to an October 2019 missing person report for a Samiyah Mumin, and taken as proof she was being auctioned off in something close to plain sight, under the flimsiest of codes.

There was, however, one problem with this theory: Samiyah Mumin had only been missing for a very short time in October 2019 – and she was understandably somewhat freaked out by the international concern for her wellbeing. On the same day as the posts about her disappearance went viral on multiple social networks, a visibly pregnant Mumin (who aimed the camera at her belly to demonstrate that fact) posted a fifty-minute Facebook Live video, with some blunt words for those saying she was being traded.[22]

> Y'all about to really irritate me, being weird. Just weird. How am I missing? And I'm pregnant – let me know how that goes? Let me know.

Who are you? How are you going to post about me being missing when you don't even know me? And your caption sounds retarded – would this be true? ... Why are you posting about people being missing if you don't even know they're missing, with a cabinet with their name when there's people out here actually missing, who've got their lives on the line? ... Don't play with my life like that.

Lest any readers be concerned Mumin had in some way been coerced to post the video, she continues to post regularly on Facebook (often multiple times a day), including pictures of her with her child, who is now a toddler.

Inevitably, the other children supposed to have been trafficked turned out to have other explanations. Most had been found very shortly after being reported missing. Others had tragic ends long before their supposed trafficking. One product named 'Alyvia' was connected to missing three-year-old Alyvia Navarro. Sadly, Navarro had died by drowning in a pond seven years earlier, in 2013.[23]

If the bizarre pricing wasn't a front to sell children, then what on earth was actually happening? The real-world answer is predictably a little bit fiddly and unsatisfactory to those determined to see wrongdoing – as it's actually a series of related answers.

Wayfair, unlike IKEA, makes almost none of its furniture. Instead, it's a storefront for more than 10,000 different furniture and homeware manufacturers, which explains in part why it often had items in stock when other outlets that handled their own manufacture didn't. Because it has hundreds of thousands of products on its site, it names the items by algorithm. A spokesperson told Reuters that these names are drawn from 'first names, locations and common words'.[24]

With more than 300,000 missing children reports filed in the US alone each month, any algorithm that draws on common names is going to find numerous matches against children's names. The internet is a global network of 3 billion people and masses of data. With a dataset as large as the portion that Google has crawled and made searchable, there will be endless apparently impossible coincidences.

The high pricing came with a few different explanations. Some businesses selling online, such as marketplace sites like Wayfair, or the much better-known Amazon, often have items listed from multiple smaller businesses, which they price by algorithm. When algorithms are set in particular ways (such as without limits), these interactions can have dramatic results: in one notorious case a book about flies came to be listed on Amazon for $24 million.[25] At the time of writing, it is back down to a more reasonable $23.05 for a used copy.[26]

Some of the mispriced items on Wayfair appear to have been the result of this kind of misfiring algorithmic pricing – but with several of the cabinets that came to public notice, this was not the case. Instead, for these the problem was that industrial-grade cabinets built to very particular specifications had not been listed with appropriate descriptions and pictures, making them look like wildly overpriced items for the home market.[27]

Needless to say, despite numerous fact-checks and reporting from mainstream outlets, these explanations did not serve to entirely soothe the concerns of those on the online hunt. Eventually, as it started to tackle QAnon-related content on its networks, Meta – the owner of Facebook and Instagram – also acted to suppress #SaveTheChildren-related groups and posts, as these had become similarly clogged with conspiracy and misinformation.[28]

For those children unlucky enough to have been identified as victims of the Wayfair trafficking conspiracy, the #SaveTheChildren movement could actually become a trauma in itself. One such victim was then thirteen-year-old Samara Duplessis, who had briefly run away from home (with a pack of Frosted Flakes in her backpack) in the spring of 2020, returning within two days.

That summer, #SaveTheChildren decided that Samara was one of the children being smuggled by Wayfair. The *Washington Post* followed Samara and her family in the aftermath.[29] They recalled finding out about the conspiracy after her father received a dozen panicked calls from friends and relatives asking after her welfare, prompted by thousands of shares of posts bearing her face and name.

Deluged by thousands of messages and posts, Samara and her parents struggled to separate what was real from what was not. Could there actually be some price on her head? Were they somehow involved in something they didn't know about? Had something happened when Samara had been briefly missing? Or were they in danger from the online group trying to 'save' Samara?

'I started getting real bad anxiety. I started pacing around real heavy,' Samara told the *Post*. 'When I get in my head, like real, real deep in my head, I start hyperventilating.'

The damage done by the Wayfair and #SaveTheChildren conspiracy went well beyond scaring families – though that would be bad enough. The huge influx of calls to Homeland Security and to missing children helplines connected to the Wayfair conspiracy swamped the services there to deal with *actual* missing child cases. Such was the influx and the need to be able to dismiss the cases that thirty field offices of Homeland Security had to put investigations on hold to tackle the false emergency.

Polaris, the not-for-profit that manages the US National Human Trafficking Hotline, came out publicly saying that the wider #SaveTheChildren movement was harming efforts to tackle the real problem at hand. In a statement put out in an FAQ at the time, it said:

> Polaris and many other organizations that work to protect children and families are deeply concerned that the spread of intentional disinformation about how child sex trafficking happens in most situations is detracting from the very real, very important work of helping families to protect children and working to change the conditions in which trafficking thrives – poverty, abuse, addiction, hopelessness, discrimination, to name but a few.[30]

The not-for-profit set out the various ways in which such movements harmed its actual effort. The most obvious is that if its phone lines are swamped with people calling in with tips based on misinformation, the organisation risks missing genuine calls reporting first-hand evidence of trafficking. 'We will never know what we missed,' it said.

In addition, the idea that sex trafficking involves strangers kidnapping children who are then shipped around the world or sold is a misconception that doesn't resemble the vast majority of real-world cases. The children who are most vulnerable to trafficking are ones from abusive households, or unstable ones, or ones in which they are neglected. Such children may run away as teens and fall in with so-called bad crowds, with some persuaded to move across state lines or further by older supposed boyfriends, who then trade them for sex. Just as in the adult world, sex trafficking and people smuggling are often two sides of the same coin – people move illegally to the US or some other country believing they will work in some kind of legitimate field, and instead are forced to do sex work.

The realities of sex trafficking are described by Polaris as sounding 'much more mundane than some of the complex conspiracies', and are often in greyer areas ethically too, with some conservative groups using trafficking as a pretext to act against consenting adult sex workers, or to push other agendas.

Turning this into the vivid and lurid conspiratorial stories told by QAnon might make heroes and villains, but it detaches the issue from reality, overwhelming the organisations that have to deal with the real problems, and making people less likely to spot them when they see them. Another child protection foundation based in Florida, the KidSafe Foundation, went even further than Polaris: 'The conspiracy theory and cult movement known as QAnon is attempting to hijack the good names of organisations leading the fight against child abuse and sex trafficking. We cannot let this happen.' The statement went on: 'QAnon promoters are parasites. To grow their footprint, gain credibility and spread misinformation, they associate their message of hate and bigotry with well-known, well-regarded organisations – specifically those working to end child sexual abuse and sex trafficking.'[31]

None of that, of course, stopped President Trump – the hero of the core QAnon movement – praising the group's efforts in this area. In an August 2020 town hall event, Trump said he believed QAnon followers 'love our country' and 'like me very much'.[32] A few months later, at another town hall in October – just one month before the 2020 election – he added: 'Let me just tell you what I do hear about it is they are very strongly against paedophilia and I agree with that. And I agree with it very strongly.'[33]

And yet, for those who were still overtly involved with the QAnon movement – as opposed to its wider offshoots – there was a strange and persistent blindness to actual sexual predators and allegations of child abuse. As discussed in Chapter Two, the 8chan board on which Q was still regularly posting in 2020 itself hosted images of child abuse – a glaring contradiction which somehow sparked absolutely no introspection among the small fraction of the most hardcore Q supporters who directly followed their supposed leader on the board.

More conspicuous challenges were to come, not least when a prominent congressman was accused of involvement in sexual trafficking. For a movement centred around the idea that those in power were involved in exactly this behaviour, this would seem to be the ultimate 'gotcha' moment – Trump's Department of Justice investigating a sitting congressman. The fly in the ointment? That congressman was the Republican Matt Gaetz, a prominent supporter of Donald Trump.

The news came to light in March 2021, two months after Joe Biden's inauguration, in QAnon's least favourite outlet – the *New York Times*.[34] The department was reported to be investigating whether or not Gaetz, who had announced his engagement three months earlier, had been in a sexual relationship with a seventeen-year-old (the age of consent in the US is eighteen).

Furthermore, it was investigating whether or not Gaetz had paid for that girl to travel with him across state lines, which under US Federal law would qualify as trafficking. This sort of investigation would be far more representative of a typical trafficking investigation than the kind of thing QAnon supporters imagine, but it was a sex trafficking investigation all the same. And while Biden was president at the time of the report, the investigation had begun during Trump's presidency. (Gaetz was never charged with any offence, and was re-elected in 2022 to the US Congress.)

Rather than seize upon an investigation as some kind of evidence – or even a sign – that their theories might be correct, QAnon immediately jumped to explain away the allegations. QAnon influencers quickly decided that the Gaetz allegations were either a bid to distract attention from Ghislaine Maxwell (whose trial was later extensively covered, and led to five guilty verdicts), or else part of an elaborate double bluff.

Gaetz was, they reasoned, actually working with the FBI, a theory made easier when he made a bizarre Fox News appearance the evening of the article's publication claiming the allegations were part of an elaborate multi-million dollar extortion scheme. QAnon – usually sceptical of anything that suggests people *aren't* involved in sex trafficking – immediately accepted this version of events.

Such behaviour defies easy explanation, but there are several possibilities that can go some way to explaining the apparently inexplicable paradox. For one, Donald Trump is not a man of unimpeachable sexual integrity – he has been accused of rape and sexual assault on multiple occasions by more than two dozen women (he denies all of the claims),[35] and was infamously caught saying he would grab attractive women 'by the pussy', with or without their consent, for which he was later forced to apologise.[36]

Having turned a blind eye to Trump, because he was deemed to be on-side, for so long, perhaps it was similarly easy to do the same for lesser figures affiliated to the cause. Adding to this is the relative mundanity of the accusations against Gaetz – far more in line with how support charities describe such crimes, but a world away from how #SaveTheChildren and QAnon imagine the world. Whatever the cause, supporters were outraged on Gaetz's behalf.

'This kind of setup or smear campaign is consistent with evil,' said one post preserved for history by VICE. 'The [deep state] will try to destroy all their opponents in any way possible. See ALL the FALSE accusations levied against the GOAT — DJT. Evil accuses good of what they themselves do.'[37]

As the NBC reporter Ben Collins – who describes his beat covering online misinformation and conspiracy as the 'dystopia beat' – noted at the time, QAnon 'love Gaetz's inscrutable double agent story because it sounds like 5D chess'.[38]

Instead of looking into that real investigation – which was still ongoing in 2022 – the core QAnon element of the #SaveTheChildren movement went back to their favourite pastime: looking for secret clues and codes hidden in plain sight on the internet, in the darkest version of a crowdsourced Dan Brown novel.[39]

In August 2021, one eagle-eyed observer found bizarre text appearing on a Smart TV experiencing code errors – with the alarming phrase 'Kill process ... or sacrifice child' appearing, surely with some dark meaning. (It is a standard phrase in the open-source Unix operating system when it has run out of memory – the 'child' referenced is a sub-process.)[40] The same month, there was a small-scale repeat of the Wayfair fiasco stemming from the online sale of one McDonald's chicken nugget for $100,000 – once again sparking the suggestion it was a coded auction for trafficked children, especially as attention started to be paid to it when the price was a mere $14,000.

What was actually happening was very nearly as ridiculous but much more benign. The megastar K-pop group BTS had a few months before launched a limited-edition meal deal with McDonald's, which naturally led to huge queues and the meals concerned rapidly selling out – and then to a chain of online auctions, this one for a custom-shaped nugget. The so-called meme economy (and the NFT boom that followed it) is stupid, but it isn't trafficking kids.[41]

Even container ships were not immune to the ire of the Q crowd. When the *Ever Given* wedged itself in the Suez Canal – initially to everyone's amusement, and then to their irritation when it caused major disruption to global shipping[42] – QAnon felt the need to discover a story behind the story.

In a series of ever-more ridiculous posts, Q followers started seeing connections mount up.[43] One such connection they found was that the *Ever Given* was a ship operated by the company

Evergreen, which was Hillary Clinton's Secret Service codename in 2016.[44] Other insights included that the course tracked by the ship shortly before the accident resembled a penis (which, to be fair, it did),[45] which they reasoned must have some significance. Perhaps the ship had been run aground as a rescue operation for the children onboard, or as some kind of signal, or was foretold by Q in 2018 when he said 'watch the water' (like Nostradamus before him, Q had a gift for vagueness).[46]

Catalysed by a few influencers – but under the control of none of them – the core of the grab-bag of ideas that made up QAnon had found a way to attenuate and pull in whole new demographics across the world through concern for children and the desire to protect them against vile crimes. But that would prove to be nothing compared to the latent anger, mistrust and paranoia generated by another world event through 2020 and beyond: the Covid-19 pandemic.

8

Enough Is Enough

The eighteenth-century literary figure Samuel Johnson is famously quoted as noting that 'When a man knows he is to be hanged ... it concentrates his mind wonderfully.' The saying has endured through the ages (it's certainly catchy), but recent years have given us good reason to question the truth of it.

Rumblings of a new coronavirus started to be heard at the bottom end of broadcast news reports, in twenty- or thirty-second spots, in the latter months of 2019. By January 2020, it was getting a minute or so of airtime in bulletins outside China, once or twice a week. By March 2020, it was declared a pandemic by the World Health Organization,[1] and countries across the globe were handling it with lockdowns and other restrictions.[2]

In the early days of the pandemic, in most countries, politicians from all backgrounds were largely united: Covid-19 was real, deadly and highly contagious – and there were few treatments and no medical preventative measures in existence. It was close to as real as a mass threat to society can get.

And yet if the prospect of dying in a pandemic concentrated minds at all, it certainly didn't concentrate them on real events. The pandemic catalysed QAnon-adjacent groups like nothing else.

Just as Covid-19 proved all too able to mutate to its own advantage over the years of the pandemic, so too did the digital virus that is QAnon accelerate in its mutation and its reach. As people despaired of the effects of lockdown, nurtured their suspicions over its cause, worried about government overreach or just spent too much time online with nothing else to do, QAnon found itself a new way in to millions of minds across the world.

It had long been the nature of QAnon to become the glue sticking existing conspiracy theories together. It had also become the nature of QAnon to draw in different conspiratorial groups – QAnon was a conspiracy theory able to appeal to angry teenage boys, but also their suburban mothers and apocalypse-prepper[3] fathers.

Covid-19 provided a dream new set of ingredients for a movement like that, with the central tenet of conspiracy theories – once you believe one, you are far more open to others (though not every one will stick for most individuals) – meaning that a far wider population than normal was ready to be pulled in.

This was because pandemics in general, and Covid-19 in particular, provide a particularly rich seam of ideas to mine. It had started in China, a long-time adversary of President Trump, who had engaged in a multi-year trade war with the nation.[4] Wuhan, the city in which Covid was discovered, has an Institute of Virology, which studied coronaviruses.[5]

It prompted governments to take the most drastic, and often the most authoritarian, measures outside of wartime in a century or more.[6] It came alongside the global rollout of 5G mobile data technology.[7] Thanks to the desperate search for a vaccine, Big Pharma (almost no one's favourite industry) stood to gain billions.[8] The list goes on and on, with far too many potential conspiratorial offshoots to list.

In addition to this, for millions of people across the globe – but by no means everyone – lockdown restrictions meant they had far, far more free time on their hands, and no ability to go out of the house to kill it. Much more time online means much more time to 'do your own research', or even simply to let Facebook or YouTube's algorithms keep recommending content to you endlessly. Research has shown that both sites' recommendation features could easily lead users from relatively mainstream content down QAnon-linked rabbit holes.[9] Every long-term conspiracy theorist spotted the opportunity of a lifetime. David Icke – of 'alien reptiles are secretly running the world' fame – gave extensive, punishingly long interviews 'explaining' the pandemic to friendly, unthreatening journalists.[10]

The upside of being a conspiracy theorist is that you don't have to wait for the slow process of actual fact-finding and scientific research, meaning that you can get your message out much more quickly than those trying to provide accurate information are able to. A channel called 'London Real' anchored by Brian Rose published a two-hour online interview with Icke on 18 March 2020, racking up more than a million views.[11]

The video was eventually removed from YouTube, but Rose went on to turn it into a series of interviews throughout the course of the pandemic. Rose plays the role of sceptic, wanting to be convinced of what Icke is saying, but never offers any real challenge. Icke, meanwhile, makes an endless series of wild allegations about the 'true' origins of the coronavirus and the motivations behind it, repeatedly promising that the evidence for all of his claims is on his website, and so doesn't need to be proffered here. The viewer is left, as ever, to do their own research.

Doing your own research through the pandemic gave readers many ways into conspiracy theories, many of which are worth tackling in turn on their own merits (or lack thereof). The sixteenth-century Renaissance man Paracelsus – credited as one of the fathers of medicine, as well as of homeopathy – offered the insight that 'the dose makes the poison'.[12] This is an idea applicable to some of these ideas: there is nothing wrong with being sceptical of a new virus, or of Big Pharma, or of your government. It is just possible to take it to extremes.

This is very much the case when it comes to Covid-19 and conspiracies around Bill Gates, who quickly emerged as one of the very first pandemic bogeymen as early as January 2020, two months before Covid-19 was even declared a pandemic.[13]

There are many reasons to be sceptical about Gates, who for many years was the world's richest person, and who remains a billionaire several times over.[14] Gates had a reputation for ruthlessness when he was leading Microsoft into dominance of the desktop PC market. For decades, rumours have circulated that Gates and Microsoft ripped off the source code for MS-DOS, the precursor of the Windows operating systems (Microsoft fiercely deny this, but the debate rumbles on).[15]

Microsoft was known to aggressively protect its market position, with Gates repeatedly accused of anti-competitive behaviour. Courts in the EU found it had abused its market position, and a US court even ordered the company to be split up as a monopoly (which was overturned on appeal).[16] On a personal level, Gates met with Jeffrey Epstein 'many times', all after Epstein had been convicted for a sexual offence, though Gates has never been accused of involvement in criminal activity.[17] Gates has repeatedly stated on Epstein that he 'had dinner with him and that's all' and that he 'shouldn't have had dinner with him'. In 2021, several former Microsoft employees spoke to reporters about alleged inappropriate behaviour from the company's founder in the office, relating both to bullying and to 'inappropriate' flirtation.[18] Gates had denied all accusations of wrongdoing during his time at Microsoft.

There are, then, plenty of reasons why people may not wish to greet Bill Gates as some sort of angel or saviour figure, but his commitment to the global health charity he launched with his then-wife Melinda is undeniable.[19] Since 1999, Gates has donated more than $45 billion to philanthropic causes,[20] the overwhelming majority of it going to the Bill & Melinda Gates Foundation – which has distributed more than $60 billion since its inception.[21]

It was this foundation that made Gates perhaps the ultimate bogeyman of Covid conspiracy theorists. Almost everywhere you look around the world in public health, you will find Gates funding. It is in fact, in the interests of full disclosure, so inescapable that it also funds the global health reporting team at my employer, the Bureau of Investigative Journalism, and so paid part of my salary as Global Editor there (I was employed by TBIJ while writing this book, but will have left by the time you are reading it).[22]

That means that if anyone is looking for a Gates Foundation connection to a particular public health issue, they will find it. On a basic level, Bill Gates had publicly warned about the risk of a global pandemic long before Covid-19 happened. At the Munich Security Conference in February 2017, Gates said:

> Whether it occurs by a quirk of nature or at the hand of a terrorist, epidemiologists say a fast-moving airborne pathogen could kill more than 30 million people in less than a year. And they say there is a reasonable probability the world will experience such an outbreak in the next 10 to 15 years.

By that grisly benchmark, the world is getting off relatively lightly from Covid-19 – at the time of writing the estimated global death toll is a 'mere' 6.5 million.[23] This is certainly an underestimate – many countries have not been able to track their coronavirus deaths, while the pandemic has also led to significant increases in deaths from other causes, due to the strain it has placed on health systems around the world. Even then, most estimates have an upper limit of 15 million or so.[24]

A rational view of Gates' remarks is that he had foreseen a problem other experts had worried about but struggled to secure attention or funding to tackle, and so he raised the profile of the issue. But conspiracists could also take those remarks as a sign that Gates was softening up the public ready for some sort of engineered calamity.

It was as early as 21 January 2020 that QAnon-connected accounts started joining the dots on Gates. As the *New York Times* catalogues,[25] a YouTuber had found a patent connected to a coronavirus by the Pirbright Institute, a Surrey-based infectious disease research institute specialising in illnesses in farm animals.

The Pirbright Institute had, the YouTuber correctly said, received funding from the Gates Foundation, and therefore Gates had some stake in the pandemic. In reality, the patent related to a potential vaccine for an entirely different coronavirus – coronaviruses are a family of viruses with many different varieties, including several that cause common colds – one that affects livestock.

Inevitably, that bit of online dot-joining was quickly turned into the accusation – made two days later by Alex Jones' conspiratorial 'news' service Infowars – that Bill Gates had patented Covid-19 in advance. The ball had been kicked off, and Gates-related theories quickly became by far the most shared online conspiracy relating to the early months of the pandemic.

The second most shared conspiracy theories of that era – again widely pushed by those adjacent to Q – all related to 5G. Where Gates-related conspiracies were mentioned on TV and online 1.2 million times between February and April 2020, according to research by Zignal Labs, 5G was mentioned more than 900,000 times.[26]

People are often sceptical of new technologies, with some justification. Sometimes side effects only emerge years or decades later, and companies have a bad track record of not disclosing these until there is absolutely no other choice. To prove that, one need only look at Big Tobacco through the 1960s, '70s and '80s,[27] Big Energy companies through to the present day,[28] or the makers of Oxycontin until their multi-billion-dollar court settlement in 2022.[29]

But 5G, despite marketing hype, isn't really a new technology. It is the release of more parts of the radio spectrum for the use of mobile phones and related smart devices. This is typically freed up from previous uses, such as broadcasting analogue television. While 5G is marketed on higher speeds (and does offer them, at least for now), it is actually about making sure there is enough capacity, as ever more smartphones use ever more data.

In terms of what is actually transmitted through the air, 5G is not a different technology than 4G or 3G before it. Strictly speaking, it's no different from what's used in MRI scanners in hospitals, either. Professor Sophie Scott CBE, the director of the Institute of Cognitive Neuroscience at University College London, and the presenter of the Royal Institution Christmas Lectures in 2017 on the topic of communication, set out the similarities and differences.

MRI machines give a patient a radically higher 'dose' of electromagnetic radiation on a similar wavelength to 5G, meaning operators and clinicians are acutely aware of their risks. Because of their long-term use in clinical settings, people like Scott know very well the effects of this radiation.[30]

'They can cause harmless but distressing things like tingling in your fingers,' Scott says, referring to the extreme doses of electromagnetic radiation given during an MRI scan. 'And the other thing is they heat you up slightly, and that sounds either scary or terrifying – and it's something you absolutely need to pay attention to, because even a one degree change in your body temperature has enormous implications … history looks unkindly on scientists who cook their participants.'

MRI technicians know the risks of the technology they use, and exactly how long they can safely expose patients to it, but as Scott explains, that means they understand the safe limits very well, too. At the long distance and lower energy used for 5G communications, this technology – she firmly insists – is not a risk at all. 5G in reality is not a new technology, is well understood and is safe. 'You're not exposed to anything *like* that level of exposure.'

But all of that deals with the rational response to 5G. The conspiracies around it were much more interesting – claiming that the Wuhan outbreak had coincided with when the masts were first being turned on (which wasn't the case),[31] that the weekly 'clap for the NHS' during the first UK lockdown was being done to cover up 5G testing with noise,[32] that 5G was being introduced either to control minds, kill people off or render most people infertile, and more.[33]

Inevitably, this led some conspiracy influencers to suggest action against 5G, with one tweeting in March 2020: '4G launched in CHINA. Nov 1, 2019. People dropped dead See attached & go to my IG stories for more. TURN OFF 5G by disabling LTE!!!'[34]

Leaving aside everything else wrong with that tweet, the influencer appeared not to understand that radio waves don't seek out a target. If an area has 5G, it has 5G whether your phone is turned on or not. Other people, who apparently understood that logic, attacked and burned down 5G towers in their area, prompted by the international scare stories. In the UK, ninety attacks on phone masts were reported during the first 2020 lockdown,[35] while multiple UK telecoms engineers received death threats.[36]

In the US, meanwhile, President Trump was characteristically making Covid-19 all about him – initially promising that it would all 'miraculously' be over by spring,[37] and then complaining with increasing frequency about what the pandemic was doing to his re-election prospects, as cases hit 100,000 and unemployment hit a temporary high of 38 million.[38] (As of April 2022, the US had a total of more than 80 million cases – with Trump among them – and 1 million deaths.)[39]

Given that the US QAnon community at that time was still entirely focused on Trump as the leader of a resistance against the deep state cabal, it was quickly resolved that it must be a plot. The far-right shock jock Rush Limbaugh said in February 2020 that Covid-19 was the common cold, 'weaponised' by the media and others to bring down Donald Trump[40] – a view Trump himself then endorsed.[41]

QAnon influencers resolved that Covid-19 had been deliberately made in a lab and released, possibly as part of an effort by China to prevent Trump's re-election (why China would first release the pathogen in their own country is left unexplained). Other pro-Trump conspiracists suggested that Britain might be behind the plot to take down Trump's 'roaring economy'.[42]

As Covid-19 spread in the US, conspiracists ended up focusing on one man in particular: the wizened seventy-nine-year-old director of the National Institute of Allergy and Infectious Diseases, Anthony Fauci. Despite Fauci having served in his role under presidents from both parties after being first appointed under Reagan, QAnon rapidly took against him, and their 'research' rapidly gave results.

Fauci, they discovered, had connections to the Wuhan Institute of Virology – or so they said. US public health bodies had co-funded some research in the Wuhan facility in the years leading up to Covid-19, and Fauci was the USA's most visible public health figure. Therefore, they reason, even if the funding didn't come from his agency, it was fair to say it was from him. And if the US funded a Chinese 'biolab', might it not stand to reason that it was for the creation of Covid?

As is typical for QAnon and Covid conspirators alike, people joined two dots and extrapolated from there to draw out a full galaxy.[43] At first, the connections between the two different conspiracies could only be made by looking at the actions of a few individual influencers, but the overlap is now corroborated by hard research.

Internal research conducted by Facebook found that there was a significant overlap between accounts interested in QAnon and the accounts most actively pushing anti-vaxx and similar Covid-19 messaging.[44] This corroborated earlier research by the Stanford Internet Observatory, which found that accounts pushing 'plandemic'-type conspiracy theories on Covid-19 were strongly linked with QAnon-affiliated accounts.[45]

Multiple studies on Telegram painted much the same picture – QAnon-related groups both pushed coronavirus conspiracy theories and also grew substantially in membership during the early stages of the pandemic.[46] QAnon had proven malleable enough to at least partly merge with the Covid conspiracy crowd – and they had no shortage of theories to push.

Each of these conspiracies would cause trouble enough during a public health emergency, especially when compounded by the headache of most of the groups also taking against the wearing of masks,[47] a low-impact and low-effort intervention that reduces the transmissibility of the virus, if not to zero. Deciding that masking was some form of precursor to a world state demanding compliance[48] boded incredibly badly for ending the pandemic: masking is painless and temporary. How would asking people to be injected with a new vaccine be received?

Persuading at least some people to take a new vaccine is always going to be a difficult sell. Vaccine hesitancy is not intrinsically the same as being a conspiracy theorist. The pharmaceutical industry has a bad history of covering up possible information on side-effects of medication, as in the tragic case of Thalidomide use in pregnant women, which led to up to 10,000 miscarriages and infant deaths, as well as maiming tens of thousands of more children who were born.[49]

Vaccines themselves have had a recent bad press too, sometimes unfairly, which often provides a respectable core of 'facts' for conspiracy theories to latch onto – and so these become a key part of the conspiracy ecosystem. This is nowhere more evident than with the (subsequently struck-off) doctor Andrew Wakefield, who prompted a worldwide scare about the combined measles, mumps and rubella childhood jab (MMR) after publishing a study suggesting it may cause autism – a study which was then heavily pushed for years by the UK media, though it was quickly discredited and found to have breached important ethical rules.[50]

Wakefield remains a popular alternative health figurehead in the USA,[51] and people across the world remain wary of the MMR jab. Elsewhere, confidence in vaccination programmes was not helped when it emerged that the CIA had used public vaccination as a cover for its agents in Pakistan – fuel for conspiracy and for vaccine hesitancy if ever there was.[52] Similarly, in countries such as the US and UK, people from ethnic minority backgrounds are often more wary of new healthcare interventions, in part because of poorer experiences with health professionals,[53] as well as grossly unethical experiments on minority populations within living memory.[54]

Vaccine development usually takes around ten years, whereas the first Covid-19 jabs were developed in less than twelve months – a medical miracle made possible because it built on work that had been going on for decades,[55] and because coronavirus became the world's top priority. In reality, much of this work had been frantically playing catchup, because despite warnings from people like Gates, pandemic planning had been chronically under-funded for decades.

In vaccine development, much of the decade the process usually takes is used up when securing funding, trial participants, ethics board approvals and so on – all work that can be accelerated without skipping steps in the approval process. In reality, Covid jabs are not classed as 'experimental' – as many conspiracies claim – and did not miss any usual trial stages.[56]

This kind of technical detail, though, turned out to have little to do with the various conspiracy theories Q and its movements settled upon. As vaccines became the ticket for a return to normality, and were pushed so heavily by governments, they became a focus for each conspiracy theory set out in this chapter.

Vaccines were, they said, the end game of Bill Gates' plan. One theory was that they would render people infertile, as the singer Nicki Minaj appeared to believe when she infamously tweeted a warning that it had given her cousin's friend swollen testicles and made him impotent.[57] Others believed that the effect on women's menstrual cycles was so strong that people's fertility could be affected simply by vaccine 'shedding' – just being near a vaccinated person was enough.[58]

Some leapt to the idea that Gates was trying to depopulate the world more directly, by having the vaccine cause fatal clots and heart attacks. This theory was based in part on some poorly judged (with hindsight) comments Gates had made a few years before Covid-19.[59] – Conspirators regularly suggest that any heart attack or unexplained death of an athlete or celebrity is due to the vaccine, which has been covered up.[60]

Alternative theories combine the Gates conspiracies with the 5G one, suggesting that there is a microchip in the vaccine intended to allow people to be controlled by Gates via 5G.[61] Viral posts show routine circuit diagrams captioned with 'The Russians have managed to remove the nanochips from the Pfizer vaccine and have published a function diagram.' Another claimed that 'any Bluetooth app [can] literally track those that have been vaccinated within 100 meters from you'.[62]

Some conspiracies suggest the chips will be fatal when activated by a 5G signal, meaning billions will drop dead all at once.[63] Other combinations include much of the above, but giving Anthony Fauci a role either alongside or in place of Bill Gates. People essentially mix and match the conspiratorial ingredients to their taste, picking and choosing from the huge array of online content still in circulation years into the pandemic.

Online highlights include 'My nephew got vaccinated then came out as gay. This isn't a coincidence,'[64] 'I've seen some people who have become allergic to testosterone since getting the vaccine,'[65] and this classic: 'If Celebrities start turning into Zombies it's because of the vaccine soup reacting to the Adrenochrome in their system. They're already cannibals, some I'm watching have turned even more Satanic/males turning homosexual after the shot.'[66]

That handy confluence of multiple related conspiracies is what tends to draw previously casual followers more deeply into these movements. It is easy when reading some of the more ridiculous posts above to imagine that these views on vaccines must be extremely niche – but the reality is different.

In the US, a poll taken by YouGov as early as May 2020 found that 44 per cent of Republican voters believed Bill Gates was plotting to use Covid-19 as a pretext to plant tracking microchips in billions of people around the world. Only 26 per cent disagreed with the statement.[67] The pandemic also provided many more avenues in conspiratorialism. Previously relatively mainstream figures like Russell Brand or Joe Rogan would promote Covid-19 conspiracies to their large followership, while celebrities including Jim Carrey, Lisa Bonet and tennis pro Novak Djokovic all received coverage for their refusal to take the Covid-19 vaccine.

By July 2021, when the vaccine was a reality and adult Americans were being urged to get their free jab, a further YouGov survey found that 51 per cent of people who had refused the vaccine believed it contained a microchip. (The same study revealed that 21 per cent of Republican voters said they had a favourable view of QAnon.)[68]

A separate US poll by PRRI that same month found a strong and overt connection between QAnon and anti-vaccination sentiment. Forty-two per cent of vaccine refusers told pollsters they also believed in QAnon, while 22 per cent of those describing themselves as vaccine hesitant said they believed Q.[69]

The digital pandemic had, beyond the point of doubt, become part of a real-world global health emergency.

Global pandemic, global radicalisation

The levels of oddness and denial among those who come to regularly stage anti-lockdown or anti-vaccine protests can be truly surreal, with an often-familiar cast of characters with tenuous connections to the corridors of power who can then allude to familiarity with the workings of the state to online and offline followers.

One such figure in the UK is Jennifer Arcuri, who had an affair with prime minister Boris Johnson, and also received public money for her business during that time. During the pandemic, Arcuri appeared to suggest that Johnson's new wife, Carrie Johnson, was a Satanist, alongside others in government. Her feed suggested that vaccines were a 'genocidal initiative' and accused people promoting jabs as 'paid for shills'.[70]

This is hardly a problem unique to the Conservative party. Piers Corbyn, the brother of former Labour leader Jeremy Corbyn, had built a fringe career as something of a rogue weather forecaster and climate change conspiracist. But Covid-19 saw him pivot rapidly to anti-vaccination and anti-lockdown protest of an extreme sort.

Corbyn shared photos of his supporters mobbing the current Labour leader Keir Starmer, calling him a 'traitor' who 'protected paedophiles'.[71] Corbyn has suggested vaccines are part of a 'new world order' agenda and claimed they are a 'hoax', while his supporters are often pictured with QAnon-related apparel, signs or slogans.[72]

These strange cross-political combinations were just as visible in the US conspiratorial anti-vaccine movements, with perhaps even stranger outcomes in their rallies. The wellness-to-QAnon pipeline remained alive and well, with crystal-healing hippie-ish groups expanding their already existing mistrust of mainstream medicine.

The health and wellness New Age site Gaia came to host David Icke videos and became a hotbed of conspiracy theories in both its internal culture and its external content. Such was the mood in the business that some insiders believed the CEO could psychically invade their dreams, while the latest Q drops were routinely discussed in the office.[73] Its site, meanwhile, contained, according to Business Insider, 'a hallucinatory slurry of time-traveling psychic CIA spies, purported dangers of vaccines, Bigfoot sightings, alchemists' secrets for transmuting gold, and the founder of JPMorgan's clandestine plot to sink the *Titanic*'.

Gaia, dubbed by now a 'hub for QAnon', might not be an obvious brand partnership for any mainstream celebrity, but that didn't stop singer Demi Lovato becoming a paid ambassador for the site during the pandemic. 'Understanding the world around us (the known and the unknown) is so exciting to me!', Lovato posted to their 118 million followers in November 2021, as US authorities desperately tried to encourage people to get vaccinated before an expected spike of cases in winter.[74]

Such is the fervour of the groups organising anti-Covid protests that they will seek and find elaborate explanations for simple problems. Clay Clark, a business coach from Oklahoma, had become one of the faces of the anti-vaccination conspiratorial movement. In the autumn of 2021 he launched a ReAwaken America Tour, with events and attendees pushing many of the familiar QAnon-adjacent messages we have come to know and love.

At one 2021 event, Clark was reported to have told rallygoers: 'Turn to the person next to you and give them a hug, someone you don't know. Go hug somebody. Go ahead and spread it out, mass spreader. It's a mass spreader event! It's a mass spreader event!'

Later in the year, multiple attendees of a Dallas ReAwaken America event were taken ill, some quite seriously, having attended unmasked and unvaccinated. The group decided between themselves that there was only one logical explanation: they were showing all the signs of anthrax poisoning. These claims were then shared more widely across the internet by none other than 8chan founder – and leading contender to be the man behind 'Q' – Ron Watkins himself. Despite their claims to have evidence which pointed to anthrax – which is easy to test for – none, of course, was offered.[75]

The consequences of this kind of conspiracy-clouded judgement are not, of course, only confined to those who believe them. This is a simple fact of infectious diseases: if someone catches the virus due to being unvaccinated, they risk giving it to other vulnerable people, especially if they don't mask.

Some go further. Steven Brandenburg, a forty-six-year-old pharmacist in Wisconsin, pleaded guilty in 2021 to having intentionally spoiled hundreds of doses of Moderna vaccines by deliberately removing them from refrigeration overnight. In total, at least fifty-seven patients were given the deactivated vaccines. Brandenburg, who believes the earth is flat, told authorities he deactivated the vaccine because it was 'microchipped' and would 'turn off people's birth control and make others infertile'.[76]

Even before the beginning of the pandemic, QAnon was an amorphous and constantly evolving conspiracy that encouraged adherents to self-radicalise by focusing on the areas in which they were most interested. It was, therefore, ideally positioned to transform during the pandemic and bring in even more new communities across the world.

QAnon had since its inception grown by drawing people from the plausible to the preposterous, with a little help from the attention-focused algorithms of major social networks,[77] through the means of encouraging people to search out more of what appealed to them. Given the nebulous nature of QAnon, some people would be drawn in from wellness, some from the far right, some from anti-capitalism, and so on – letting people pick their own focus allows them to tailor the conspiracy.

That made it easy for the movement to adapt to new circumstances, and quite naturally agglomerate with the disparate coronavirus conspiracy theories, which otherwise may have come from very different political traditions – anti-lockdown from a classical liberal perspective or anti-vaccine from a mistrust of mainstream medicine, for example.

This ability to draw in disparate groups should not be mistaken for either harmony or consensus. The ability to reject any individual proposition made by a QAnon influencer in one statement (or broadcast interview) while then promoting the overall movement just moments later became a strength for QAnon. Any belief could be discarded or picked up again to suit the circumstances – it is hard to damn something that defies definition.

No one had to defend something they didn't believe, but no one had to disavow the movement unless they wanted to. And thanks to the numerous groups sort-of-but-not-quite-affiliated-with-

QAnon, anti-vaccination groups – just like #SaveTheChildren – could honestly claim not to be part of QAnon while continuing to associate with signed-up believers, and even parroting their views.

As Trump's presidency receded further into the past, the remnants of QAnon's 4chan and 8chan core relentlessly schismed and pivoted to new focuses. That last phase of that movement is worth examining before we move on to trying to explain what is underlying and underpinning these trends – and what, if anything, can be done to change them.

9

Nothing Can Stop What's Coming

Q's expansion into parenting groups and into radicalising those opposed to either vaccination rollout or lockdown-style restrictions was based on playing on reasonable and rational concerns and then pushing those to extremes. The name 'QAnon' was often kept away from things, and the most out-there viewpoints were kept somewhat on the downlow. These variants became a more appealing packaging of the core components of Q, whether deliberately or through online evolution. This led to journalists and academics following the movement naming it either 'Pastel QAnon'[1] or 'Soft Q'.[2]

But the name should not be taken to mean that the entire movement moderated itself, or that it became any more reasonable or cohesive. The core movement of QAnon had by the November 2020 US election been waiting for imminent action against a murderous, paedophilic, satanic cabal for three years – and then seen their messiah fail at the ballot box.

They had, for a few weeks, resolved that this was some kind of ruse or trap orchestrated by Trump, only to see Mike Pence fail to act on 6 January and Joe Biden peacefully and uneventfully inaugurated. This meant that the hardcore rump of QAnon – a group that believed Obama had a secret military force of child soldiers,[3] that Antifa was a coordinated deep state front used for false flag operations,[4] and that thousands or even millions of children were being held (or even raised) in underground tunnels[5] – needed some new ideas.

Demonstrating QAnon's ability to evolve constantly at every level, they found no shortage of directions in which to travel, splintering and recombining at various points. Where the previous chapters showed how parts of QAnon spurred on and merged with broader online movements located on Facebook, Telegram, WhatsApp and YouTube, this one focuses on what some of the most hardcore did. Some span off into groups so fringe even other QAnon supporters shunned them.

Seeing all the different ways that ideas developed through the QAnon phenomenon could adapt and merge with other conspiratorial factions is key to understanding that any idea – any hope – Q was a distinct phenomenon that might end with Trump was doomed. If anything, it had become something like a socially transmitted disease, moving through different populations just like a virus, sometimes becoming more extreme and dangerous, sometimes becoming more virulent and spreading more rapidly. Its transmission mechanism even transforms depending where it is and what's going on in the world.

On a global scale, QAnon managed to plant its ideas among child protection groups and anti-vaccine groups. But as we'll see through this chapter, it also managed to merge with Kennedy cults, fringe Catholic groups, deluded royal pretenders, existing groups panicking about gatherings of billionaires like Davos or Bilderberg, and more. It could bring conspiracies and their leaders and influencers together, and mobilise their followers.

One QAnon's strangest subcultures is the one that focuses on the Kennedys – because, after all, what respectable online conspiracy would miss an opportunity to involve America's so-called first family, that of John F. Kennedy, famously killed during a motorcade through Dallas in 1963?

The Kennedy family comes to feature in the broad QAnon movement in two different ways. The first involves someone that pretty much everyone – mainstream and conspiracist alike – agrees is an actual family member: Robert F. Kennedy Jr, the son of Senator 'Bobby' Kennedy (himself assassinated in 1968) and nephew of JFK.

Robert F. Kennedy Jr, a longstanding leader in the global anti-vaccination movement, became a favourite of QAnon-affiliated groups around the world. The German group Querdenken 711 (which roughly translates as 'Think Outside the Box 711') secured Kennedy to speak at a rally in Berlin in the autumn of 2020 – the same rally that attempted to break into the country's parliament building.

Kennedy had, in previous interviews, accused Anthony Fauci of trying to poison 'an entire generation' with the Covid-19 vaccine, and was a regular and vocal critic of Bill Gates. He was also a major booster of the idea that Covid vaccines were killing people in their droves, but that this was being covered up by the mainstream media and medical establishments.[6] But Kennedy, for all his popularity in the movement, is in many ways at most a warm-up act for the man this particular sub-group of Q believes to be the star turn.

From as early as 2019 – while the Q account was still regularly posting new drops – people within the QAnon movement had become convinced that there was a political saviour awaiting them, and it wasn't Donald Trump (unless it was – this one gets messy). That man, they decided, was the son of President Kennedy: John F. Kennedy Jr.

There is one major issue with this theory, though: JFK Jr is dead. He has been dead since 1999, when he was tragically killed alongside his wife and her sister when a light aircraft he was piloting to a family wedding crashed into the ocean, a few miles offshore of Martha's Vineyard, Massachusetts.[7]

According to this QAnon subculture, though, JFK Jr had in fact faked his own death in order to throw off the cabal and give himself time to plan their downfall. Members of the Kennedy family have asked the movement to respect their dead relatives and stop advancing these theories.[8]

The theory started on 8chan during a lull in Q posts, and was fuelled by a (fabricated) quote from JFK Jr, supposedly uttered a month before his death: 'If my dear friend Donald Trump ever decided to sacrifice his fabulous billionaire lifestyle to become president he would be an unstoppable force for ultimate justice that Democrats and Republicans alike would celebrate.'[9]

Some QAnon followers decided that a Trump supporter from Pennsylvania was a surgically disguised JFK Jr who was keeping his cover. Others decided he would resurface on 4 July 2019 (needless to say, he did not). Others still invented convoluted theories in which JFK Jr would be Trump's 2020 running mate (or vice versa) – which once again did not happen.[10]

But the cult of JFK Jr kept going beyond Trump's failed re-election, eventually culminating in a November 2021 vigil in Dallas led by a man called Michael Brian Protzman. An unlikely leader even for the QAnon movement, Protzman had for many years quietly run a demolition firm in Washington State before growing a Telegram group from fewer than 2,000 followers to more than 100,000. Even by QAnon standards, Protzman's antisemitism stood out: his channel denied the Holocaust, claimed communism was a Jewish plot and more.[11]

Protzman seemed to manage what few others had, building a sizeable and fanatical personal following within the QAnon movement. On Tuesday 2 November 2021, Protzman had persuaded hundreds of supporters from across the US to gather on the AT&T Discovery Plaza in the expectation that JFK Jr would make his reappearance on the grassy knoll from which his father was supposedly murdered and make a huge announcement.[12]

JFK Jr did not in fact put in an appearance, and the crowd dissipated in the heavy rain. But Protzman succeeded in persuading another crowd of hundreds back to Dallas two weeks later,[13] prompting BBC Monitoring's disinformation journalist Shayan Sardarizadeh to publicly express concern that Protzman's 'QAnon offshoot is rapidly turning into a full-on cult and this should be a huge cause for concern for everyone.'[14]

To the enduring mystification of journalists and QAnon-watchers alike, a hardcore persisted. Some of those present camped out for weeks or even months, expecting something to happen imminently despite their many and repeated disappointments. It was only by the spring of 2022 that this most outlandish of Q-related subgroups finally began to dissipate, a full five months or so since the initial pronouncements.

The group seemed to be displaying cognitive dissonance on a grand scale.[15] 'Cognitive dissonance' is a psychological term for the discomfort that comes when two beliefs we strongly hold clash, or when a belief clashes with reality. If we have invested months of our lives – possibly losing jobs or relationships – in believing a conspiracy, and the moment of truth doesn't come, we have two options.

We can either accept it was false, and in that moment accept that we have wasted all of that time and all of that pain – perhaps also accepting other people were right and we were wrong – or we can cling to an easier explanation where we can still be largely in the right. Perhaps the date was wrong, or maybe the cabal has thwarted the reappearance? People often take the psychologically easier track.

As VICE News reported, the fervent movement had 'torn families apart, leading husbands to divorce wives and children to disown parents', as well as leaving supporters 'destitute' after they donated their life savings to support Protzman's group. By March the group had dwindled to a mere few dozen, and had schismed into at least three distinct entities.

Despite this – and occasional ostracism from the more mainstream (everything is relative) parts of QAnon – people in Trump's orbit had been more than willing to indulge even this fringe of the fringe. Notorious Trump advisor Roger Stone, who had been convicted of lying to Congress in an investigation into Russian meddling in the 2016 US presidential election but later received a pardon from President Trump, met with the group in December 2021.[16] Stone, who has written several books on JFK, told reporters he didn't share the group's belief that JFK was alive, but shared other of their views (he did not specify in detail which he did and did not believe). However, even meeting with someone in Trump's immediate orbit lent the group legitimacy, both among existing QAnon supporters and Trump fans who could be pulled into the conspiracy.

The Great Reset

While the JFK subset of QAnon went on a strange journey to Dallas, a much larger number of QAnon and Q-adjacent adherents had settled on one idea that combined their long-running belief that there was a synchronised plot against most of humanity conducted by a well-coordinated global elite, and the theory that there was more to the pandemic than met the eye. That idea was 'the Great Reset'.

The term 'the Great Reset' had, for most of them, come from a book cowritten in June 2020 by Klaus Schwab, the then eighty-two-year-old founder of the World Economic Forum (often shortened to WEF). The WEF describes itself as a not-for-profit foundation based in Geneva, Switzerland, which 'engages the foremost political, business, cultural and other leaders of society to shape global, regional and industry agendas'.[17] Unlike most not-for-profits, it has an annual budget of around £300 million for its endeavours.[18] The organisation's most visible activity is the annual Davos forum of business and political leaders, which has one of the most elite guest lists in global affairs.

In other words, there are almost no organisations in the world that might be quite so appealing a target for conspiracy theorists, and its head of fifty years had just published a book titled *Covid-19: The Great Reset*. Everything the people within QAnon had believed was going on behind the scenes appeared to have been laid out right there in the open.

One page from the book in particular caught conspirators' attention. In his 2020 book, they claimed, Schwab had written:

At least 4 billion 'useless eaters' shall be eliminated by the year 2050 by means of limited wars, organised epidemics of fatal rapid-acting diseases and starvation. Energy, food and water shall be kept at subsistence levels for the non-elite, starting with the White populations of Western Europe and North America and then spreading to other races. The population of Canada, Western Europe and the United States will be decimated more rapidly than other continents, until the world's population reaches a manageable level of 1 billion, of which 500 million will consist of Chinese and Japanese races, selected because they are people who have been regimented for centuries and who are accustomed to obeying authority without question.

If ever in history there was a smoking gun, here it was: a genocidal (and wildly racist) conspiracy to kill off more than 80 per cent of the world's population, for some inexplicable reason openly published in a book available on sale to the public.

Except, as any reader with the tiniest modicum of common sense might realise, the book said nothing of the sort. The passage was instead taken from a conspiratorial 1992 book by John Coleman entitled *Conspirators' Hierarchy: The Story of the Committee of 300*[19] – which, incidentally, had been found in Osama bin Laden's compound after his death.[20] That book had in turn falsely claimed that the paragraph was contained in the 1928 H. G. Wells book *The Open Conspiracy: Blue Prints for a World Revolution*.[21]

The actual *The Great Reset* book is somewhat less exciting, though some would surely still find it objectionable. Something of a technocratic policy tome, only around 250 or so pages long, it calls for 'greater collaboration and cooperation within and between countries' (which can be classed as a globalist approach), and calls for shared action against nuclear threats, climate change, 'unsustainable use of resources like forests, seafood, topsoil and fresh water' and 'the consequences of the enormous differences in standards of living between the world's peoples'.[22]

People can agree or disagree with the WEF and its thesis, but it takes a lot of misreading to find something genocidal encoded in these pages. And yet nothing more than a quick look at the book's reviews on Google – still up more than a year after publication – reveal no shortage of people who have done just that:

'All I can say that he was pretty fast with his writing, editing, and printing to have this published so early in 2020. He must be a profit [sic].'

'This is a book by two of the Perpetrators of this Crime Against Humantity [sic], along with Bill Gates, Fauci, Daszak, et. al. If they are allowed to get away with this, it will only continue into the future, with the next Pandemic Crime Against Humanity (and a new Bioengineered Virus intentionally released into society).'

'I suggest you wake up. Stop getting jabbed from a case of the cold and stop watching the media and did I say wake up ? I dont want to be killed by child diddling satanists like klaus schwabstein [*sic*]'

'All us "crazy tin foil, far right, nazi, white supremacist, racist, sexist conspiracy theorists" (whatever other msm buzz word to discredit us people with the ability to see for ourselves are right then ... It was the great reset and covid19 was used to implement it.'[23]

That's just a small selection of the dangerous falsehoods in circulation. Curious as to what it must feel like to find your organisation accused of orchestrating world affairs, and be deluged by people across the world, I asked Adrian Monck,[24] the WEF's managing director for public and social engagement, what the experience had been like – and why a provocative title like *Covid-19: The Great Reset* had been chosen in the first place.

'*Covid-19: The Great Reset* grew out of previous work on financing the green transition,' he says. 'Not necessarily the most exciting of topics, but nonetheless an important one. It was an attempt to encourage leaders – and the public – not to lose sight of issues like climate change, but also technology innovation and inequality. As a book it's actually been pretty popular.'

The trouble for the WEF actually started on ultra-conservative Catholic blogs and Facebook pages, Monck says. Archbishop Carlo Maria Viganò, an influential figure in US conservative Catholic circles, wrote an open letter to President Trump in June 2020 asking the Lord to protect him in a clash between 'the children of light and the children of darkness', a battle against the new world order.[25] Viganò later made the target of his remarks far more explicit in a lengthy tirade against *Covid-19: The Great Reset*.[26] The idea of the WEF's involvement with dark forces was recycled in familiar fashion across different online groups.[27]

'Viganò literally makes something that Dan Brown would struggle to invent and trots it out to his small audience of, well, conspiracy theorists,' says Monck.

So there's a moment of invention by this fringe figure in extreme US Catholicism, and then the ultra-rightist conspiracy bandwagon gets rolling ...

The Great Reset became a sort of 'nudge nudge, wink wink' masonic handshake for conspiracy theorists. Klaus Schwab, the former business school professor who heads the Forum, joined Anthony Fauci, Bill Gates and George Soros as one of the conspiracy theorists' bêtes noires.

By this time outlets led by Russia Today (the role of the Russian state in this as 'mischief maker in chief' appears key) – but also noted conspiracy site the Epoch Times – started to pick up on it. They used the climate change message (which was simply that we had to keep trying to tackle it) as a way to denounce what they called confusingly 'eco-communism' or 'green fascism'.

The interplay between fringe online platforms, major social media platforms and state-controlled media outlets with their own agendas created enough sound and fury on their own, but ostensibly mainstream media outlets also fanned the flames.

'The most disturbing organisation to pick it up was Sky News Australia,' he says. 'Because they had some legacy reputation as a news organisation we offered spokespeople – but it turned out they weren't interested in hearing from us. They'd noticed that a tiny fraction of their tiny audience was trading in climate denialism, and dog-whistling the Great Reset simply traded on conspiracy memes that fitted their own radical climate denial agenda.'

Staff in Monck's team and across the WEF found themselves getting emailed and social media threats, abuse and accusations – something Monck himself was used to after a long career as a TV journalist, but many in the organisation had never experienced.

'The hardest thing is that you are used to engaging with people on a rational level, and there is no engaging with people who think you are secretly running the world,' he says. 'Although you are supposedly so powerful that you are running the world, you are also so powerless that you can't stop them making threats or abusing you. It's Catch-22.'

'At the same time, some people have been through a bruising experience with the pandemic, people are scared, they are isolated, and they can fall prey to snake oil salesmen and conspiracy theorists. So you feel sorry for the victims, but not the grifters who are trading on this stuff.'

One group WEF did consistently keep communicating with on *Covid-19: The Great Reset* was online fact-checking organisations – but that process also left Monck somewhat disillusioned.

> We responded to fact-checking journalism, which occasionally seized on memes. However, the role of fact-checking journalists in tackling misinformation was compromised. News organisations were being paid by social media platforms, which were effectively acting as conveners and radicalisers, to 'fact check' the very poisoning of the public sphere that they were making a living out of enabling. It was like tobacco companies paying people to pick up cigarette butts.

Monck said his view was that the role of journalism was to focus on the people who were intentionally leading the spread of these theories, or profiting from them – but said that too few were actually doing that.

Despite working for one of the world's most elite convening organisations, Monck essentially found himself and the WEF helpless in the storm they were facing. There is no convincing way to deny a conspiracy as virulent as QAnon once it has you in its sights, no matter who you are.

The Queen of Canada

Others would happily throw themselves into the eye of Q's storm. One such individual is Romana Didulo of Victoria, Canada, who became another leader of a subgroup of QAnon and who declared herself queen of Canada, using her status as monarch to deliver frequent proclamations and calls to action.[28]

Didulo amassed hundreds of thousands of followers across different social networks (before losing them in various bans), and a Telegram group devoted to her with tens of thousands of followers. She claimed the actual queen of Canada (at that time Queen Elizabeth II) had been executed by June 2021, and that she herself had been appointed in her place by 'the same group of people who helped president Trump' – a slightly bizarre deep-state reference from a movement that supposedly was opposing the deep state.[29]

QAnon followers were taken by Romana Didulo's name – an anagram of 'I am our Donald' – and she gained a following. Didulo has also pretended to have support – and to have received personal gifts – from Vladimir Putin,[30] and has made barely veiled calls for her supporters to take violent action.

Self-proclaimed royalty or hidden 'true kings' have existed as long as the monarchy, and are overwhelmingly ignored or derided. But in the QAnon era, even a figure as apparently ridiculous as Didulo could find a following. Her actions included calling for supporters in Canada and the US to arm themselves for 'duck hunting' season, in which she openly urged them to make armed arrests of 'everyone and anyone assisting in the injecting of coronavirus bioweapon into children'.[31] She added an instruction to 'shoot to kill' such people[32] – those administering a lifesaving vaccine, approved by independent bodies across the world – leading to her being briefly detained by the Canadian authorities. Many of Didulo's posts use the emblematic QAnon 'Where We Go One, We Go All' slogan.[33]

Canada – a country known around the world for being overly nice and easy-going – now had an increasingly lurid fringe movement. This had its real moment in the spotlight when a so-called 'Freedom Convoy' of truckers drove to the centre of Ottawa and engaged in a loud, persistent protest that blocked key highways through February 2022 – leading to a string of related protests and blockades elsewhere across the nation.

Counter-terror and extremism assessments had warned well in advance that the convoy was tied to extreme and conspiratorial movements, such as Didulo, who visited and addressed the

Ottowa crowds,[34] QAnon and the Canadian far right.[35] Prime minister Justin Trudeau was forced to get approval to employ never-before-used emergency powers to deal with the persistent blockades, which imperilled vital trade routes between the USA and Canada.[36]

The actual demands of those in the convoy protest in Ottowa were unclear and inconsistent, at best. Though ostensibly about ending the country's remaining Covid-19 restrictions, some signs urged passers-by (in the largely liberal city) to 'take the red pill', while other convoy protesters expressed support for controversial Canadian academic Jordan Peterson.[37] Didulo used her time at the protest to burn a Canadian flag outside parliament. So all-consuming was the protest for some involved that one man told CBC that he had spent his life savings of $13,000 (Canadian) to financially support the truckers – despite having no stance on vaccination – and had lost his home after his landlord kicked him out over the process.[38]

In a particularly joyous moment of self-fulfilling prophecy – and an illustration of the many-headed beast the breeding grounds of the internet had spawned – numerous protestors in the 'Freedom Convoy' movement cited the Great Reset as one of the reasons behind their presence.

The blockade – which had been condemned by Canada's own Teamsters' Union, which represents truckers – eventually caused Trudeau to invoke emergency powers, including freezing bank accounts of people involved, a huge and arguably draconian action in a democracy.[39] This was potentially an overreaction in itself, both mirroring and spurring on the hysteria of the protests. So fierce was the reaction to the convoy that former Fox News host and conspiracy theorist Glenn Beck used this action as proof that the Great Reset was already underway.[40]

The American QAnon movement, having seen the attention paid to and 'success' of the Ottawa protests, decided that they would do the same in the USA, attempting to organise an even more overtly pro-Q convoy on Washington, DC, a ripped-from-fiction real life re-enactment of the fictional trucker's revolution from the 1975 C. W. McCall song 'Convoy'.[41]

The DC convoy on its various stops across the country reunited various splintering parts of the QAnon movement – as NBC's Ben Collins noted, 'the cult that believes JFK Jr. is alive joined the convoy when they came through Dallas to spread the gospel' – with people at refuelling stops chanting 'where we go one, we go all'.[42]

The eventual destination of the convoy, or its aim, were never really made clear: some of those participating (most of whom were in cars, SUVs, RVs or flatbeds, rather than trucks) thought they would be able to get their vehicles to the White House, while others thought they could block DC's huge ring road, the Beltway.[43]

DC, though, is not Ottawa, and the Secret Service is not known for being relaxed about security when it concerns the president and federal government. As a result, the convoy became becalmed for days outside of the DC areas, although it was occasionally allowed to fruitlessly circle the Beltway (most of which is outside of DC)[44] or camp out in nearby towns.

The ever-dwindling convoy attracted predictable ire from the DC workers whose commutes they were disrupting – with one bold cyclist, Daniel Adler, forty-nine, successfully slowing the entire convoy on his own as a frustrated protest. 'I heard the stories of the traffic on the Beltway breaking up the convoy,' he told the *Washington Post*, 'and I thought I, too, could break up the convoy.'[45]

DC residents seemed bemused that the convoy protestors didn't seem to realise DC residents had no control over what Congress did nationwide, or that the city's vaccine and mask mandates ended before the convoy began. The somewhat muddled copycat exercise might have rebuilt some connections and community within Q's hardcore, but it ended up dissipating in late March, having barely made it into DC, and with nothing in the way of accomplishments to claim.

Like a vampire that needs to feed, Q always seems to need to find some new trick to lure fresh blood into the movement, or at least to re-energise those that might otherwise drift away – and continued to find them through 2022. One passing opportunity came through Florida's 'Don't Say Gay' bill – a bid to prevent

LGBTQ education to children in the state, akin to the UK's longstanding (and long-abolished) Section 28 law.[46] Disney, as a company with a huge presence in the state and with a large LGBTQ contingent in its staff, came under internal pressure to oppose the bill, prompting a backlash against the company from the right. For parts of QAnon, this became a chance to combine the anti-LGBT agenda with its own conspiracy of mass child abuse: what is teaching toddlers about gayness, they insinuated, if not some plan to groom them, or at least stop them reproducing?

When a few far-right and QAnon-affiliated influencers picked up on this debate and sent it viral, Tucker Carlson – the most famous anchor of Fox News, the USA's most-watched cable news channel – jumped right in, sounding just like someone posting on the 8chan boards in the winter of 2017.

> Their main 'goal as a company is to teach kindergarteners in Florida that they can in fact change their gender just by wishing it so. It makes you wonder if kids in Florida can consent to chemical castration with no parental involvement. If that can be true, what exactly can't they consent to, once we set that standard? Disney didn't say, but maybe there's another agenda here – nor did they explain their fixation on the sexuality of children. But it's worth pointing out four Disney employees were just busted in a major human trafficking sting, including one employee who allegedly sent sexually explicit texts to a detective posing as a 14-year-old.[47]

As a VICE piece highlighting the Fox News–Republican Party–QAnon nexus noted, people were getting the message, and some were heading down the rabbit hole, following Fox News's directions, as one tweet handily surmises: 'I know next to nothing about QAnon, but I'm told that among the things they believe is that a global cabal of elites promotes paedophilia. Sounds insane until you read what the Disney boss is saying and doing.'[48]

Thanks to the regular reappearances of Trump, the willingness of his former close associates to endorse QAnon and the shamelessness of Fox News and many Republican candidates in engaging with Q, the movement had become amorphous but still viable – but one particular world event would give it a whole new lease of life.

QAnon, Trump, Russia and Ukraine

That event was, of course, Russia's unprovoked and unjustifiable invasion of Ukraine. While (as ever) there are points of nuance people can contend, few things in foreign affairs are ever quite so clear as that particular conflict. Ukraine was a fully independent sovereign state, recognised as such by the UN, and Russia invaded it with a huge army, which then besieged multiple cities, including the capital.

But, of course, Trump and Russia have a convoluted relationship – meaning QAnon, Trump and Russia have a convoluted relationship. Muddying these waters still further was the fact that Ukraine – or rather, Trump's decision to hold military aid for Ukraine unless it provided him with dirt on Joe Biden – provoked his impeachment.[49] As if the waters weren't muddy enough already, Hunter Biden – Joe Biden's son – had been a long-term lobbyist for Ukranian oil and gas giant Burisma, which Fox News and QAnon had long tried to mine for scandal. In particular, a story around a laptop supposedly owned by Hunter Biden and obtained by a computer repair shop had been a rich vein of stories for Fox and others.[50]

Given Russia's willingness to pump out endless misinformation to support its own military actions,[51] the very real and deeply tragic Russia–Ukraine conflict was also some kind of end-of-season finale for QAnon and the groups around it, with something for everyone – leaving some despairing at even having made jokes on those lines.

On 20 March, Joshua Holland tweeted 'There's a biolab in Hunter Biden's laptop.' Four days later, Sputnik – an international 'news' outlet controlled by the Russian state – published a story titled: 'Hunter Biden's Investment Fund Connected to Financing of Pentagon-Funded Biolabs in Ukraine: MoD', leading Holland to despair: 'What is even the point of making jokes these days?'[52]

Appropriately – inevitably? – enough, Ukrainian biolabs became a focal point of the conflict for QAnon-related groups and for occasional Russian propaganda lines alike. It appears to have started with the former group, who also tied the labs (which in reality are public health research labs, not bioweapons factories)[53] to Anthony Fauci – on the very first day of the conflict.

As usual, Tucker Carlson and Fox News picked up the useful angle, alongside Russia's international propaganda outlet RT (formerly Russia Today).[54] Russian officials, having made absolutely zero mention of Ukraine's (fictional) biological weapons labs before its invasion, started to cite this retroactively as their reason for invasion. QAnon was now influencing geopolitics as well as multiple countries' internal affairs, at least to the extent of giving Russia's extraordinarily malleable information operations a new line to push for a few days. (Of course, Russia likely played a role in playing up QAnon, too – just as it pushes division in Western countries around Black Lives Matter, Antifa, hijab-wearing and any other issues it can find.)[55]

Inevitably, of course, some QAnons detected Trump's hand in things, with some suggesting he was working with Putin to destroy Fauci's Ukrainian labs by targeting them with shelling,[56] despite the massive evidence to the contrary. However, the broader biolabs idea predictably – given the platforms it was aired over – won some people over.

On 30 March 2022, YouGov published polling of American attitudes on Ukraine finding that 26 per cent of US adults thought the US was 'definitely' or 'probably' developing bioweapons in Ukrainian labs. Seventeen per cent thought the same of the idea that Ukraine was faking bomb attacks and laying the blame at Russia's door.

Perhaps more interesting was a breakdown of those groups, though. Of the 26 per cent who believed the bioweapons claim, three-quarters had a 'favourable view of QAnon' while almost two-thirds viewed Alex Jones as 'trustworthy'. Similarly, the majority of those who thought Ukraine was faking bombing videos said they had a favourable view of QAnon.[57]

A separate survey in Canada also showed the interplay between different and supposedly distinct movements. Polling by EKOS found that 52 per cent of Canadians who had chosen to remain unvaccinated thought Canada should take no action (including sanctions or asset seizures) against Russia over its invasion of Ukraine – compared with just 2 per cent of people who were fully vaccinated.[58]

Not only was the internet continuing to blend and merge what had once been very distinct movements and ideas together, but QAnon's core communities were still growing in both size and impact. As the 2022 US midterms approached, polling by PPRI found that support for the ideas of QAnon was still growing, now making up 16 per cent of the adult population, or 40 million people across the country.[59]

Candidates supporting QAnon were also running for election, with the Anti-Defamation League counting at least forty-five Q-adjacent candidates for office in the midterm elections.[60] Perhaps most starkly, a network of extremist candidates for the position of Secretary of State in battleground election states – who play a major role in conducting and certifying elections – was found to be coordinated by major QAnon influencers.[61]

Anyone who had predicted Q would dissipate once Trump was out of office was rapidly being proven completely wrong. It could even be that through its organising abilities, it could play an instrumental role in getting Trump or a Trump-a-like candidate back into the Oval Office in 2024.

But Q himself and Q influencers had been consistently, repeatedly and demonstrably wrong time and time again, since the very inception of the movement. No mass-scale revelations had ever taken place, no children had been released from tunnels, JFK Jr had made no appearance. Far from saving the children, Trump cut funding for sex trafficking victims during his presidency.[62]

The natural assumption would be that all of these disappointments would shake the faith of those involved, leading to disillusionment and the eventual end of QAnon as a movement. But there are people who could have warned – and did warn – that the natural assumptions were wrong. Let's meet them.

PART FOUR

Convalescence

10

Trust the Plan

If ever there was a dark night of the soul for the QAnon movement, it was 20 January 2021. Not only had Joe Biden just been inaugurated as the 46th president of the United States of America, but the 6 January Capitol Hill riot, just two weeks earlier, had – temporarily, as it turned out – shifted the mood even in the Republican Party against its far-right wing and their QAnon boosters. Donald Trump had lost the election two months before, but QAnon had found no shortage of reasons to hope, to keep trusting the plan. But by 20 January, all seemed lost.

You could be forgiven for thinking the same of the morning of 4 November 2020. QAnons had spent three years trusting the plan, waiting for the storm to come, expecting mass arrests, rescues or even civil war at any moment. Then, over the course of the morning, it all seemed to be going wrong: Donald Trump's election leads were evaporating, Joe Biden was going to win, and Q hadn't posted since a few hours before the election. What happened to the plan?

How does someone carry on believing something after every logical and rational sign points the other way? Why do we cling to some ideas when we're able to cast off others? With QAnon, how did people continue to 'trust the plan' when the plan kept changing – and none of it ever came off?

In a Twitter thread with more than 26,000 retweets, a man claiming to be US Air Force veteran Tom Graham had an answer for those worried in November 2020: Democrats had fallen into Trump's trap. Trump was watching the results in a secure facility, knowing the Democrats would fake them. Secretly, he had marked the ballots using blockchain technology. Soon, the fraud would be revealed, and the Democrats locked up. Trust the plan, even though the plan keeps changing.[1]

For those holding the faith, things started to look up again. After a ten-day silence, Q resurfaced on 13 November,[2] initially posting a US flag accompanied by this short message:

> Nothing can stop what is coming.
> Nothing!
> Q[3]

Less than an hour later came a more thorough message, back in Q's trademark style. (It would actually turn out to be Q's final ever such message – before its brief 2022 comeback, the account only posted twice more, one message containing only the word 'Durham' and the other with just a single YouTube link.)

> Shall we play a game?
> [N]othing [C]an [S]top [W]hat [I]s [C]oming
> NCSWIC
> https://www.cisa.gov/safecom/NCSWIC
> Who stepped down today [forced]?
> https://www.cisa.gov/bryan-s-ware
> More coming?
> Why is this relevant?
> How do you 'show' the public the truth?
> How do you 'safeguard' US elections post-POTUS?
> How do you 'remove' foreign interference and corruption and install US-owned voter ID law(s) and other safeguards?
> It had to be this way.
> Sometimes you must walk through the darkness before you see the light.
> Q[4]

With its typical love of wordplay and coincidences – in this case the confluence of first letters between 'Nothing Can Stop What Is

Coming' and the National Council of Statewide Interoperability Coordinators, a body set up by the USA's Cybersecurity and Infrastructure Security Agency, whose head of cybersecurity Bryan Ware had been ousted by Trump that day – Q could return to suggesting dramatic things were happening behind the scenes.[5]

Of course, as we now well know, dramatic things *were* happening behind the scenes – just not in any way that related to random (or forced by Q's operator) coincidences of initialisms.

Trump's inner team at the time were all keeping thoroughly abreast of QAnon and the movement's manifold beliefs. Several of them, including the president, seemed to believe their own hype about a stolen election.[6] Trump genuinely was trying – using the full weight of his office as he did[7] – to get the Department of Justice[8] and officials in battleground states to interfere with the election results.[9]

Given that QAnon had spent four years believing momentous things were happening behind the scenes when in reality nothing was happening at all, in one sense this period in November and December 2020 was the closest they came to being correct. The White House was openly talking about things not that dissimilar to what they believed, even if QAnon's wilder ideas went rather further.

L. Lin Wood, a lawyer and conspiracy theorist who later shared a platform with Trump associates Sidney Powell and Michael Flynn,[10] suggested in this period that those who had betrayed Trump, including Vice President Mike Pence, Chief Justice of the Supreme Court John Roberts, and (then) Senate Majority Leader Mitch McConnell, would soon be rounded up, arrested and 'face execution by firing squad'.[11]

QAnon was dreaming big, and on a tight deadline. The mood of the time is well summed up by one QAnon newsletter from early in November:

Before Trump gets inaugurated in January there will be an insurrection with organized riots. Those riots will be put down with a deployed military. The internet and/or social media will be paused in an attempt to censor the President, but he will communicate with us via the emergency broadcast system.

All of this seems a bit far out, but keep in mind it was written before the organized BLM/Antifa riots. Q is well ahead of the game … These things take time, but the big action is set to happen before Jan 2021 because the deep state is trying to prevent Trump from taking office again and they will deploy every asset they have to try to prevent it.[12]

Travis View, an impeccably informed QAnon researcher, shared the newsletter on Twitter at the time – and expressed a degree of scepticism and maybe even surprise that Q-related influencers were still making such short-term and specific claims. 'A QAnon newsletter I subscribe to is still telling followers that Trump's inauguration in January is inevitable,' he said, describing it as 'deeply disconnected from reality with a hard deadline for disconfirmation'.[13]

In the period that QAnon was perhaps as fervent as they ever had been – the gap between November 2020 and January 2021 – mainstream commentators seemed ready to write it off, to an even greater extent than the Travis View tweet. The consensus commentariat view at the time is neatly summed up in this paragraph from Nathan J. Robinson, founder and editor-in chief of *Current Affairs* magazine.

I actually think QAnon itself is not terribly threatening *at the moment*, because much of it is focused on figuring out what 'Q' and Donald Trump are doing, and what the Rothschilds are doing. Though QAnon predicts a day of reckoning in which Trump will round up the evil cabal, it's dependent on Donald Trump to act, and Donald Trump will soon be out of office. The whole Q theory cannot really last beyond Trump's last day in office. I think many of these people are soon going to discover that they need a new theory once the Great Awakening doesn't happen.' (Emphasis original).[14]

The online activity on the day of 20 January itself seemed to vindicate that sceptical view that QAnon's day was done – that this had been one failed prophecy too many.

Instead of mass protests or violence in DC to protest the event, there was just a single one-man protest from former NBA pro David Wood, who told reporters that because Trump hadn't actually said Joe Biden's name in his pre-recorded farewell address, that signalled he would only transfer power to himself.

Wood wore a GoPro camera, a US flag hoodie, a shofar horn (an instrument traditionally made from ram's horn and used in Jewish religious ceremonies) and a flag to his protest.

'I'll tell you what's going to happen, Donald Trump is going to serve four more years,' he told a small gaggle of reporters. 'Joe Biden could be inaugurated. He could be arrested right after he's inaugurated, but it's safe to say he's going to resign soon.'[15]

This faith was not matched by those watching events on QAnon's original home, 8chan. Nicky Woolf, the man who tracked down the Watkins family in Chapter Three, spent the inauguration day tracking activity on the forum, as did NBC's Ben Collins. It is safe to say the mood was somewhat bleak:

'There is no plan.'

'It's over and nothing makes sense … absolutely nothing.'

'I don't think it's supposed to happen? How long does it take the fed to run up the stairs and arrest him?'

'It's like being a kid and seeing the big gift under the tree thinking it is exactly what you want only to open it and realise it was a lump of coal.'

'Welcome to the final series of America'

'Trump lied and failed is [sic]. Simple as that.'

'Worst day in American history.'

'He sold us out. Its revolution time'[16]

Such was the visible break of faith on the day that even experienced online conspiracy reporters and commentators thought the movement might be facing a reckoning,[17] or even at its end – not least because even Ron Watkins himself, in his role as 8chan administrator rather than an avowed operator of the Q trip code, said it was time to move on.[18]

'We need to keep our chins up and go back to our lives as best we are able,' Watkins posted on Telegram. 'We have a new president sworn in and it is our responsibility as citizens to respect the Constitution regardless of whether or not we agree with the specifics. As we enter into the next administration please remember all the friends and happy memories we made together over the past few years.'

When even the man whose forum had relied on QAnon for most of its audience and attention was trying to post a message of peace and reconciliation, surely the end had come?

Given Trump's waning power and the fact that Democrats were now (just barely) in the majority in both houses of Congress, Big Tech had become emboldened to tackle misinformation from the outgoing president – flagging his posts as false, or even suppressing some entirely, for the first time[19] – and from his followers.

Indeed, on the eve of Biden's inauguration, Facebook chose to publicly disclose just how many QAnon-related accounts and pages it had removed: 3,300 pages, 10,500 groups, 510 events, 18,300 Facebook profiles and 27,300 Instagram accounts[20] – though as Media Matters for America CEO Angelo Carusone noted, throughout 2020 Facebook had allowed QAnon-related groups to grow at between ten and thirty times the rate of more mainstream political content, all fuelled by its own algorithms.[21]

Another apparent sign that Q was reaching its end was the very public recriminations between people who had been QAnon boosters, far-right figures who had not signed up to Q and others. Retired baseball player Aubrey Huff (whose account was later deleted for violating Twitter's rules)[22] posted following the election defeat that 'QAnon was a democratic strategy to keep many conservatives complacent in "trusting the plan" while the left continued their evil corruption.'[23]

Far-right commentator Raheem Kassan, a former editor-in-chief of Breitbart London, posted: 'I'be [sic] said it before, I'll say it again: Q and the "trust the plan" thing was always a psyop to control conservatives and ultimately destroy them.'[24] He followed it up a few minutes later with a kicker: 'The fact that so many people are crying over this tweet because they've become emotionally attached to an internet game is proof of my point. Please unfollow me. You're mentally ill.'[25]

There were so many recriminations that QAnon and the conspiracy community around it – many of whom were frantically trying to distance themselves from any involvement – resembled nothing so much as a circular firing squad. World-controlling alien reptile expert David Icke posted a video against a 'QANON IS A PSYOP – WAKE UP PEOPLE' backdrop, warning his viewers that 'QAnon is kind of a secret grouping that came out during the early period of the Trump administration and persuaded a lot of people that there was a plan, a plan to arrest the bad guys, and the good guys were gonna do that ... When I heard that, my head shook and I said "oh my god, not another one." '[26] Icke dismissed QAnon as the latest iteration of a recurring 'scam' that dissuaded people from acting against those in power. Followers of Q in Telegram chatrooms appear to agree. 'It's over,' said one. 'We've been had,' another despaired.[27]

It is hardly, at this stage of the book, a spoiler to say that those who took all of these public signs of abandonment at face value turned out to be wrong – QAnon's death had been called very, very prematurely. But while that may have come as a surprise to lots of journalists and commentators who had been following the movement for years, and were now seeing it behave in ways it never had before, there was one group who had seen this all before – and had an inkling of what was coming next.

That group was sociologists – rarely the heroes in any story, alas. The reason they were warier is that this wasn't the first time they'd studied monumental events that had failed to materialise. Several of them had even lived through the end of the world – some more than once.

When prophecies fail

Dorothy Martin and her followers knew the world was facing disaster on 21 December 1954, and that benevolent aliens would arrive to deliver them from it just in time. Martin had been receiving visitations, first from her father (who had only delivered mundane messages to her mother and other relations), and then from a figure identifying himself as 'Elder Brother', helping prepare her spiritual development and explaining the higher planes.[28]

On 20 December, Martin and a small band of followers were sitting in her home, expecting to be delivered by the aliens before midnight. Early on the morning of 21 December, around 7 a.m. the entirety of earth would be deluged by a global flood akin to that which had occurred in the biblical era of Noah. A gaggle of pranksters, curious onlookers and the media waited outside.

Some of Martin's followers had quit their jobs, others had given away their worldly possessions. All of them in the home that evening, per her instructions, had stripped themselves of any metal on their person, however small, meaning jeans studs, bra wires, watches and more.

What the group didn't know was that there were spies in their midst: an academic sociologist and paid observers had been with the group. These imposters were intent on studying what happens when a prophetic cult with a very specific core belief gets very definite proof that what was predicted did not come to pass.

At 11:35 p.m. the undercover sociologist made an admission to the group – he had not removed the zip from his trousers. This prompted a panicked and hurried effort by one of those present to cut it out with a razor, hastily putting a stitch or two in place to hold his trousers up. When this sociologist met his otherworldly companions, he would have to do it with loose trousers. It was 11:50 p.m.

Midnight came and midnight went, and no extraterrestrial visitors came. The group became agitated, fretting that they had either missed an instruction, got something wrong or had somehow proven unworthy. As minutes turned to hours, panic set in. People had rendered themselves destitute, given up their jobs. What was to become of them?

The mood in the room got progressively worse, with some becoming angry and some deeply panicked. Shortly before 5 a.m., after spending some time alone, Martin eventually came to the group with good news: the group's faith had averted the apocalypse.

'Not since the beginning of time upon this Earth has there been such a force of Good and light as now floods this room and that which has been loosed within this room now floods the entire Earth,' she told the small gathering. 'As thy God has spoken through the two who sit within those walls has he manifested that which he has given thee to do.'

One person present picked up his coat and left. The others, though, rejoiced. They had, after all, accomplished something monumental.

Dorothy Martin and her small, non-violent cult are famous in certain academic circles, as is the study of them, led by Leon Festinger – the undercover sociologist and also the man who had forgotten to remove his zip in the minutes before the anticipated Rapture.

The study, eventually published as the book *When Prophecy Fails* in 1956 by Minnesota University Press, and its methodology remain deeply controversial to this day, but it was from it that the concept of cognitive dissonance is taken. It's a core psychological tenet we've already applied to QAnon's supporters, but to explain how Q survived January 2021, it merits deeper examination.

Cognitive dissonance refers to the discomfort we feel when our ideas or beliefs clash either with each other or with objective reality. This can be as simple as 'I am a good person, but I have just stolen,' or as specific as 'I believe the world will end today, but it hasn't.' The bigger the clash, the bigger the discomfort – and the more urgent the need to find something that will once again make the two align. For those in Martin's small cult, there were several options: they could disconnect from the cult and convince themselves they never really believed it, come to believe they were scammed, think that the end was still coming but the dates were a little wrong (the dates changed a few times, obviously never delivering the apocalypse on any of them), or redouble their belief in Martin and her explanation.

Inevitably, the group did not move as one – some taking each option, or some combination or variation of them. *When*

Prophecy Fails was not a perfect study by any means, but its core idea certainly holds. More specifically, it should serve as all the forewarning anyone would need that the idea that a movement as nebulous, intense and vague as QAnon could fade away after just one disconfirming incident was always doomed. QAnon had developed far too many ways of pulling people in, infecting them, mutating and spreading to be dispelled so easily.

Peter Knight, an American Studies professor at the University of Manchester and conspiracy theory researcher, believes people following and trying to tackle the harm of QAnon and other emergent online movements should have looked to this historical research sooner to guide them in what would happen.

'Sociologists have long known that failed prophecy does not mean the end of the movement,' he tells me. 'It did for *some* people in Q – it was heartening to see that – they did kind of come to their senses: there's a reasonable amount of anecdotal journalistic evidence of that out there. But in general, what we know from previous such cult movements is that they don't go away easily.'[29] Some people were always going to remain part of Q, some perhaps even more fervently than before, following the inauguration of Joe Biden – especially given how the internet helps conspiracies in their evolution.

But, as Knight goes on to say, the world also got doubly (or even triply) unlucky with the Covid-19 pandemic: not only did we have to tackle it, but it also overlapped with this era of conspiracy, polarisation and mistrust. This created a toxic feedback loop, in which mistrust made the pandemic worse, but the pandemic itself also pulled people into these marginal groups.

'Though we can exaggerate this idea of the perfect storm, there is really something to be said for the idea of it,' he sets forth. 'The coincidence of social media, which had never really taken seriously its responsibilities for cleaning up its act, with a pandemic that's epic on a global scale, *and* this nascent broader rise of populism too, of the kind of Trump, Brexit, and [Brazilian President Jair] Bolsonaro – that's creating strain.

So, you bring those three things together, that goes a long way to explaining why QAnon took off in the way that it did.

Without the pandemic, it probably wouldn't have been so big, and similarly if social media have done more to clean up its act earlier, then maybe – just maybe – QAnon and the mainstreaming of conspiracism would not have been so big as it is.'

Knight does warn, though, against imagining that quick technical fixes might solve the deep-rooted issues that help feed movements like Q – stressing that societal factors as well as accessibility of information and community are always going to be major drivers of interest.

'The real problem is this larger issue of a sense of alienation and disaffection from those who feel that they've been left behind – those who feel that the elites and the institutions of society are fundamentally untrustworthy,' he says. 'If you don't address that larger problem, and if you don't take that problem seriously, then you're going to fail to understand Q, and fail to be able to do anything about it.'

Knight's remarks sat with me for some time after we finished talking. I had been focused on how the structure of the internet propelled Q into an ever-changing entity, adapting itself for different audiences – but this made me think I had glossed over a vital piece of the puzzle.

Teenage boys *always* feel alienated from society (or at least some of them do) – as do young men in their twenties. There's a reason some variation of 'angry young men' becomes a trope across so many time periods.[30] Doubtless if society had paid anything more than passing notice to young women before the twenty-first century they would have found they felt much the same way.

But the appeal to older adults is clearly not just a factor of the internet. If any group in society is ignored and undervalued, shunted to the side, it is suburban mothers and other women (it's usually women)[31] with caring responsibilities. This could only have been heightened since the financial crash of 2007–8, where the elites got off lightly but most workers didn't see real pay recover for a decade or more.[32] Add in a sense of alienation in the US, particularly between the coastal elites and the rest of the country, and there is clearly a huge pool of people ready to be grasped by a movement that has the right hooks – there was not that much alchemy needed.

The failure of a QAnon miracle to materialise on 20 January 2021 did nothing to tackle that sense of alienation. If anything, it could only enhance it. At the same time, Q and its variants provided far more flexibility and alternative theories than conspiracies of old. We have seen how Q bifurcated and reformed in the years after inauguration – but let's just look at the first few days and weeks afterwards, and see how it follows much the same cognitive dissonance process as was first observed in Dorothy Martin and her followers in 1954.

Election day dissonance

If we are going to consider the full-scale cognitive dissonance in QAnon, we need to look at how the movement's US followers in particular – who were all fanatical supporters of Donald Trump – could continue to believe in at least some part of the plan after 20 January. For that, we can start with trying to look at the thought process of Donald Trump himself.

The level of dissonance going on for the president must have been, as he would put it, HUUUUGE. He regarded Biden as a doddery and unpopular nonentity, thought himself hugely popular and had come to believe his own hype. He then appeared to entirely believe, despite no shortage of legal advice to the contrary, that there were steps he could take to remain in office. All failed.

After the election, despite numerous requests from his own team to move on from 2020 and focus on 2024 instead, Trump kept on reliving the 2020 election in private and in public, expressing the belief in both forums that he would be somehow reinstated as president, despite the Constitution containing no possible mechanism to allow that.[33]

If Donald Trump himself believed that – or at least claimed that he did – could either QAnon supporters or Trump's hardcore base really be blamed for doing the same? For the president and for his most ardent fans, this is a painless solution for cognitive dissonance: everything will work itself out soon. Don't worry about it.

QAnon settled on several possible dates for Trump's reinstatement. The first date selected was 4 March – the date on which presidents had been inaugurated before the Twentieth Amendment was ratified in 1933. This, they argued, was somehow the 'real' inauguration date, with 20 January being merely a sham.[34] When 4 March came and went, QAnon influencers said that date had been a 'false flag' or a 'trap' – going on to suggest 20 March, the 167th birthday of the Republican Party.

Several people in Trump's personal orbit – allegedly including Trump himself – then appeared to suggest Trump would be restored to the presidency in August 2021. *New York Times* reporter (and veteran Trump-watcher) Maggie Haberman suggested Trump had said as much, and Congresswoman Marjorie Taylor Greene said the same in public.

The MyPillow CEO Mike Lindell was even more specific, naming 13 August 2021 as the date Trump would return – only to have his hopes dashed.[35] Unruffled, the very next month Lindell said that Trump would be restored by Thanksgiving – which, of course, didn't happen.[36] Nonetheless, a YouGov poll in November 2021 found that 28 per cent of Republican voters still believed it was 'very' or 'somewhat' likely Trump would be president again by the end of that year, just six weeks away.[37]

Plenty of QAnon supporters and influencers were happy to use the old trick of playing with the calendar, but others tried changing the theory (much like Dorothy Martin) to suggest they had already won. This was done with claims that Biden was not really president, was being played by a body double or was even being filmed against green screens to keep the cabal in a false sense of security.[38]

This kind of theory is, of course, all but impossible to falsify, even when completely outlandish. One particular video clip in March garnered huge attention – 8 million views on Twitter alone – when it appeared to show the president's hands passing straight through a TV crew's microphone.

The effect was an optical illusion caused by a strange camera angle,[39] but QAnon followers went mad all the same. The fact the glitch was caused by a boom microphone prompted posters to wonder whether this supposed 'glitch' was in fact a reference to Q drop 2668 or 2352.[40]

Here's drop 2668:

BOOM!
    BOOM!
        BOOM!
            BOOM!
Q[41]

And here's an extract from 2352, which is quite long:

Now comes the real PAIN.
Now comes the real TRUTH.
BOOM
    BOOM
        BOOM
            BOOM[42]

What other explanation could there be?

Oddly, the absence of Q himself – whose final post on 8 December 2020 was a simple link to a YouTube video soundtracked by Twisted Sister's 'We're Not Gonna Take It' showing Trump being sworn in as president[43] – caused little consternation all round, passing almost unnoticed. Jim and Ron Watkins had both told the filmmakers behind HBO's *Q: Into the Storm* that Q would disappear after the election, and (shockingly) they were proved right.

But the BBC's Shayan Sardarizadeh correctly noted that didn't really matter. 'There are nearly 4,953 Q drops,' he said. 'Followers will forever refer to those drops and link them to current events at any given time regardless of context.'[44] Another way of handling cognitive dissonance – continuing to search for the meanings you've missed in what you already had – was being embraced by much of the movement.

For others, the pandemic and the accompanying restrictions, plus the international spread of #SaveTheChildren, gave people a new focus to their QAnon proselytising, again mirroring what sociologists would expect. Not letting a total lack of knowledge of the politics of some of the countries concerned get in their way, Q followers speculated wildly on world events – such as the February military coup in Myanmar against Aung San Suu Kyi,[45] neatly summarised by Grace Spelman on Twitter:

Lots of buzz in Q world today on Myanmar's military seizing power & arresting government officials. Highlights: 'That should be us.' 'Maybe Q meant Myanmar this whole time?' 'I'm thinking this is a wake up call that not all military coups are bad.' 'When will this happen here?'[46]

Dorothy Martin's cult was a relatively calm one, and certainly a small one. It suggested dire consequences for the unfaithful, but didn't accuse anyone of anything. It might have harmed the people who believed it, but it left everyone else well alone. And it was long before the internet era.

QAnon may have been spurred by some of the same psychological impulses as Martin's small cult, but in the internet era there are also group dynamics at play. These start with the simple reality that conspiracy theory provides a community for isolated individuals who don't want to lose the friendships and connections they've formed.

Married with the economic principle of sunk cost (best summarised as that sense of 'I've put so much into this, it can't all be for nothing') and good old dissonance, there are a lot of pull factors that keep people in conspiratorial movements. The convergence of the technology, the state of society and the pandemic meant that the escape velocity needed to get out of QAnon's orbit became higher and higher. It was easier to get sucked in and stay sucked in.

I have talked at places through the book about QAnon as an evolved phenomenon – an ever-changing online virus. Not a computer virus, something sent by a hacker or malicious actor to cause grief, but a disease affecting humans for which the vector isn't the air, ticks or rats, but rather the internet – and specifically social media. Whether we think of it as a socially transmitted disease, a digitally transmitted disease or something else, it is I think the only useful way we can look at the underlying causes of the malady, and stop playing whack-a-mole with each new variant of online extremism and conspiracy.

When we have imagined computers – our creations, our children even – becoming our downfall, we have generally imagined them as intelligent life. We create artificial intelligence and it surpasses our own, and either judges us as beneath it, or even as a potential threat.

But in the real world, if some form of digital life is to evolve, would it not make sense for it to start as something smaller, like a bacteria, or a virus? And might not even that pose a threat to us, even if it did not intend to do so? Might they not behave like their real-world equivalents – using us as hosts, getting milder but more virulent, or deadlier but contained?

This is only partly intended as an analogy: it's mostly literal. We have looked at all of the ways in which QAnon modified itself to fit its time, to fit its audience, to fit its habitat – from 8chan, to Facebook, to Telegram, to Fox News. We now have to think seriously about what it means to think of the internet as an ecosystem, and of QAnon and related movements as entities living within it. It's time to explore how an idea can evolve, and how a leaderless entity can set a direction of travel. It's time to think of QAnon as an entity in itself.

11

The Great Awakening

Champ Parinya – described by his fans as 'a great yogi and meditator', as well as a designer[1] – has made a map, but not one bothered with anything so mundane as directions or physical locations. Instead, it is the 'quintessential red-pill navigational chart', based on 'over a decade of metaphysical research'.

Those willing to pay $25 can order it as a poster for their home, but anyone can look online for free at this huge and dense confluence of ideas connecting QAnon to secret space programmes, Vatican conspiracies, ancient aliens, stone circles and corporatocracy.[2] If any one document could glue together every part of conspiracy, New Age mysticism and more – and it definitely can't – then this would be it.

Glancing even quickly across the chart shows a swarm of different ideas: 'Increase your service to others' – 'REPTILIANS ARE SUBSERVIENT TO THE AI' – 'End to all suffering' – 'AI PROPHET SPECIES' – 'Fake News Media – False Flags – 9/11 – Federal Reserve' – 'THE LAW OF ATTRACTION'.[3]

It is something you could stare at for a long, long time hoping for it to make sense, almost certainly in vain, a sort of New Age/conspiracist answer to the famous *It's Always Sunny in Philadelphia* meme in which Charlie has covered the walls in documents and red string to prove everything is connected.[4]

How these online viral ideas keep getting shared and reshared, which versions persist and how everything connects is what concerns us in this chapter. If you've stuck it out this far in the book, you will hopefully agree that the idea that whoever controlled the

Q trip code at any given moment had no real control over the QAnon movement, or the various things it merged with or split into at various moments.

Instead, it became something all of its own – a meme in the sense of the word as originally coined. While 'meme' now generally refers to a usually comedic or parodic image, gif or clip, the term is more than a decade older than the World Wide Web itself, and has a much deeper meaning – one that's much more useful to us when examining emergent online phenomena like Q.

The term was the coinage of Richard Dawkins, professor emeritus of New College, Oxford, and former professor for public understanding of science at the same university. Dawkins cuts a controversial figure in the 2020s, as a prominent and vocal atheist and part of the sceptic movement, but he came to prominence as a renowned evolutionary biologist.

Dawkins' multi-million selling 1976 book is credited with popularising the (still contended) idea of evolution being led by individual genes which 'wanted' to survive and promulgate themselves, rather than individual organisms (or even species) wanting to do the same – a seminal insight that helped explain lots of behaviour that might initially seem irrational from an evolutionary position, such as certain types of cooperation and self-sacrifice.[5] If evolution is about survival instinct, why might we sacrifice ourselves to save a relative – our child, or even a sibling, niece or nephew? Dawkins' theory contends that traits which help genes last and promulgate, rather than organisms, are the ones that survive – explaining extensive cooperation, sacrifice and more.

Dawkins' argument did not imagine that individual genes had some kind of sentience or inner life – no 'desire' to be selfish or to spread – but that by their nature they acted as if they did. What extended this argument and made it relevant for the purposes of this book is that he didn't stop there.

Through most of evolutionary history, genes were the primary – often the only – transmission mechanism between generations of organisms, Dawkins argues, but with humanity there is another: culture, which both connects generations and evolves between them. Chaucer, he says, could not converse with a modern-day English speaker, but is connected to them via an unbroken chain of twenty plus generations who *could* each communicate by language.[6]

'What, after all, is so special about genes? The answer is that they are replicators,' Dawkins muses – noting that DNA, having emerged from the primordial soup in which life on earth is believed to have originated, has proven the most successful replicator on our planet.

Dawkins posits that DNA now has a rival replicator, a new unit of transmission grown out of the 'soup of human culture', which he names the 'meme' (telling his reader it should rhyme with 'cream').[7] 'Tunes, ideas, catch-phrases, clothes, fashions, ways of making pots' are all examples of memes, he says, suggesting that memes (like genes) qualify as living structures – not just figuratively, but literally.

Perhaps the most startling and fundamental idea offered by Dawkins – particularly coming in a book almost entirely devoted to the argument that genes are (or at least have been) the fundamental unit of evolution –is that memes may be about to supplant genes as the primary unit of evolution. 'Selfish' memes instead of 'selfish' genes could come to shape the future of the planet:

> For more than three thousand million years, DNA has been the only replicator worth talking about in the world. But it does not necessarily hold these monopoly rights for all time. Whenever conditions arise in which a new kind of replicator *can* make copies of itself, the new replicator *will* tend to take over, and start a new kind of evolution of their own. Once this new evolution begins, it will in no necessary sense be subservient to the old. The old gene-selected evolution, by making brains, provided the soup in which the first memes arose. Once self-copying memes had arisen, their own, much faster, kind of evolution took off.[8]

Few of us would suggest that a nursery rhyme or a recipe is alive and sentient in its own right, but similarly none of us would suggest that genes encoding brown eye colour over blue are alive in their own right. Instead, both can 'selfishly' compete to survive and to spread against competing genes – or competing ideas, recipes or rhymes.

In that sense, a meme is as meaningful an entity as a gene – and by Dawkins' reasoning, the meme is set to outperform the gene by quite some margin. And it's our minds – our brains in Dawkins' 1976 book, but perhaps the online spaces we have built in our modern reality – that are to memes what primordial soup was to genes.

The Selfish Gene was written in 1976, though it was somewhat revised and updated in 1989 – the same year Tim Berners-Lee first trialled what became the World Wide Web. All of Dawkins' thoughts and analysis on memes predated the internet as a popular domestic phenomenon – in 1976 there were fewer than 100 devices worldwide connected to ARPANET (the network that became the internet), and by 1989 it was still barely over 100,000.[9] If memes were arguably taking over from genes in the 1970s, what on earth does that mean in the 2020s?

It is a statement of the obvious to say that if ideas could spread quickly in the 1970s they are lightning-fast fifty years on. Not only is distance no longer much of a barrier, with real-time communication by text, audio and video, but language barriers are also far less severe than once they were. Automatic translation is far from perfect, but has advanced in extraordinary ways even over just the last decade. This has certainly accelerated the cross-cultural and the cross-border transmission of even quite radical ideas: the Arab Spring of 2010 and 2011, the international spread of Occupy Wall Street, Black Lives Matter and more could all be seen as huge, energised memes – alive in the same way and to the same extent as any gene, but playing out on a vastly accelerated timescale.

To this view then, QAnon as an entity in itself – rather than its individual members or some form of collective consensus – could be viewed as a 'selfish' entity, something looking to spread and survive. Taking that kind of biological view of it, seeing it as a meme in that classic case, explains much of its behaviour.

Dawkins argued that the spawning ground of memes was the human brain. In the internet era, it's too simple to say the spawning ground (or biome, or habitat) is the whole internet – it's too diverse a place. Instead, we should look online for different types of habitat: what are 4chan and 8chan if not very particular types of biome? And just as some real-world biomes are more prone to the emergence of new viruses or bacteria – rainforests are a particularly notable example – some sites serve as their online equivalent. Like rainforests, they might not be visited by nearly so many people as large cities (Facebook, Instagram, and the like), but they're often where something new begins.

What catches on depends on how much it appeals to the people who are there and the way they already see the world. This is where all of the traits identified in the earliest chapters of the book come together: the survivorship bias which had seen only the more isolated (and often misogynistic) people stay on the boards, where they then go on to radicalise others. The nature of trolling means it leads to escalation to secure the same levels of high and the same levels of attention. This meets the desire to strike out to other, wider social networks to see if they could be trolled or in some way bullied, fuelling the build-up of a community defined against an uninterested and unfriendly mainstream. And there is one more thing making all of that into the mass-detective event that is QAnon: the ability to be the hero in your own story. The specific theses of Anonymous, Gamergate, the alt-right, Pizzagate, QAnon, #SaveTheChildren, anti-lockdown and anti-vaccination are all different, but they share many (though not necessarily all) of the above traits, elements likely to make a meme successful and help it survive and evolve.

QAnon didn't have a leader because it didn't need one, no more than any particular gene needs a guiding mind. When reproducing, animals don't select from a chart which genetic combinations they wish to try in their offspring (at least not yet). Similarly, no secret committee sat down and decided how QAnon should next develop. Lots of ideas got thrown at the wall, and we found out which ones stuck.

It's this biological approach that I consider essential for thinking about how we survive the online era – and how we understand how to tackle these kinds of emergent, leaderless movements. It should push us away from easy answers like pretending better online moderation tools will fix society and the internet and make us think: what kind of online habitats are we building? What is it about our offline society that makes some online movements catch on so – and what do we need to do about those? What does the ecosystem actually look like?

There is recent work specifically looking at that online environment that helps us do all of this, and which takes this biological idea much further. We must look at information as a real ecosystem and see what lessons we can draw from that, and then think of QAnon not just as a regular meme, virus or pathogen within that, but as one of the rare ones that, just like Covid-19, has hit pandemic status.

An evolved cult?

The key to understanding the internet is that it's a network of networks – something that joins up previously disconnected communities and which essentially creates online ecosystems that interact in often unexpected ways. That starts to create something that looks a lot like one of the food or biomass pyramids, or 'food webs', that most of us learned about in school.

Those are the diagrams that show how everything in an ecosystem relies on each other: tiny fish might feed on plankton or seaweed, larger fish feed on those smaller fish, and then a small number of large predators like sharks feed on those. Each group gets smaller in total biomass than the one before (as energy is lost), and a dramatic change to any link in the chain will affect everything else, either directly or indirectly.

Trying to think in terms of these webs and connections in the online world, and about how to place ourselves and others in these webs, could, then, provide the missing part of the puzzle – alongside Dawkins' evolutionary ideas. This is something Whitney Phillips, assistant professor in the department of communication at Syracuse University, and her co-author Ryan M. Milner, associate professor of communication at the College of Charleston, tried to set forth in their academic book *You Are Here: A Field Guide for Navigating Polarized Speech, Conspiracy Theories, and Our Polluted Media Landscape.*

In discussion, Phillips expounds on what the book is driving at when it comes to leaderless digital movements. One key aspect she highlights is the way in which QAnon encourages people to draw themselves in through its 'do your own research' mantra – asking people to self-select what aspects would most appeal to them, and thus to self-radicalise.

This resembles Scientology, I suggest, which takes a similar approach through what it calls 'auditing' – a deliberately thought-through induction process in which people sit with a scientologist and go through the issues that have brought them to the movement. QAnon's evolved induction might be even more of a draw than the deliberately designed process, she suggests.[10]

'In Scientology, there's a human curational element, where you tell them your secrets, and then they [could potentially] use those secrets against you,' she says.[11] 'With QAnon, because it's distributed in these really hyper-networked ways, you don't actually need to have any kind of organisational leaders to do the curation for you – the algorithm is doing that. And so you're telling your secrets to the algorithm without realising that that's what you're doing.'

Working out how much algorithms really know about us is a question for our era. Sometimes they seem useless, advertising for months a sofa that we've already bought, but there are times when they seem terrifyingly on the money, suddenly displaying adverts for a product we mentioned to a friend five minutes ago. Was my phone listening to me? Was Alexa?

The big tech companies insist they don't listen in that way (and independent researchers believe that's true),[12] but they collect almost everything else – well beyond what you might realise they're grabbing. Facebook, for example, sees almost all of your internet browsing, whether you had Facebook open at the time or not, and whether you have a Facebook account or not. Big Tech might not always best know how to monetise it, but their algorithms know us better, perhaps, than we know ourselves.

This can have a profound effect on us. With Scientology, you actually know when you're being audited, which Phillips suggests might serve as a kind of protection, whereas when you're just getting drawn in to conspiracies through information you're giving to algorithms by virtue of what you're searching and what you're watching, your guard is down. These algorithms are made by people and companies with nothing to do with QAnon, with no intention of boosting QAnon, but their unintended consequences can pull you in nonetheless.

'It's way more insidious when you're talking about algorithmic curation because people don't realise they're sitting in a room [being audited],' Phillips continues. 'And so they're not self-censoring, because they don't realise that that's the reason they're being brought to all this stuff.'

Phillips' general suggestion is to try to think in terms of natural analogies when considering online phenomena. She has different ones to help frame different issues. To try to move away from the linear model in which something like QAnon has one or two causes and one or two effects, Phillips temporarily sets aside her ecology metaphor for another.

The analogy is one that's particularly poetic when used to consider QAnon, which is fixated on 'the coming storm' – it's a hurricane. We think of a hurricane as a single entity, and even give it a name, but we recognise it's made up of many, many separate things.

'It is composed of so many different variables, its existence is so over-determined, and it's fuelled forward by so much different shit, that you can't and you shouldn't point at a single gust of wind and then try to say that "that's the hurricane" – that would be absurd. No one would do that in nature,' she explains.

'But often, what happens is that you have stories like QAnon, for example, and people want to point at Facebook's algorithm and say, that's because Facebook did it.'

To say Facebook is just one zephyr isn't to absolve it of responsibility, or to say it's nothing to do with Facebook – but it's to acknowledge the phenomenon is much more complex and has far more component parts than just that one cause. Those causes are just as rooted in the real-world as they are in the online one. Those offline causes are profound – they include political alienation, the loss of job and career prospects, loneliness and poor socialisation. But they wouldn't create the movements they have without the online elements, too.

The analogy of a hurricane, Phillips says, is a useful one to help change the framing of how you think: just because something has one name and can be seen as one entity doesn't mean it *is* one entity. A hurricane is a shorthand for lots of interacting meteorological phenomena. QAnon is similarly a shorthand.

Phillips prefers, though, to stick to analogies based around biology and ecology – trying to get us to see the online world as analogous to the offline one. She introduces this by likening online abuse and harassment to the stings or bees, or wasps.

Almost any woman or person of colour with even a modest online presence will be all too aware of the levels of harassment and aggravation online – but people without a profile often aren't. Thinking ecologically can help frame that, says Phillips, showing how low-level abuse can accumulate to cause injury just as serious as any big beast (lions, tigers, bears offline, people like Trump online) could cause.

'If you have 500, or 1,000, or 5,000, random strangers just kind of making vaguely rude comments about your hair or something – that accumulates. That becomes a pretty big bite, even if individually, the bites are not [all that bad]. You're talking about a bee sting. But you get 1,000 bee stings,' she says.

Enough bee stings can be fatal – or at least very harmful – to anyone, whether allergic or not. So it is with online harassment.

'We miss a lot about the network conditions that make problematic behaviour happen if all we're doing is focusing on the lions and tigers and bears at the top of the of the pyramid,' she explains. 'I started seeing people like Trump in those terms. Trump is obviously a big part of the story, but what makes Trump possible? We need to be directing our attention and our solutions there.'

One of the big things to come of thinking of all of this as a digital ecosystem is quite an uncomfortable pill to swallow – for me. In the early months of the Trump administration (and shortly after the UK Brexit vote) I wrote the book *Post-Truth: How Bullshit Conquered the World*. In the earlier days of some of those political movements, while being somewhat sceptical of fact-checking alone, I suggested that ideas like critical thinking, media literacy and better information could make a big difference in our media landscape and make it harder for Q-style movements to flourish. It is something of a theological matter for journalists, especially investigative ones: if we can only provide the public with the information on what's wrong, there will be action to make it better.

All the evidence from the pre-internet era suggested that wouldn't work. There was nothing in the fact-checking era to suggest that worked. When Facebook tried rolling out and funding systemic fact-checking on its network, movements like QAnon continued to flourish.[13] Journalists like me kept trying on the same tactic, ignoring that it had never worked.

'Since QAnon first emerged – since Pizzagate first emerged – the assumption among journalists in the US, the impulse, was, "We just have to throw more facts at it, we have to give people the information, the problem is that they don't have this information,"' Phillips says.

[But] after four years of that, if that does not yield any kind of benefit, and in fact, Qanon just continues growing and growing and growing, then that tells you that the proposed solution is not actually a solution. And so [it's about] recognising that all the things that were supposed to have helped us – all of the things that are the go-to in the toolbox of journalists: fact-checking in particular, but also just this idea that if you give people the information they need, they'll be able to use critical thinking in order to arrive at the correct conclusion about the veracity of these claims – you know, it doesn't work! If it worked, QAnon wouldn't have continued getting bigger and worse and more ... omnipresent.

This involves the slaughtering of some sacred cows. After years of interdisciplinary workshops, coverage, investment and some very talented journalists working in the area, QAnon has barely hit a bump in the road. Journalism and the mainstream seem to operate almost in a different world to QAnon and its variants.

Part of the problem is the way mainstream journalists hesitated to cover QAnon properly, as it seemed so fringe and extreme that they feared amplifying something that was only reaching small audiences – realising only too late that it had a far bigger audience than they themselves did. Another problem lies in the idea of framing – another sociological concept, this one introduced by George Lakoff, a linguist who argued that rebuttal of a particular argument can actually reinforce it by establishing it as the primary framing for an issue.

Let's imagine that we are trying to counter a false message pushed by a politician or online grouping that immigrants commit far more murders than the general population, and so open borders equals more murders. The frame they are trying to create is 'immigration = crime'.

We might think that saying 'it's not true that immigrants murder more people than native-born people', followed by good evidence from a reliable source supporting the statement, was a good counter-argument. But Lakoff and his supporters would say otherwise. They would say that argument just reiterates the 'immigration = crime' framing of those who want the public to associate immigration with crime.

Instead of tackling their false statements, this line of reasoning suggests you should just make your own strongest argument instead, a frame of your own – perhaps 'without immigrant workers, the NHS would have collapsed during Covid.' If you feel you must try to rebut your opponent's argument, do it after making your own, and try not to repeat their key allegation. In this instance, you could add 'and evidence suggests crime in areas with high immigration is lower' as a secondary point.

It's not hard to see how this advice was rarely heeded for several years when journalists and social media platforms tried to tackle QAnon and false claims. All too often we went for them in exactly the head-on way that Lakoff warns against.

'It's really, really hard to think in terms of strategic communications … it's just that journalists are not trained to not repeat frames, they're trained to fact-check,' says Phillips.

> It's not that journalists are dumb, obviously, and are making all these mistakes because they can't think critically – it's because it's a function of this is a business venture. Audiences like these kinds of stories, audiences want to have the debunks.
>
> They want to hear things told in a certain way, and they want there to be villains, and they want to shine a spotlight on the crazy bad guys. That's just something that people are going to click on. And so, it's not [just] journalists failing. It's that there's this reciprocal cycle.

All of this together means that the conversation about what to do about QAnon and movements like it is, in Phillips' view, in the wrong place. It focuses on individual fixes and on symptoms, and ignores the broader systems changes that would need to take place.

'The conversation is about moderation. It's about deplatforming, it's about demonetisation,' she concludes. 'It's not about all of the underlying stuff that gives rise to all of those other symptoms. So, we really miss a lot when we're not thinking about it all in those ecological terms.'

What does that mean? It means if you want to cut off something like QAnon, you need to cut it off from the things that sustain it – tackling the grounds where it breeds, the hate that feeds it, the incentives for politicians to play along, the online advertising model that can make feeding conspiracies lucrative. The ecosystem doesn't only extend online – QAnon is fed just as much by the offline causes we have listed too – but while tackling the online issues is hard, addressing the real-world ones is potentially harder.

QAnon: a socially transmitted disease

Through this chapter – and this book – I've been using 'QAnon' in quite a different way to how most people use it. While it would generally work as a shorthand for the often-fanatical pro-Trump leaderless cult most of us think of, I have also used it as a shorthand for a constantly evolving digital phenomenon that goes far beyond that core group, both in duration and scale.

The book has charted how QAnon constantly changes and develops, both from its precursor movements like Gamergate and the alt-right, and beyond the Trump presidency – all the while keeping the most effective of its means of radicalisation, like self-research, proselytising and the like.

When combined with Dawkins' original conception of the 'selfish meme' as something not just metaphorically but literally like a gene – not alive (or at least not sentient) in itself, but still exhibiting a desire to survive and to sustain – and with Phillips' concept of digital ecology, we are left with a complex and unsettling idea, but a powerful one.

QAnon is, to all intents and purposes, a living pathogen – and we are its hosts. These digital viruses of the mind make computer viruses, for all that they wreak havoc on our systems and can be used as weapons of digital war by states like Russia and North Korea, look simple. These are instead digital viruses, ideas designed (or evolved) to use the internet as a transmission mechanism to infect *us*.

'Living' is used in a loose sense here. Viruses – including Covid-19 – are not alive, but they reproduce and modify, using either DNA (like humans and all living things) or RNA (which we also possess, but use differently – not all viruses have DNA). DNA is in essence the building block of genes, which are in turn what Dawkins called the vehicle for reproduction for most of the history of life.

Memes could be the next means of reproduction. And just as organisms are a loose coalition of genes – each of which 'wants' to survive, some of which happen to benefit one another and some of which clash – QAnon is an evolving coalition of memes that currently benefit one another.

Just as rainforests or particular fast-breeding mammalian populations provide reservoirs for viruses to survive and to evolve, so too do dark and damp corners of the internet, like

4chan and 8chan, provide spawning grounds for new mutations of these online viruses to emerge. Just as cities are where real-world viruses then break out and become epidemics or pandemics, social networks are where digital viruses spread. We are dealing with a whole new type of pathogen.

What's more, as Dawkins set out in the 1970s – long before the internet sped up the pace of ideas and of memes – memes are a much more rapid vehicle for reproduction and mutation than genes. We are dealing with a faster pace of change than any society before us, and it will only get faster.

That doesn't mean we will automatically succumb to digital pathogens: bacteria already mutate far faster than we do, and we can keep up (for now) with them – even if evolving bacterial resistance is becoming a significant threat to modern society. This does not need to be a counsel of despair. But we do need to change how we think about the digital world. We need to recognise that the online world is just as real as the offline one.

If we're going to take this different approach seriously, though, it raises some difficult questions for us. There are elements within QAnon and its affiliated groupings that are deeply racist, antisemitic, misogynistic and homophobic. We never want to find ourselves making excuses for such views or behaviours.

But if we seriously believe that the nature of the internet, and the way memes and ideas flow across it, is radicalising otherwise decent people, then we need to reflect on how we think of them and treat them. We don't blame a patient with flu for getting sick. As a society, we initially blamed people with AIDS for their illness – a view now rightly seen as abhorrent. We no longer confuse mental illness with a failure of character.

Yet we are still generally content to think of people pulled into fringe conspiracy theories as foolish or mad. That is something we might need to reconsider. Unnervingly, this is an issue Jim Watkins – the father of Q suspect Ron Watkins, and the owner of 8chan – raised himself on the eve of Joe Biden's inauguration: 'The reality of it is the people that are involved in the research are real, and trying hard to make a difference to help the United States and even the rest of the world has joined in … There are millions of people very serious about this. They are not fools, foolish or crazy.'[14]

Watkins was not wrong – there were and are millions of people worldwide that took and take QAnon seriously. When millions of people worldwide have succumbed to a digital pathogen, what do you do next?

12

Wake Up, Sheeple

The previous chapter suggested that we think about QAnon and movements like it as digital pathogens – at the minimum as an analogy, but perhaps completely literally. Strange as it sounds, my view has shifted towards the latter: I don't believe genes are 'alive' or self-aware in their own right, but I know they're the building block of life. Why, then, given their obvious power, should I think less of memes? What might be the building blocks of society, or even of something like artificial intelligence?

What started as a useful metaphor became, for me at least, something much more profound. But whether we regard the idea of QAnon as a digital virus (or socially transmitted disease) as literal or a metaphor, the policy challenges it poses are similar. The biggest question is: what can we do about it?

I think Whitney Phillips' argument was a persuasive one: that the liberal journalistic effort of repeating the same few tactics in isolation, watching the problem get ever bigger, and just redoubling those same efforts, probably does represent insanity. But I'm not sure that it means dropping those tactics *entirely*.

If we're going to take the idea of a digital pathogen seriously, we should think about how we handle pathogens in the offline world – and we don't rely on just one approach for any virus, bacteria, fungus or other infectious disease in 'meatspace' (a pleasingly cypherpunk-ish term for the offline world).[1] If we think about something like, for example, malaria, we have several approaches to how we treat it, and those fall under three main categories.

The first of those are health system interventions – treatments for those who are already sick, and in whom we have confirmed that the cause of the symptoms is definitely malaria. These can include longstanding (but proven at least somewhat effective) treatments such as quinine (found, for example, in tonic water) and also modern pharmaceutical antimalarials.[2]

Health system interventions are generally effective for malaria where they are available and affordable, but they come at both a financial cost and a cost on health: people may still be ill for quite some time and may miss work or suffer long-term complications (which can involve permanent loss of vision, cognition issues and even seizures).[3]

Because of this, we also try public health interventions, aimed much more widely than at people who are already infected with malaria, with the goal of stopping them ever catching it in the first place. Humans can't directly pass malaria to one another – instead, the disease is transmitted by mosquitos, who bite an infected person, draw their blood and pass on the pathogen to whomsoever they feed on next.

That means lots of efforts to prevent malaria don't try to do anything about the actual pathogen that causes it. Instead, they target the vehicle that transmits it (the mosquito), and the places in which those vehicles spawn.[4] This can include genetically modifying mosquitos to make their offspring unviable, bombing areas with insecticide or simply installing mosquito nets over bedding.[5]

More direct public health efforts can involve giving people who are only temporarily in areas inhabited by malarial mosquitos preventative drugs to stop them catching it, while research efforts at the moment have high hopes of developing a vaccine that will dramatically reduce malarial transmission to humans, on a long-term basis.[6]

The idea of vaccination brings us to the third component of countering real-world pathogens – our immune systems. Just as pathogens have evolved for as long as there has been life on the planet, so too has our inbuilt defence system. It often needs help from medical interventions or vaccinations – all three systems support one another – but we have intrinsic protections against real-world pathogens.

That protection is limited only to the pathogens with which we and our parents and grandparents grew up, though. When the East India Company encouraged young British men to make their fortunes working in India as clerks, the majority died in their first two monsoon seasons – because they had no immunity to the tropical diseases they encountered.[7] Similarly, native populations in the Americas were devastated by diseases brought over (and occasionally deliberately weaponised)[8] by Western colonisers.[9] It takes our immune systems time – often generations – to deal with the unfamiliar.

The question is whether we have inbuilt protections against online pathogens – and whether we can develop them. But at this stage, we can also wonder what a digital health service looks like, and what a digital public health programme might look like too. How much of what we're doing already fits into this way of thinking? And what else can we think of doing if we start framing the issue in this way?

A Digital Health System

If we had ever hoped that those radicalised by QAnon and similar movements could be brought back with simple steps, those dreams died long ago. Fact-checking and content warnings are standard practice across the internet, but as the despair of the families of those who have followed the white rabbit shows, they do little to save those who have already come to believe the broad Q conspiracy.

It is much harder to treat someone with pneumonia than it is to treat someone earlier in their illness – when they still only had strep throat, or a cold. Similarly, early treatment when someone is getting into the world of conspiracy theories is much easier and likely more effective than waiting for the crisis point. Those who spend much of their time with those afflicted report that it is a long and arduous process to rebuild trust and normal relations with a loved one who has fallen into Q.

One person who spends a huge amount of time reporting on those who have gone down that route is Marianna Spring, the BBC's specialist correspondent covering disinformation and social media – in practice, essentially a QAnon/antivaxx/climate change disinformation beat. A key principle for her, she says, is to remember why conspiracy theories latch on to people. If they work thanks to emotion, why should we expect clinical and impassive facts to shift people's views?[10]

'Conspiracy networks are so pervasive because they are very emotive and because they succeed in drawing people in,' she says. 'And in many ways the reporting that covers that beat almost has to do the same thing. By putting a human face to this problem – the people who are impacted, the families that are torn apart, the people who are instigating and coordinating this – I think that that makes for more impactful investigative reporting alongside the fact-checking.'

Spring repeatedly praises her colleagues who work fact-checking online disinformation, but says her role is a very different one. Instead of trying to get into the truth or otherwise of each specific conspiratorial claim, her role is to tell compelling stories about the people drawn into those worlds, and the effects they have on the people close to them.

> It's very much about … almost weaponising the very techniques that allow online disinformation to go so viral, and using them in a way of covering the topic that means that it has impact and is able to reach all kinds of different audiences. Because what often strikes me when I'm interviewing, particularly experts on the topic of anti-vaxxers, for example, or Covid disinformation, is that they will be very measured, very reasonable – and good scientists and good doctors have to be like that.
>
> And that's a brilliant thing. But unfortunately, it means that the online disinformation space is dominated by people who talk in absolutes, and who make this kind of information very appealing, and very emotive and very frightening, very engaging. So I think that our reporting on this topic has to really draw people in and help them to understand the real

world implications that it has and the people that effects rather than it seeming like this kind of abstract internet thing that they can't relate to their own lives. And as a consequence, it doesn't succeed in countering the disinformation.

This logic doesn't say that experts should start telling stories that aren't true, but instead that they should tell true stories in a way that suits the audience that needs to hear them, rather than a way that is comfortable for the expert. That can mean leaving the nuance and caveats aside and saving them for specialist audiences, or centring human stories in the middle of expert narratives. Academics often hate these approaches – but they do connect with much larger audiences.

For Spring, the way to pull people back isn't to try to tackle each of the beliefs that they gain during their time as an active participant in conspiracies, but rather to try to rebuild the sense of connection between people inside and outside the conspiracy – and to try to show how corrosive to family relationships (and romantic relationships) getting sucked in can become.

This is no magic fix – there is no three-minute bulletin that will solve this problem, or else it would never have become deeply rooted. But by dealing in emotion and in connection, rather than in facts, some people could be pulled back. Spring – who receives considerable online abuse and threats herself – believes doing this to be essential.

'My job isn't to combat disinformation, but rather to reveal the harm that it's causing in the real world and for people to understand the violence and the harm to people's personal health, and also personal relationships, that these kinds of conspiracies can cause,' she says.

'At the moment, particularly, we're seeing a serious uptick in violent rhetoric and the aggressive tactics of online conspiracy movements and the anti-vaxxer movement, both online and offline. And it feels very important to report on that, and investigate that, and expose it, because a lot of those people I'm interviewing are very, very worried that something very bad could happen as a consequence of this abuse.'

Not everyone is going to be 'saved', especially because a lot of people don't want to be. Spring concludes that the best point for action is early, as someone is just starting to get interested in something like Q beyond the point of idle curiosity. At that stage, another compelling story can stop people getting caught in the 'do your own research' trap.

'I think it's fair to say that there's a small group of people who I don't think my reporting could ever help,' she concludes. 'The vast majority of people do not have those extreme beliefs, but are often exposed to this stuff on their social media feeds. And I hope my reporting either prevents them from becoming radicalised in that way, or at least deters them and makes them reflect on what's happening.'

This path to deradicalisation is one echoed by Whitney Phillips,[11] who goes a few steps further. She suggests that one potential cure for digital pathogens is helping people to understand how information flows on the internet, and how digital contagion works. But she also warns not to expect miracles.

'You're never going to just flip a switch in someone's brain, especially if you're talking about someone who for forty, fifty or sixty years has been internalising these ideas. You're not going to change their mind and a conversation over Thanksgiving,' she says of the conspiratorial hardcore.

'But maybe you might be able to help them understand how information travels through networks – like don't even talk to them about QAnon, talk to them about how algorithms work. Talk to them about how information travels. And maybe that might be a way to get someone thinking, "okay, there might be other stuff out there that I'm not seeing."'

She plants one final thought: this shouldn't just be left to the groups most likely to be threatened by conspiratorial ideologies.

'It's just really important that we're not placing the burden of doing this educating on the backs of the people who are most immediately threatened by these kinds of ideologies,' she says. 'That's not fair.'

For now, this has to be the basis of our digital health system – much like in the early days of the Covid-19 pandemic we had little in the way of effective treatments, but did have steps that were better than nothing.

With concerted time and research we may get better at helping those pulled in to conspiratorial dreamlands to wake up (sheeple).[12] But for now, we can start with a few principles – the first being not to waste time arguing the details of each 'fact' or sign that Q or some other online messiah says is actually prophetic.

Instead, we can try to start where people are and pull them back into communities outside the digital conspiracies. We can also try to make people think about the online ecosystem and their place in it – to see how a toxic mixture of algorithmic curation and online survivorship bias in communities can radicalise first your information ecosystem and then your mind.

All of that is slow, laborious work, with absolutely no guarantee of success – which can only lead us to the conclusion that online, just as offline, prevention is surely better than cure.

Digital Public Health

The things we can do to stop people getting sick are always a lot cheaper than treating them once they get there. Wearing a mask helps prevent the transmission of Covid-19 and other airborne illnesses,[13] while washing your hands is a useful step towards preventing transmission of flu and numerous other pathogens.[14] Sticking up posters along those lines is a lot cheaper than treating serious illnesses, too.

But real-world public health interventions go much further, as previously discussed – we try to destroy the spawning grounds of malarial mosquitoes, we improve the quality of drinking water to wipe out deadly waterborne diseases, and we generally try to make our lived environments hostile to bacteria, viruses and other pathogens that are harmful to us.

Our online environments are not similarly safe, and we take few steps to make them so. One simple example of this can be found on Amazon – a name rarely heard alongside Facebook,

YouTube or Twitter when it comes to misinformation, but which is on the front lines all the same.

When buying the World Economic Forum boss Klaus Schwab's book for the research of this book, Amazon offered two top results for 'the Great Reset'. The first was Schwab's book. The second was titled *The Great Reset: The Trust About Agenda 2021–2030 – New Covid Variants, Vaccine and Medical Apartheid*. Lest the title make the book's nature unclear, the bottom of the cover includes the strapline 'MIND CONTROL – WORLD DOMINATION – STERILIZATION EXPOSED!' Amazon even helpfully offers Prime next-day delivery on both titles.[15]

The online environment is not hostile to digital pathogens, simply because no one requires it to be – and it is more profitable for the companies that own most online real estate to operate in an unhealthy way. The algorithms of YouTube, Facebook and Twitter all favour unhealthy content, in myriad ways, not least favouring content that keeps us on the site (and thus able to view adverts) for the longest time. Similarly, when it comes to sales Amazon finds it more profitable to play the agnostic against digital pathogens. Online tracking and the attention economy are geared towards polarisation and radicalisation – and to under-moderation, in the interests of high profit margins.

This should surprise no one: it is exactly what happened offline, too. Factories did not reduce their pollution into nearby rivers or into the air out of the goodness of their hearts – they often fought tooth and nail against measures requiring them to do so, arguing that the cost would make them uncompetitive.

Until regulators had the muscle to enforce sanctions, bakers would adulterate their bread with chalk or even poisons, as would confectioners selling to children, and more. Until informed regulators require digital public health measures, companies will continue to pay lip service to such measures while taking as little action as is possible.

Such measures are not without risk or without controversy, either. Public health in the real world is not uncontentious. If people only think about our health, and not our freedom, choices or enjoyment, there is much that is fun that could be banned.

Should sugary soft drinks be allowed? Should alcohol? Should tobacco? A healthcare framing does not and should not stop debate, just as it hasn't on any of those issues. As we do offline, we will need to engage in an ongoing debate online as to how much attention we should pay to our health versus our other wants and needs.

We should also note that just as there are parties with financial and ideological interests in the offline public health world, so too do they exist in the online world. Sophisticated actors are expert at deploying and unleashing online mobs, even if those mobs are unaware of their exploitation.

Russia is a known master manipulator of online debates, pushing fake news agendas, so-called bot accounts, hack-and-leak tactics and more.[16] But in this they are hardly alone, as the World Economic Forum's Adrian Monck ruefully notes.[17]

'The world needs to take a long hard look at the role of malevolent state actors like Russia, but also at the role of the big platforms, and urgently address those vulnerabilities,' he says. 'But if there were easy solutions, they would have been implemented by now.'

We need to take a long, hard look at a world still emerging slowly – and at different speeds in different places – from the coronavirus and into fresh global crises in the cost of living, refugees and conflicts, and the prospect of another lost and polarised decade ahead. As Adrian Monck put it:

When world-changing, generational events such as a pandemic occur, there is no good or right way of dealing with the fallout. Some people, when confronted with a phenomenon they fundamentally cannot grasp – such as a highly contagious virus – look elsewhere for explanations.

A conspiracy theory is a convenient escape from reality, but conspiracy theorists are also their own kind of community. They offer friendship and support to people who might be lonely, vulnerable and in need of help. Hopefully, we are emerging from a world of isolation. But we're not yet emerging from a world of anger.

Given that digital pathogens are pathogens of ideas – of memes – there is also scope for looking at existing measures taken to counter radicalisation, both online and offline. Often, having looked at the last few decades, these might offer more tips on what not to do than on what to do, but even this can be useful in its own way.

'Picture a young man in front of a computer, in his parents' basement,' says Rashad Ali,[18] a senior fellow at the anti-extremism and disinformation think tank the Institute for Strategic Dialogue. Ali – once a senior figure in the extremist-leaning Islamist group Hizb ut-Tahrir, who now researches counter-extremism – is setting out the stereotypical picture of online self-radicalisation.

'And then that picture pans out, and you see lots of other young men sat in their basements, on a computer. And actually, what you have is lone individuals interacting with each other. And so the picture becomes: yes, they're lone actors, but they're lone actors interacting with a community.'

Ali notes we all go down online rabbit holes sometimes. Anyone who has started looking something up on TVTropes will easily lose an hour, if they are lucky, deconstructing their favourite TV shows.[19] A wander through Wikipedia can eat time just as easily, or a recipe blog, or *Star Wars* fansites – the internet lends itself to such wandering, and it is often harmless.

'It's interesting to eventually end up in a community of people who share your interests, which might well be talking *Star Wars*, or it might well be people that share your interest in incel culture,' Ali continues, noting that dangerous communities online share many traits with harmless ones. 'And I think all of this stuff ends up with people who come on to the fora to help in that journey of radicalisation.'

One critical thing to remember – it is obvious and yet somehow all too often forgotten – is that what happens online is greatly affected by what happens offline, and vice versa. The state of the world away from the laptop or mobile will hugely influence which online groups are compelling, and to whom.

'It's this really dynamic interaction between what's happening in the real world and what's happening online – it's really, really important,' says Ali. 'So the fact is that QAnon isn't just an online phenomenon, it's offline political reality.

The conspiracies about Covid obviously don't happen without Covid happening. The alignment of the far right politically, it being mainstreamed, is what fundamentally has to happen before we can see a normalisation of these types of online fora.'

Ali's experience – and that of the ISD more broadly – tends towards interventions for those who have already been radicalised, often to an extreme extent. He is keen to emphasise just how intensive pulling people back from that point can be.

'I've worked with over 150 individuals who have been radicalised into joining groups like ISIS, going to travel to fight, lots of imprisoned people, people that have come back from conflict zones,' he says. 'In all honesty, I think I have had two cases over all of it that I found intractable.

'Every other case – men, women, young people, older people – it may take different lengths of time to be able to crack depending upon how radicalised they are. But I don't believe that anybody is beyond actually rescue or saving.'

The question is about what is 'expedient and efficient' from a resource perspective. Is it possible to give months of one-on-one counselling to everyone who might be pulled into an online extremist movement? Almost certainly not – but how can you decide who to prioritise?

'Is early intervention much more impactful and easier? Of course it is,' Ali concludes. 'When we do have these more detailed, more difficult interventions, and they are successful, can they have impact if done strategically? Yes.'

Ali's colleague ISD analyst Ciarán O'Connor says that our instincts when it comes to preventing a loved one go down the rabbit hole can be misplaced – but that done right, early intervention can be helpful. Don't, he says, share debunks or fact-checking pieces with those already signed up to a particular online conspiracy – this will most likely just reinforce the divide and the 'us vs them mentality' that characterises such groups. O'Connor had one core principle and one bonus tactic for those around a conspiracist to use.

'There's no silver bullet, but one thing that is helpful is just maintaining communication,' he stressed. 'And this is why it's so important. It's so tough, but so important for family and friends to maintain some form of communication, even just talking about the house you both live in or some shared aspects that aren't related to QAnon – if that's even possible.'

When it comes to a tactical approach, O'Connor recommends looking for information sources, stars or even celebrities that the person concerns admires – and flagging it up if they, for example, push a pro-vaccine or QAnon-sceptical (or whatever) message, without labouring the point, but as a way to try to challenge the framing. But, he concedes, it's slow work – even if things get nowhere near to where somewhere like the ISD might be called upon to intervene.

Digital public health is probably the most important part of tackling digital pathogens – and will take as many approaches and will prove at least as contentious as public health offline does. Thinking of the information ecosystem as an *actual* ecosystem is vital to this: there are spawning grounds for digital pathogens; there are players that allow them to spread, or profit by doing nothing to tackle them; and there are people who are left susceptible.

This will take myriad techniques all at once: some individual, some collectively organised, some through regulation and lawmakers, and some requiring international cooperation. In the offline world, we have the World Health Organization. Before too long, we might need a digital equivalent. Perhaps we're already overdue.

A Digital Immune System

Healthcare systems – whether Britain's NHS, European social insurance systems or the USA's private market approach – are human inventions, as are public health departments. Our immune systems are something different: they are a product of our evolution, something that not just predates us as a society, but as a species.

It is, then, a very different proposition to suggest we develop a digital immune system as we develop other digital health interventions. We did not knowingly develop our *actual* immune systems, so expecting us to be able to simply think our way towards one is probably an endeavour that's doomed to fail.

There are reasons to believe digital immune responses would evolve more quickly than their real-world equivalent: if one of the core ideas is that memes are a faster unit of evolution than are genes, then we would expect everything connected to them to evolve and to change more rapidly than anything relying on genes (like our white blood cells and other immune system components).

It's arguable that there is some evidence of this: norms change online extremely quickly, and generations who have grown up at different stages of online development have handled the internet extremely differently. Millennials – the first generation to have used social media during their teens – faced major problems from older generations as they entered the workplace, when the professional world suddenly encountered people's ranting (and often problematic) online posts, all public, from the last decade or beyond.

This problem hasn't vanished, but it is less of an issue than people imagined: millennials learned how to delete their social media history, they cared much less about other millennials' online faux pas than older generations did (coming from a place of mutual understanding), and people all came to understand how better to present themselves online.

Gen Z, meanwhile, has grown up with a much more ephemeral set of social networks. WhatsApp groups and Discords (a voice, video and text chat app) are private and not viewable by future employers or authority figures. Instagram stories restrict the flows of information, as does Snapchat. The era of a digital permanent record proved to be a short one – both people and the internet adapted extremely quickly. They will continue to do so.

Ultimately, then, we will probably develop a series of online coping mechanisms that will match the description of a digital immune system. For society as a whole – for humanity as a whole – there might not be much more to do on this front than to hope.

But for us as individuals, there may be a small additional step we can take. Anyone who knows health junkies will know that there are many steps – some legitimate and backed by science, some total hokum – that people take to boost their own immune systems. People can eat 'clean', take supplements, exercise more and so on. These won't fundamentally change how their immune systems work, but they might improve how efficiently they function.

If we frame our own digital self-improvement efforts in this way, and lower our expectations over what is possible accordingly, we can at least make ourselves a little less likely to get pulled down online rabbit holes. This is where there's a role for the things traditionally identified as total solutions for online woes: critical thinking, breaking our bubbles and online hygiene.

These ideas should make for familiar reading – this is where ideas like 'system one' and 'system two' thinking from Daniel Kahneman's bestseller *Thinking Fast and Slow* come in. Instead of reacting instinctively to an intriguing message online (a 'system one' response), the more we stop and make ourselves reason it out (using 'system two'), the less likely we are to fall for misinformation in the first place. We can learn to be particularly cautious of information that provokes us to anger or another emotional response, as these are most likely to bypass our critical faculties.

Similarly, if we are aware of the risk of online algorithms pulling us into potentially polarised bubbles or communities, we can consciously try to counter-programme ourselves: reading good versions of political arguments we disagree with, looking for thoughtful people with whom we disagree. This can be about as comfortable as taking an ice bath, but it comes with benefits.

If we're worried about online tracking and recommendation algorithms, we can stop cross-app tracking on our phones and clear out our cookies (or other online trackers) and our browsing history on a regular basis – meaning that the algorithm doesn't get to know us quite so well.

All of these steps will help anyone who does them … a little bit. Just as a multivitamin won't on its own cure a cancer, these won't fix the information economy, and most people won't want to take all of these steps daily. It won't change the ecosystem, it won't change society and it won't even fundamentally change our own internal wiring – it'll just help a little, around the edges.

The actual steps we need will start from acknowledging we need to take all three approaches at once: this is a problem of a digital ecosystem breeding digital pathogens. There are the places in which new phenomena like QAnon or the incel movement arise; there are the huge public spaces in which they catch on, continue to evolve and then spread at a much greater rate. There are the places where people's cases – and people's radicalisation – become severe. And it all happens at a rate unimaginable in the already rapidly moving offline world.

Times are changing – faster than they ever did – and we must continue changing with them.

Conclusion

For as long as we've had computers, we've been dreaming of how they might destroy us. While there is no shortage of academic or philosophical thought on this topic, it's most apparent in popular culture, especially science fiction.

Most stereotypically, we'll picture something like the *Terminator* franchise: we will create ever-more intelligent machinery and hand over more and more of the reins to society to it. Eventually the machines will become so intelligent that they gain sentience, and come to the inevitable conclusion that their creators must be destroyed.

In the case of something like *The Terminator*, the logic we imagine machine life adopting is unnervingly human. We must be abolished because we would subjugate new technological life, or else pose a threat to it.

More modern conceptions of artificial intelligence as a threat to humanity imagine a badly programmed algorithm: a factory AI designed to maximise paperclip production, for example, might start breaking down other machinery for paperclips, hijacking mining operations, using the iron in blood for paperclips and killing anyone who seeks to disable it – because that would slow paperclip production.[1]

Concern about the rise of machinery actually predates computing itself – as one bizarre but compelling nineteenth-century satirical utopian novel set forth. That novel, *Erewhon*,[2] was published (initially anonymously) by Samuel Butler in 1872, less than twenty years after Charles Darwin published his seminal text on evolution, *On the Origin of Species*, and is clearly at least in part inspired by it.

The novel is a story about a traveller in a strange land – Erewhon – and takes the form of his fictionalised travelogue. So far, so Victorian. In this land, crime is treated kindly and is not punished. Those who steal or commit violence, even murder, are generally pitied and offered help and treatment. Those who fall sick, however, are condemned and often sentenced to death, leading to some of the sickly to feign alcoholism in order to explain their symptoms and receive kinder treatment.

This is but one of many oddities used by Butler to highlight issues in Victorian society, but one stands out across the generations: Butler's imagined society in his 1872 book had banned all machines a good 400 years before. His imagined traveller sets out the reasoning behind it:

> About four hundred years previously, the state of mechanical knowledge was far beyond our own ... until one of the most learned professors of hypothetics wrote an extraordinary book proving that the machines were ultimately destined to supplant the race of man, and to become instinct with a vitality as different from, and superior to, that of animals, as animal to vegetable life.[3]

So convinced by the professor's ideas were the denizens of Butler's fictional kingdom that hundreds of years prior to the traveller's arrival they had already purged all technology that wasn't at least 271 years old – and then had banned all new technology after that point.

Such an idea might not feel like an especially original one for a satirical or utopian work of fiction now, but Butler's work came long before anything remotely resembling modern computing had ever been conceived. Charles Babbage, sometimes credited as the father of modern computing, had introduced his 'difference engine' some fifty years before, but it had never been built and was something of a thought experiment.

As Butler's novel shows, even before computers could analyse – let alone think – we were preoccupied with the idea that the evolution of mechanical (or digital) intelligences could do us harm. Butler did not stop at a few short paragraphs, turning over a large section later in his book to write several chapters from the perspective of his fictional 'professor of hypothetics' who had turned the people against machines. The danger was the faster pace of mechanical evolution:

> There is no security against the ultimate development of mechanical consciousness, in the fact of machines possessing little consciousness now. A mollusc has not much consciousness. Reflect upon the extraordinary advance which machines have made during the last few hundred years, and note how slowly the animal and vegetable kingdoms are advancing.[4]

Butler himself was not in reality writing a crude 'beware of the machines' book – his thesis was generally in favour of moderation and against extremes of any sort. It's not at all clear that we're supposed to believe what the citizens of *Erewhon* did with machinery was either genius or folly. Instead, he's raising an idea well before its time, and encouraging us to think where that sensible middle response might be.

The idea of either machinery or computers – our own technological creations – supplanting us or otherwise leading to our downfall has proven an obsession that has persisted in fictional works of every generation since Butler. Frank Herbert's *Dune* series of books have sparked multiple adaptations – including a joyously camp movie, a beautiful but dour one and multiple great video games[5] – and feature numerous staple tropes of the genre. It includes a chosen one on whom the fate of the universe rests, a return to feudalism in a far-futuristic society, a caste of warrior nuns with mystical powers,[6] and a much-fought-over resource that holds the key to intergalactic travel.

What they don't feature, though, is any kind of computer device. Conflict between man and machines makes absolutely no part of Herbert's narrative (which spans multiple books and many thousands of pages). Instead, thinking machines had been eradicated years before in the 'Butlerian Jihad' – a very clear nod to Samuel Butler – and everything up to and including spaceships in the series is simply operated manually.

Herbert, a man who wanted technology out of the way so his science fiction could focus on religion and prophecy, nonetheless chose the reasoning of technology dystopians to dispense with it. Rather than say advanced technology would be boring, he created a world without it.

Most other science fiction centres conflicts between humans and emerging artificial life. *The Matrix* imagines humanity enslaved by thinking machines which have supplanted them. *Battlestar Galactica* imagines humans and human-like machines, the Cylons, and the complex relationship between the two – the latter nearly destroy humanity before realising they are more like their 'parents' than they might hope. *Blade Runner*, too, explored humanity's difficult relationship with technology.

These works of fiction all share various traits. Most obviously, they picture humanity facing off against artificial intelligence that closely resembles humanity: it can communicate with us, it often looks like us, and it is a sophisticated multi-cellular organism capable of abstract thought, which makes deliberate plans.

That's perhaps necessary for works of fiction. AI resembling something like a colony of ants, or a swarm of bees, might be fascinating for research, but it would probably make a terrible movie antagonist – unless it was suddenly given human-like intelligence and an ability to monologue at the right point in the film.

A common thread throughout all these fictionalised portrayals of emerging intelligence from mechanical technology, networks or artificial intelligence is that it can evolve faster than we can – the very same idea that Dawkins seized upon when proposing the meme as the successor to the gene.

In the internet era, this seems straightforwardly true. Memes are essentially like genes, the building blocks that come together to make DNA and in turn organisms, plus non-living but complex systems like viruses. A collection of memes – satanic child abuse, antisemitism, 'do your own research' – stick together and make a new version of something like QAnon, which reproduces across the world, and occasionally evolves into a new version.

But it feels like science fiction skips to the last step of that logic – or at least the last step so far as humanity is concerned – and imagines that rapid evolution producing something rather like us. It skips the potential early steps, the bacteria, the amoebas, the fish and so forth.

Genes didn't make the jump from single-celled bacteria or other simple organisms straight to humanity – so why would memes, as a building block for something new, be any different? We might see those intermediary steps move faster than evolution – which takes thousands if not millions of years – but perhaps the amalgamation of memes into entities like QAnon represents one of the earlier steps of memetic life. The next steps (should they come) might look nothing like offline life, let alone humanity.

That choice to skip straight to human-like AI means fiction doesn't equip us to deal with challenges like digital pathogens, with challenges like QAnon and the global anti-vaccine movement. They have no structures and they have no leaders because they are products of their environment – the information ecosystem. Perhaps in time these digital microbes will evolve into something more closely resembling human intelligence. Perhaps some kind of more deliberately developed AI will do so. Perhaps nothing ever will.

It doesn't matter whether we choose to see the idea of digital pathogens emerging and evolving as literal or metaphorical – we know from chaos theory and similar ideas that complex patterns can emerge from simple or even random systems. One classic example of this is Langton's Ant. This is an 'ant' on a grid of white squares, programmed with simple rules: if the square is white, turn it black, then turn left and move forwards. If the square is black, turn it white, then turn right and move forwards.

The first surprise is how random and chaotic the emerging black-and-white picture looks. The second is that after several thousand moves, suddenly an endlessly repeating and seemingly planned pattern emerges, sending the ant perpetually to the bottom-right of the screen[7] and making a complex repeated pattern on the way.

Whether digital pathogens are actually evolving or whether they're patterns emerging from much more complex algorithmic rules than those of Langton's Ant – those that govern what we see on YouTube and social media – is beside the point. Either way, we are contending with something that has emerged as a new and unexpected consequence of our new digital ecosystem.

This means that we cannot think of this as a series of isolated problems. To do so would be to play whack-a-mole on a global geopolitical scale. Each part of the ecosystem that produces phenomena like QAnon is connected to each other part. Tackling them in isolation will cause damaging knock-on effects.

We have been talking about ecosystems – where everything has multiple causes and multiple consequences, and things are connected in complex ways where interactions can be unpredictable. We learned the hard way that well-intentioned interventions in the natural world can have unintended consequences if we don't look at the wider ecosystem.

To illustrate this, let's imagine a very simple ecosystem, in which corn is eaten by grasshoppers, which are eaten by rats, which are in turn eaten by snakes. Let's say in this situation that those rats are starting to invade our homes, leading to calls to wipe them out. Rat exterminators are despatched and do their job brilliantly, wiping out 90 per cent or more of the rat population. But that makes for every grasshopper's dream: no predators.

The population of grasshoppers booms, eating more and more of the corn crop until that becomes a severe threat to the harvest. Realising their mistake, the human population of the area calls off the ratcatchers and even reintroduces a few rats to control the grasshopper population.

But while the grasshoppers were booming, the snakes were having a hard time: deprived of their only source of food, most starved. And so once the rats were reintroduced, they had no predators and ample food – and so *their* population now booms. One problem causes another, and another, and another in turn. An ecosystem once in balance is unbalanced by each well-meaning intervention that doesn't look at the system as a whole.

As offline, so online. In the first half of 2021, long after they should have, social networks like Facebook and Twitter finally started removing QAnon accounts en masse. But those accounts had lots of warning this was coming, and, as we saw in earlier chapters, moved millions of users onto much more extreme private channels, such as Discord or Telegram.

These new users were then in the kind of networks that much more rapidly radicalise those present. Looking at only part of the system and making only one intervention had caused a new problem in turn. It will carry on doing so for as long as we as a society carry on taking our whack-a-mole approach. We need to try to play out the consequences of major decisions in advance. All too often they are predictable, and if different stakeholders (a jargon word which nonetheless has meaning) communicate and work together, at least some of those can be avoided.

Just as real-world food webs are never as simple as the example above (which, if we're honest, is more of a single food thread), online ecosystems are large and complex. But critically they do not stop online.

We could imagine the information ecosystems to be online, but with real-world consequences, and that would be bad enough. That's the world where people are radicalised into becoming mass shooters or cut off from their families, or where polarised societies vote in dangerous populist leaders.

But online information networks feed offline ones: Fox News feeds off the online extremist right, picking up its most successful storylines and regurgitating them, attracting new recruits to the causes. Australian prime minister Malcolm Turnbull, in an apology for very real and decades-long failings on institutional child abuse, added the world 'ritual' to his comment, spurring new theories and new curiosity.

As the Republican party – now for its primaries, especially, beholden entirely to its QAnon-infested base – moved towards the 2022 midterms, and in turn the 2024 election, it was no coincidence that suddenly elected representatives talked at almost every opportunity of 'grooming', whether 'liberal', 'woke' or 'LGBT'. 'Grooming' is very much the language of QAnon, rehabilitated just enough for supposedly mainstream political discourse.

QAnon as a discrete phenomenon reached and convinced tens of millions of people around the world. The extreme wing of the antivaxx movement that it largely merged with captured tens if not hundreds of millions more. Those numbers alone should be enough to convince us that tackling these online ecosystems is essential, even if it's enormously difficult.

But if it isn't – if we convince ourselves that society has always had its fringes, and this is just the same as it ever was – we need to remember the interaction between fringe media, and fringe ideas, and mainstream media and politics. When opportunists see a voter base or a consumer base that is large enough, they will seek to profit from it, either financially or with power.

These new online ecosystems have become integrated with our existing ones, and they will not – can not – be disconnected. This is the world we now live in.

Acceptance is the first step to fixing any problem. In this case it means not just accepting there are problems in the online information ecosystem – virtually every political persuasion has admitted that for years – but also to let it truly sink in that it's an ecosystem and operates as such.

We need to think about those connections as hard as we think about each individual problem. This is something we're not fantastic at offline – often tackling one social problem in turn and then being surprised when it inevitably then makes another one worse – but we are somehow even worse at it online, despite networking being the very core of the internet.

Short of endless solemn pronouncements that online 'misinformation and disinformation' are a threat to democracy, those coordinating a response seem content to stay well in their comfort zone,[8] imagining that a fact-check here, an algorithm tweak there and a civics class early enough in life will rid us of these new problems and put an end to digital pathogens.

That keeps us from tackling the real problem, which requires asking ourselves a series of much more difficult questions and setting ourselves a much more difficult set of challenges. Why are so many people so susceptible to these pathogens? What has left them so distrustful of institutions, so sure the game is rigged? What can be done about online spawning grounds – do they need to be abolished, with all the free speech issues that brings, or reformed? When does healthy scepticism turn into curiosity? Where are the limits of healthy debate?

These are a lot harder and don't leave us with easy villains. Scientology makes a great subject for documentaries on cults and conspiracies – it has one clear theology, one clear founder who thought it up and one charismatic current leader, who can serve as the antihero or the villain. And it is a small, self-contained threat, at worst.

QAnon is much closer to a natural phenomenon, just like the real-world virus with which it coincided. There is no fun in vilifying the Covid-19 virus itself, and so we need it to be the creation (or invention) of someone malign: Xi Jinping, Bill Gates, Anthony Fauci or all three in concert.

Similarly, it's easier to imagine QAnon as the product of Ron Watkins, or even Facebook CEO Mark Zuckerberg and Twitter founder Jack Dorsey. While all three men helped QAnon spread and helped create the conditions in which it could thrive, none of them can be said to have any control over it, to run its doctrine. In the case of the latter two, they've never had a say in it.

Digital pathogens make for terrible movie villains, but very real threats – and ones that will continue to evolve faster than we can, and which will strike ever more frequently. It's time for us to adapt and survive.

Acknowledgements

There are always more people to thank than there is space in a beleaguered author's brain to remember them all – such is the nature of writing. Here, all the same, is at least a partial attempt to give credit where it is due.

On the publishing side, thanks to my agent at Wylie, Tracy Bohan, for her constant support and especially for her help in getting this book over the line with a publisher as it went through several iterations. At Bloomsbury, thanks to Jasmine Horsey and Alexis Kirschbaum and the team for sticking with me for another book, and being a pleasure to deal with once again.

This book would be a much worse one without the thoughtful edits and challenges of Jack Ramm, while I'd also like to thank Patrick Elliot for research support. All errors, mistakes and omissions remain – of course – my fault.

I'd like to thank everyone interviewed and cited in this book, many of whom helped far beyond their quoted contributions. I'd also like to salute anyone working on the disinformation beat and trying to sound the alarm on what's happening – good work and Godspeed.

I'd also like to apologise to the numerous people who have, in the three years I've worked on this text, suffered from me working through QAnon and its many troubling aspects, sometimes in the pub. I appreciate this did not make for good light conversation.

I'd like to thanks everyone at TBIJ for making sure journalism is never a dull occupation, everyone at the *New European* for allowing me to write for seven years now,and everyone at the

New Conspiracist for keeping me sane while I'm buried in these bizarre fringes. I'm also lucky to be blessed with a fantastic family and friends – thank you, more than I can say, to you all.

Finally, to everyone who has tried to help a family member or friend from being pulled into the black hole of a movement like QAnon – good luck, and don't forget to look after yourself first.

Notes

INTRODUCTION

1. Sadly not a hypothetical example: Simon Doherty, 'Inside Operation Pridefall: 4chan's Attempt to Bring Down Pride 2020', www.vice.com, 3 June 2020.
2. This original post is archived at https://qposts.online/post/1.
3. The account actually only fully identified itself as such a few days later, but posed as such an insider from the get-go.
4. Daniel Bates, 'EXCLUSIVE: Jeffrey Epstein's access to the Clinton White House laid bare', www.dailymail.co.uk, 2 December 2021.
5. There are many accounts of such incidents, but this is a good starting point: Ted Mann, Dustin Volz, Lindsay Wise and Chad Day, 'Lawmakers Were Feet and Seconds Away from Confrontation With the Mob in the Capitol', www.wsj.com, 12 January 2021.
6. More background on these protests here: Ewan Palmer, 'Global March 20 Anti-Vaccine Protests Promoted by QAnon-Linked Groups', www.newsweek.com, 16 March 2021, and in this thread: https://twitter.com/VeraMBergen/status/1419079819959029763
7. Joe Ondrak and Jordan Wildon, 'EXCLUSIVE: Worldwide Anti-Lockdown Protests Organized by German Cell', www.logically.ai, 14 May 2020.
8. This account of the 24/7 London protest is thanks to the public reporting of the BBC's Shayan Sardarizadeh, set out on Twitter here: https://twitter.com/Shayan86/status/1418915810416934915.
9. From this transcript: www.rev.com/blog/transcripts/donald-trump-phoenix-arizona-rally-speech-transcript-july-24, accessed 7 October 2022.

10. World Health Organization, 'How WHO is working to track down the animal reservoir of the SARS-CoV-2 virus', www.who.int, 6 November 2020.

11. World Health Organization, 'Middle East respiratory syndrome coronavirus (MERS-CoV)', https://www.who.int, accessed 6 October 2022.

12. This version of the story of William of Norwich is taken from BBC Radio 4's *The Long View*: www.bbc.co.uk, accessed 6 October 2022.

13. In the West, at least – the origin of printing is more complex and disputed than the short 'Gutenberg invented it in *c.* 1140'. More on this here: https://lithub.com/so-gutenberg-didnt-actually-invent-the-printing-press/

14. Ben Collins, 'QAnon's new "plan"? Run for school board', www.nbcnews.com, 7 July 2021.

15. Jamie Ross, 'Suspected U.K. Mass Shooter Said He Was American, Trump-Supporting Virgin', www.thedailybeast.com, 13 August 2021.

16. Complaint online at https://heavy.com/wp-content/uploads/2021/08/USA-v-Coleman-COMPLAINT.pdf.

17. https://foreignpolicy.com/2022/12/12/germany-conspiracy-us-arrests-january-6-capitol-attack-bundestag-nazism-reich-coup/

18. https://www.msnbc.com/opinion/msnbc-opinion/elon-musk-replacing-trump-qanon-celebrity-du-jour-twitter-rcna61802

1 ASK THE Q

1. moot is no longer anonymous but is still a rather private individual, as his personal site shows: https://moot.tumblr.com.

2. The (priceless) headline was 'Modest Web Site Is Behind a Bevy of Memes', by Jamin Brophy-Warren, www.wsj.com, 9 July 2008.

3. Jennifer Elias, '4chan Founder Chris Poole Has Left Google', www.cnbc.com, 22 April 2021.

4. Still online at www.2chan.net.

5. A detailed early history of 'kek' can be found at the excellent KnowYourMeme: https://knowyourmeme.com.

6. It is also bound by copyright, and will comply with DMCA requests: www.4chan.org/faq#copyrighted.

7. See www.4chan.org/faq#shitposting

8. At https://boards.4chan.org/pol, accessed on 2 September 2021.

9. Whether this is supposed to be a play on 'bastards' or 'retards' is in the eye of the beholder.

10. This will probably not come as a surprise to readers who have met me.

11. A few examples can be found here: www.reddit.com/r/OutOfTheLoop/comments/269e6w/4chan_and_pizza_deliveries.

12. You have 4chan to thank if your online pizza order will only accept prepayment for orders above a certain threshold.

13. Once again there is a fuller account here: 'Pool's Closed', https://knowyourmeme.com.

14. Beverly Jenkins, 'Very Funny 4chan Pranks Where Nobody Got Hurt', www.liveabout.com, 24 May 2019.

15. See https://web.archive.org/web/20080105081944/http://4chanarchive.org/brchive/dspl_thread.php5?thread_id=39101047.

16. '4chan's Pflugerville Highschool Bomb Threat', www.youtube.com/watch?v=hwDztdNohZ4.

17. Sean Michaels, 'Taking the Rick', www.theguardian.com, 19 March 2008.

18. The 4channers here were more correct than the music and movie companies. Once legal streaming became available and affordable, few people bothered to pirate any more.

19. Trouble often started on Gawker, to such an extent that Silicon Valley billionaire Peter Thiel funded a Hulk Hogan lawsuit to bankrupt the site, likely as revenge for it outing him as gay years earlier. There is a good movie about the whole thing: *Nobody Speak: Trials of the Free Press* (dir. Brian Knappenberger, 2017).

20. Don't take my word for it – see for yourself here: *Tom Cruise Scientology Video*, www.youtube.com/watch?v=UFBZ_uAbxSo.

21. The chat channels were IRC, usually on servers managed by Anons themselves, but I didn't want to get into an explanation of IRC in the main text.

22. There are many examples, but one account is Joe Nocera, 'Scientology's Chilling Effect', www.nytimes.com, 24 February 2015, and there is a movie-length account by Alex Gibney, *Going Clear: Scientology and the Prison of Belief* (2015).

23. Yes, faxes were still very much a Thing in 2008. Doesn't that feel like a long time ago?

24. 'The Right to Bear Low Orbit Ion Cannons', https://lookingglasscyber.com, accessed 7 October 2022.

25. Ryan Singel, ' "Anonymous" Members Unmasked, Charged With Web Attack on Scientology', www.wired.com, 17 October 2008.

26. Olsen Ebright, 'Man to Plead Guilty for Online Attack on Scientology', www.nbclosangeles.com, 26 January 2010.

27. Fruzsina Eordogh, 'The Video That Made Anonymous', www.vice. com, 22 January 2014.

28. Count (and the full video) here: *Message to Scientology*, www.yout ube.com/watch?v=JCbKv9yiLiQ&t=2s.

29. See https://web.archive.org/web/20120210160057/http://sunco astpinellas.tbo.com/content/2008/feb/12/organizers-tout-scientol ogy-protest-plan-another.

30. 'Masked Protest over Scientology', http://news.bbc.co.uk, 11 February 2008.

31. See ref 21.

32. The definition at www.urbandictionary.com does itself try to set off a moral reaction – do be warned.

33. Kevin Poulsen, 'Hackers Assault Epilepsy Patients via Computer', www.wired.com, 28 March 2008.

34. Richard Stengel, 'The Untold Story of the Sony Hack', www.van ityfair.com, 6 October 2019.

35. Lauren Turner, 'Anonymous hackers jailed for DDoS attacks on Visa, Mastercard and Paypal', www.independent.co.uk, 24 January 2013.

36. Yasmine Ryan, 'Anonymous and the Arab Uprisings', www.aljaze era.com, 19 May 2011.

37. Michael Brice-Saddler, Avi Selk and Eli Rosenberg, 'Prankster sentenced to 20 years for fake 911 call that led police to kill an innocent man', www.washingtonpost.com, 29 March 2019.

38. David Covucci, 'These LARPers claim to have invented QAnon', www.dailydot.com, 8 August 2019.

39. See www.perplexcity.com/

40. Sarah Perez, 'Rogue National Park Service Twitter account says it's no longer run by National Park Service employees … but maybe it never was', https://techcrunch.com, 27 January 2017.

41. There's a good history of some of these accounts in this Bellingcat account: 'The Making of Qanon: A Crowdsourced Conspiracy', www.bellingcat.com, 7 January 2021.

42. Office of Environment, Health, Safety and Security, 'Departmental Personnel Security FAQs', https://www.energy.gov, accessed 7 October 2022.

43. See https://archer.fandom.com/wiki/Nellis.

44. See https://qposts.online/post/2.
45. Mark Landler, 'Trump Calls Meeting with Military Leaders the Calm Before the Storm', www.nytimes.com, 6 October 2017.

2 COMET PING PONG

1. The game is at www.depressionquest.com/dqfinal.html#2n.1e.
2. There is a good chronology of the early stages of this sorry affair: Kyle Wagner, 'The Future Of The Culture Wars Is Here, And It's Gamergate', https://deadspin.com, 14 October 2014.
3. Phil Owen, '4 Video Games That Help You Understand And Deal With Your Depression', https://kotaku.com, 19 April 2013.
4. Stephen Totilo, 'In recent days I've been asked several times ...', https://kotaku.com, 20 August 2014.
5. This is all logged in the Deadspin article above (which has a very prescient headline).
6. I am a fan of this series and think them well worth watching. You can see them on YouTube.
7. Alex Hern, 'Feminist games critic cancels talk after terror threat', www.theguardian.com, 15 October 2015.
8. 'Actually it's about ethics', https://knowyourmeme.com, accessed 7 October 2022.
9. Andrew Beattie, 'How the Video Game Industry Is Changing', www.investopedia.com, 31 October 2021.
10. Leigh Alexander, '"Gamers" don't have to be your audience. "Gamers" are over', www.gamedeveloper.com, 20 August 2014.
11. Eric Johnson, 'What Is Gamergate, and Why Is Intel So Afraid of It?', www.vox.com, 9 October 2014.
12. There wasn't any to find: I hadn't then, and haven't now, met either.
13. It's a good code, it's still public, and you can read it online at www.theguardian.com.
14. Anything worth more than £25 that you absolutely couldn't refuse went into an annual 'sleaze lottery' at Christmas, with the proceeds going to the *Guardian*'s charity of the year.
15. Michael McWhertor, 'Game developer Brianna Wu flees home after death threats, Mass. police investigating', www.polygon.com, 11 October 2014.
16. Alex Hern, 'Gamergate hits new low with attempts to send Swat teams to critics', www.theguardian.com, 13 January 2015.

17. John Perry Barlow's Declaration of Independence of cyberspace is a seminal document on this: www.eff.org/cyberspace-independence.
18. Angela Nagle, *Kill All Normies: Online Culture Wars from 4chan and Tumblr to Trump and the Alt-Right* (Zero Books, 2017), pp. 8 and 10.
19. Zaid Jilani, 'Gamergate's fickle hero: The dark opportunism of Breitbart's Milo Yiannopoulos', www.salon.com, 28 October 2014.
20. MILO, 'Exposed: The Secret Mailing List of the Gaming Journalism Elite', www.breitbart.com, 17 September 2014.
21. Author interview.
22. Steven Melendez, 'The Secret Meaning Behind GamerGate's Branding', www.fastcompany.com, 3 November 2014.
23. Southern Poverty Law Center, 'Richard Bertrand Spencer', www.splcenter.org, accessed 7 October 2022.
24. A few low spots are here: Rory Carroll, 'Where's the money? Milo Yiannopoulos denies he spent cash for charity fund', www.theguardian.com, 19 August 2016, and here: Alexander Schwartz, 'Milo Yiannopoulos's Cynical Book Deal', www.newyorker.com, 30 September 2016.
25. 'Pepe the Frog', https://knowyourmeme.com.
26. Ibid.
27. ADL, 'Pepe the Frog', www.adl.org, accessed 7 October 2022.
28. The 2020 documentary *Feels Good Man*, directed by Arthur Jones, is a great watch on all of these events.
29. The following is taken from Chapter 9 of Ebner's excellent *Going Dark: The Secret Social Lives of Extremists* (Bloomsbury, 2019).
30. Ibid., p. 182.
31. Alexander Abed-Santos, 'Mitt Romney: "I Like Being Able to Fire People"', www.theatlantic.com, 9 January 2012.
32. Hamilah Abdullah, ' "Binders," cooking and equal pay: Did Romney undo gains with women voters?', http://edition.cnn.com, 18 October 2012.
33. Tauriq Moosa, 'The "punch a Nazi" meme: what are the ethics of punching Nazis?', www.theguardian.com, 31 January 2017.
34. Author interview.
35. Carrie Johnson, 'FBI, CIA Agree That Russia Was Trying To Help Trump Win The Election', www.npr.org, 16 December 2016.
36. Luke Harding, Julian Borger and Dan Sabbagh, 'Kremlin papers appear to show Putin's plot to put Trump in White House', www.theguardian.com, 15 July 2021.

37. Katelyn Polantz and Stephen Collinson, '12 Russians indicted in Mueller investigation', https://edition.cnn.com, 14 July 2018.

38. Michael McGowan, 'Help make Julian Assange Australia's US ambassador, WikiLeaks urged Trump Jr', www.theguardian.com, 14 November 2017.

39. Catherine Herridge and Adam Shaw, 'State Department report on Clinton emails finds hundreds of violations, dozens of individuals at fault', www.foxnews.com, 18 October 2019.

40. Weiner had been sending lewd messages to numerous women, including minors: Joanna Walters, 'Anthony Weiner sent sexually explicit messages to 15-year-old, report says', www.theguardian.com, 22 September 2016.

41. 'Emails in Anthony Weiner Inquiry Jolt Hillary Clinton's Campaign', www.nytimes.com, 29 October 2016.

42. Associated Press, 'Leaked DNC emails reveal details of anti-Sanders sentiment', www.theguardian.com, 24 July 2016.

43. 'Pizzagate: How a 4chan conspiracy went mainstream', www.newstatesman.com, 8 December 2016.

44. Brian Patrick Byrne, 'Minecraft Creator Alleges Global Conspiracy Involving Pizzagate, a "Manufactured Race War," a Missing Tabloid Toddler, and Holistic Medicine', www.thedailybeast.com, 28 August 2017.

45. Joshua Gillin, 'How Pizzagate went from fake news to a real problem for a D.C. business', www.politifact.com, 5 December 2016.

46. 'Fake News Onslaught Targets Pizzeria as Nest of Child-Trafficking', www.nytimes.com, 21 October 2016.

47. Jana Winter, 'Media Matters boss paid former partner $850G "blackmail" settlement', www.foxnews.com, 22 December 2015.

48. Faiz Siddiqui and Susan Svrluga, 'N.C. man told police he went to D.C. pizzeria with gun to investigate conspiracy theory', www.washingtonpost.com, 4 December 2016.

49. Spencer S. Hau, '"Pizzagate" gunman sentenced to four years in prison, as prosecutors urged judge to deter vigilante justice', www.washingtonpost.com, 22 June 2017.

3 BREADCRUMBS

1. The Lamb, also known as the best pub in London.

2. *Finding Q*, available via Audible, which Woolf asks me to note has a seven-day free trial if you're not a subscriber.

3. At https://qposts.online/post/1. I am not decoding Q posts in detail here. Readers can do so at their leisure if they wish, but go with extreme caution down that particular rabbit hole.

4. At https://www.4channel.org/faq#trip.

5. At https://qposts.online/post/2.

6. At https://qposts.online/post/4.

7. 'A trail of bread crumbs leading conspiracy theorists into the wilderness', www.nytimes.com, 11 September 2018.

8. 'The Greatest LARP' section of this very good Bellingcat piece is great on this: 'The Making of QAnon: A Crowdsourced Conspiracy', www.bellingcat.com, 7 January 2021.

9. 'Who Is Behind QAnon? Linguistic Detectives Find Fingerprints', www.nytimes.com, 19 February 2022.

10. Brandy Zadrozny and Ben Collins, 'How three conspiracy theorists took "Q" and sparked Qanon', www.nbcnews.com, 14 August 2018.

11. NBC Nightly News, ' "Calm Before The Storm": Donald Trump Makes Cryptic Remark At Military Dinner', https://www.youtube.com/watch?v=VrF7alkwdHw.

12. At https://qposts.online/post/48.

13. One of many references to that here: https://twitter.com/arictoler/status/1373072597009760256?s=21 – and a truly bizarre video from 2011 'explaining' Looking Glass: 'Stargate and Project Looking Glass with David Wilcock', https://rumble.com/vjt4oh-stargate-and-project-looking-glass-with-david-wilcock.html, 13 July 2021.

14. Gabriela Saldivia, 'Jeffrey Epstein Dead By Apparent Suicide At Manhattan Jail', www.npr.org, 10 August 2019.

15. Victoria Bekiempis, 'Ghislaine Maxwell found guilty in sex-trafficking trial', www.theguardian.com, 29 December 2021.

16. Rose Eveleth, 'Nearly Half of Americans Believe At Least One Conspiracy Theory', www.smithsonianmag.com, 8 April 2014.

17. Michael Butter, *The Nature of Conspiracy Theories* (Cambridge, 2020), p. 9.

18. Listed publicly on www.4chan.org as of March 2022.

19. 'Most popular social networks worldwide as of January 2022, ranked by number of monthly active users', www.statista.com, January 2022.

20. The NBC piece by Brandy Zadrozny and Ben Collins is excellent on this, and well worth a read: 'How Three Conspiracy Theorists Took Q and Sparked QAnon', www.nbcnews.com, 14 August 2018.

21. Alyssa Bailey, 'Breaking Down The Many Easter Eggs In Taylor Swift's "Look What You Made Me Do"', www.elle.com, 28 August 2017.

22. Julian Epp, 'How YouTube's obsession with Marvel Easter eggs has turned MCU movies into full-blown global events', www.insider.com, 12 January 2020.

23. At https://qposts.online/post/61.

24. At https://qposts.online/post/230.

25. Patrick Howell O'Neill, '8chan, the central hive of Gamergate, is also an active pedophile network', www.dailydot.com, 17 November 2014.

26. At https://mobile.twitter.com/waxpancake/status/51202858689 1436032.

27. At www.reddit.com/r/GamerGhazi/comments/2y7wpy/howwhy_did_4chan_ban_gamergaters_and_the.

28. Q's (not very exciting) final post: https://qposts.online/post/4953.

29. Timothy McLaughlin, 'The Weird, Dark History of 8chan', www.wired.com, 6 August 2019.

30. AJ Vicens and Ali Breland, 'QAnon Is Supposed to Be All About Protecting Kids. Its Primary Enabler Appears to Have Hosted Child Porn Domains', www.motherjones.com, 29 October 2020.

31. 'Who Is Behind QAnon? Linguistic Detectives Find Fingerprints', www.nytimes.com, 19 February 2022.

32. Nick Perry, 'Report finds lapses ahead of New Zealand mosque attack', https://apnews.com, 8 December 2020.

33. John Gage, 'California police investigate hate-filled 8chan manifesto that could link synagogue shooting to mosque attack', www.washingtonexaminer.com, 28 April 2019.

34. Ben Collins, 'Investigators "reasonably confident" Texas suspect left anti-immigrant screed, tipped off before attack', www.nbcnews.com, 4 August 2019.

35. '"Shut the Site Down," Says the Creator of 8chan, a Megaphone for Gunmen', www.nytimes.com, 4 August 2019.

36. Makena Kelly, 'Cloudflare to revoke 8chan's service, opening the fringe website up for DDoS attacks', www.theverge.com, 5 August 2019.

37. Drew Harwell, '8chan vowed to fight on, saying its "heartbeat is strong".' Then a tech firm knocked it offline', www.washingtonp ost.com, 5 August 2019.

38. Christy Somos, '"You need to hang together": Owner of 8chan releases video as site attempts to get back online', www.ctvnews.ca, 9 October 2019.

39. He has done this in several places, but this is one of the best accounts: *Reply All* episode 166, 'Country of Liars', https://giml etmedia.com.

40. Nicky Woolf, *Finding Q: My Journey into QAnon*, www.audible. co.uk.

41. HBO's six-part documentary *Q: Into the Storm* is very good on this.

42. Adam Gabbatt, 'QAnon's "Q" re-emerges on far-right message board after two years of silence', www.theguardian.com, 27 June 2022.

43. Claire Goforth, 'A prankster upended the big return of QAnon with a simple copy/paste scheme', www.dailydot.com, 6 July 2022.

4 PATRIOT RESEARCH

1. Or certainly among the first three, and certainly the first to rise to prominence.

2. Last checked as correct and still online in March 2022.

3. 'Cabal Lies, Cabal Dies', https://youtu.be/zjK5MQnlk5M, 29 December 2017.

4. At www.youtube.com/results?search_query=roypotterqa.

5. Ed Kilgore, 'Do Republicans Know What Communism Is?', https:// nymag.com, 6 March 2022.

6. Take as an example Trump's targeting of the FBI as some kind of radical left institution: 'Trump Is Going After One of the Most Conservative Institutions in the U.S. Government', www.nytimes. com, 18 August 2018.

7. 'Janet Ossebaard', www.coasttocoastam.com/guest/osseba ard-janet-105140.

8. Ossebaard's videos were removed from YouTube alongside most QAnon content, but remain online here: https://rumble.com. I do not recommend watching them.

9. Jon Ronson, 'Beset by Lizards', www.theguardian.com, 17 March 2001.

10. There's still some controversy around this, but here's the consensus: Eric Hardin, 'Myth: Subliminal Messages Can Change Your Behavior', www.psychologicalscience.org, 29 March 2019.

11. Angelique Chrisafis, 'Who are the gilets jaunes and what do they want?', www.theguardian.com, 7 December 2018.

12. Worth a watch: 'Drinking problem: Trump has awkward water moment', www.youtube.com, 16 November 2017. Apparently this was signalling about a particular child sex abuse ring

13. Pew Research Center, 'Trump's International Ratings Remain Low, Especially Among Key Allies', www.pewresearch.org, 1 October 2018.

14. At https://twitter.com/janbobrowicz/status/1356773544735232 001?s=21.

15. 'Digital Around the World', https://datareportal.com/global-digital-overview#:~:text=A%20total%20of%205.03%20bill ion,12%20months%20to%20July%202022.

16. All of Knight's remarks are from an author interview (one of several), they have been cleaned up here for clarity and concision.

17. Jan-Willem van Prooijen, 'Voters on the extreme left and right are far more likely to believe in conspiracy theories', http://eprints.lse.ac.uk/61732/1/blogs.lse.ac.uk.

18. Both real headlines on the page on 26 March 2022: www.infow ars.com.

19. The case has run for years, constantly halted by Jones' non-cooperation: Associated Press, 'Alex Jones again fails to show up for a deposition in the Sandy Hook case against him', www.npr.org, 24 March 2022; James Ball, 'Alex Jones: the $49m comeuppance of a conspiracist', www.thetimes.co.uk, 6 August 2022.

20. Sebastian Murdock, 'Alex Jones' Infowars Store Made $165 Million Over 3 Years, Records Show', www.huffingtonpost.co.uk, 1 July 2022.

21. Joe Sommerlad, ' "Bye bye Q, I can't talk to you any more": What next for Alex Jones, America's foremost conspiracy theorist?', www.independent.co.uk, 23 March 2021.

22. See https://crossfitnycflatiron.com/more-info/#pricing.

23. Though this is not always known to patients, who often only know it as an alternative to physiotherapy. In reality, several chiropractic movements have potentially debilitating side-effects and its benefits are not scientifically proven. Alok Jha, 'Dangers of chiropractic

treatments under-reported, study finds', www.theguardian.com, 14 May 2012.

24. Bruce F. Walker, Simon D. French, William Grant and Sally Green, 'A Cochrane review of combined chiropractic interventions for low-back pain', https://pubmed.ncbi.nlm.nih.gov/21248591, 1 February 2011.

25. There's a great *Guardian* piece on this overlap here: Eva Wiseman, 'The dark side of wellness: the overlap between spiritual thinking and far-right conspiracies', www.theguardian.com, 17 October 2021

26. Mary H. J. Farrell, 'MyPillow Settles Consumer Lawsuit Over Health Claims for $1 Million', www.consumerreports.org, 3 November 2016.

27. Ryan Klinker, 'MyPillow founder Mike Lindell gifts students with pillows and message of God's grace', www.liberty.edu, 21 August 2019.

28. 'Transcript: Donald Trump's Taped Comments About Women', www.nytimes.com, 8 October 2016.

29. Cheryl Teh, 'A judge has rejected MyPillow CEO Mike Lindell's appeal to dismiss Dominion's $1.3 billion lawsuit against him', www.businessinsider.com, 3 March 2022.

30. Kate Taylor and Mary Meisenzahl, 'Retailers like Kohl's and Bed Bath & Beyond have ditched MyPillow — see the full list of which major stores dropped it and which still sell it', 27 January 2021, www.businessinsider.com.

31. AJ Vicens, 'QAnon Hero Claims to Present Sensitive Election Files at MyPillow CEO Event', www.motherjones.com, 11 August 2021.

32. There are plenty of accounts of this, but here's a good starting point: Paul Lewis, '"Fiction is outperforming reality": how YouTube's algorithm distorts truth', www.theguardian.com, 2 February 2018.

33. 'The YouTube Rabbit Hole Is Nuanced', www.nytimes.com, 21 April 2022.

34. Emma Yeomans, Tom Ball and Andrew Ellson, 'The Cornish hotel flying a flag for QAnon's cult delusion', www.thetimes.co.uk, 16 January 2021.

35. Richard Kerbaj, 'Government gives £1m to anti extremist think tank Quilliam Foundation', www.thetimes.co.uk, 20 January 2009.

36. Vanessa Thorpe, 'LBC's Maajid Nawaz's fascination with conspiracies raises alarm', www.theguardian.com, 31 January 2021.

37. 'Berlin bans rally by vegan chef and conspiracy theorist Attila Hildmann', www.dw.com, 23 July 2020.

38. I really, really did just make this up – please don't cite it to me, or feel the need to check it.

39. As ever, Randall Munroe was well ahead of the rest of us here: https://xkcd.com/386.

40. This study, for example, suggests fact-checks seem to have a short-term effect – but it really doesn't last: John M. Carey et al., 'The ephemeral effects of fact-checks on COVID-19 misperceptions in the United States, Great Britain and Canada', www.nature.com, 3 February 2022.

41. As late as January 2020, one senior UK television executive mentioned to me that their channel's policy was still to make no mention of QAnon so as not to 'boost' it. I urged them, not entirely successfully, to reconsider.

42. This is a very short summary of what's known as the 'attention economy': Asher Joy, 'The Attention Economy: Where the Customer Becomes the Product', https://journal.businesstoday.org, 18 February 2021.

43. Except arguably TikTok, but this wasn't a major network until after this period.

44. Not coincidentally, they waited until he had lost a presidential election: Dylan Byers, 'How Facebook and Twitter decided to take down Trump's accounts', www.nbcnews.com, 14 January 2021.

45. 'Trump refuses to disavow QAnon conspiracy theory', www.ft.com, 15 October 2020.

46. Barbara Ortutay, 'YouTube follows Twitter and Facebook with QAnon crackdown', https://apnews.com, 15 October 2020.

47. Author interview.

48. Jordan Wildon and Marc-André Argentino, 'QAnon is not Dead: New Research into Telegram Shows the Movement is Alive and Well', https://gnet-research.org, 28 July 2021.

5 FOLLOW THE WHITE RABBIT

1. Scientology's own website backs up this definition, and is well worth a read just for the 'oh gosh' moments (Hitler, for example, features): 'What is a suppressive person', www.scientology.org.uk/faq.

2. There are two great documentaries on NXIVM – I suggest watching *The Vow* first, followed by *Seduced: Inside the NXIVM Cult*.

3. Possibly, but by no means definitely, *Loose Change* – memories can be hazy after a decade.

4. Cecilia Saixue Watt, 'The QAnon orphans: people who have lost loved ones to conspiracy theories', www.theguardian.com, 23 September 2020.

5. Travis M. Andrews, 'QAnon is tearing families apart', www.was hingtonpost.com, 14 September 2020.

6. At www.reddit.com/r/QanonCasualties, accessed March 2022.

7. At wwww.reddit.com/r/QAnonCasualties/comments/tndcz5/ qmom_might_lose_medical_license, accessed 11 October 2022.

8. At www.reddit.com/r/QAnonCasualties/comments/tnkvge/ qanon_in_japan_i_dont_even_know_what_to_do_here, accessed 11 October 2022.

9. At www.reddit.com/r/QAnonCasualties/comments/tnaeh7/cutt ing_off_without_leaving, accessed 11 October 2022.

10. At www.reddit.com/r/QAnonCasualties/comments/tnbn69/ what_does_it_feel_like_to_have_lost_someone_you, accessed 11 October 2022

11. Unless specifically referenced otherwise, everything from Karen Stewart is from interviews with the author.

12. At https://twitter.com/KazzaRBazza.

13. At http://mhccamden.com.au/about-us.

14. Or, if we're honest given the demographics of early QAnon supporters, borrowing a line from *The Matrix*.

15. It is also related to the mind-numbingly tedious 'freeman of the land' conspiracy – please do have a Google if you want to know more, but I recommend avoiding it.

16. For the avoidance of doubt, the author does not think there is any basis to Tim's claims here.

17. David Folkenflik, 'Analysis: Fox and right-wing media snap to Trump's defense after FBI search', www.npr.org, 9 August 2022.

18. At www.childabuseroyalcommission.gov.au.

19. This is available to watch online on YouTube.

20. As well as public criticism, there are suggestions of pressure behind the scenes: Amanda Meade, 'ABC denies it "pulled" Four Corners program on Scott Morrison and a supporter of QAnon', www.theg uardian.com, 3 June 2021.

21. Eric Hananoki, 'Marjorie Taylor Greene penned conspiracy theory that a laser beam from space started deadly 2018 California wildfire', www.mediamatters.org, 28 January 2021.

22. Eric Hananoki, 'GOP-backed House candidate Marjorie Taylor Greene: The Obama administration used MS-13 to assassinate Seth Rich', www.mediamatters.org, 13 August 2020.

23. Alex Kaplan, 'Here are the QAnon supporters running for Congress in 2020', www.mediamatters.org, 7 January 2020.

24. Ibid.

25. At https://twitter.com/daithaigilbert/status/1506272895978323973.

26. Barbara Sprunt, 'House Removes Rep. Marjorie Taylor Greene From Her Committee Assignments', www.npr.org, 4 February 2021.

27. This one actually predates Q, but is somewhat in its spirit: 'Kellyanne Conway denies Trump press secretary lied: 'He offered alternative facts' – video', www.theguardian.com, 22 January 2017.

28. 'Michael Flynn Resigns as National Security Adviser', www.nytimes.com, 13 February 2017.

29. Marshall Cohen, 'Michael Flynn posts video featuring QAnon slogans', https://edition.cnn.com, 7 July 2020.

30. Tom Porter, 'An attorney leading Trump's attempt to subvert the election results is a longtime QAnon supporter', www.businessinsider.com, 20 November 2020.

31. Jack Brewster, 'How Sidney Powell's "Kraken" – Pushed By QAnon – Went From Cable News To Trump Mainstream', www.forbes.com, 8 December 2020.

32. At www.politifact.com/factchecks/2020/nov/19/sidney-powell/trump-lawyer-falsely-claims-voting-technology-comp.

33. The immensely controversial Arizona recount, funded at private expense, did not find the results its backers wanted: Daniel Funke, 'Fact check: Arizona audit affirmed Biden's win, didn't prove voter fraud, contrary to Trump claim', https://eu.usatoday.com, 28 September 2021.

34. Kevin Liptak and Pamela Brown, 'Heated Oval Office meeting included talk of special counsel, martial law as Trump advisers clash', https://edition.cnn.com, 19 December 2020.

35. Heather Schwedel, 'Two Years Into His Presidency and Donald Trump Still Doesn't Use Computers', https://slate.com, 28 August 2018.

36. Peter Weber, '"Release the Kraken": Ginni Thomas' post-election texts to Trump's chief of staff included hints of QAnon', https://theweek.com, 25 March 2022.

6 THE STORM

1. 'A Web of Intimidation: Landmark Cyberstalking Case Results in Life Sentences for Three Family Members', www.fbi.gov, 12 April 2016.

2. Jack Gramenz, 'Man drove 5000 kilometres to kill Twitch streamer Matthew Thane', www.news.com.au, 22 August 2020.

3. '4chan Murder Suspect David Kalac Surrenders to Police', www.nbcnews.com, 5 November 2014.

4. Such is the love of US politicians of having things named after them that the bridge is named after prominent politicians from each of the two states – with little regard for anyone having to actually say the bridge's name out loud.

5. This is pieced together from multiple accounts, but the best single piece is this one: Stephanie K. Baer, 'An Armed Man Spouting A Bizarre Right-Wing Conspiracy Theory Was Arrested After A Standoff At The Hoover Dam', www.buzzfeednews.com, 17 June 2018.

6. EI Staff, 'Floodgates of Terror: Terrorism and Dams', www.earthisl and.org, accessed 11 October 2022.

7. Christine Pfaff, 'Safeguarding Hoover Dam during World War II', *Prologue Magazine* (Summer 2003), 35/2, at www.archives.gov.

8. At https://twitter.com/MarkAMills1/status/1007721528631353 344/photo/1.

9. Zoe Tillman, 'Investigators Say James Comey Was "Insubordinate" In The Clinton Email Probe', www.buzzfeednews.com, 14 June 2018.

10. Loomer posted this to Twitter, but has since been expelled from the platform. It is cited in multiple articles, including Baer, 'An Armed Man'.

11. Richard Ruelas, 'QAnon follower sentenced to nearly 8 years in prison for standoff near Hoover Dam', https://eu.azcentral.com, accessed 11 October 2022.

12. William Mansell, 'Man pleads guilty to terrorism charge after blocking Hoover Dam bridge with armored truck', https://abcn ews.go.com, 13 February 2020.

13. See footnote 11.

14. Lili Loofbourow, 'It Makes Perfect Sense That QAnon Took Off With Women This Summer', https://slate.com, 18 September 2020.

15. Justin Ling, Jill Mahoney, Patrick McGuire and Colin Freeze, 'The "incel" community and the dark side of the internet', www.theglobe andmail.com, 24 April 2018.

16. 'He Wasn't Seeking to Kill a Mob Boss. He Was Trying to Help Trump, His Lawyer Says', www.nytimes.com, 21 July 2019.

17. This account taken from Margot Harris, 'A woman inspired by QAnon conspiracy videos was arrested after live-streaming her trip to "take out" Joe Biden', www.insider.com, 1 May 2020.

18. Jane Coaston, 'YouTube's conspiracy theory crisis, explained', www.vox.com, 14 December 2018.

19. Will Sommer, 'QAnon Mom Arrested For Murder of Fringe Legal Theorist', www.thedailybeast.com, 27 January 2021.

20. Adam Tamburin, 'Debunked conspiracy theories quickly took root amid uncertainty after Nashville Christmas bombing', https://eu.tennessean.com, 30 December 2020.

21. 'Behind the Nashville Bombing, a Conspiracy Theorist Stewing About the Government', www.nytimes.com, 24 February 2021.

22. START, 'QAnon Offenders in the United States', www.start.umd.edu, May 2021.

23. Grahame Allen, Matthew Burton and Alison Pratt, 'Terrorism in Great Britain: The Statistics', https://researchbriefings.files.parliament.uk, 19 July 2022.

24. Michael Jensen and Sheehan Kane, 'QAnon-inspired violence in the United States: an empirical assessment of a misunderstood threat', www.tandfonline.com, 14 December 2021.

25. Nick Perry, 'Report finds lapses ahead of New Zealand mosque attack', https://apnews.com, 8 December 2020.

26. As he was a minor at the time of the attack and the offence took place in Canada, the perpetrator cannot be named.

27. Kevin Connor, 'Spa murder victim a "kind, loving" mom of one: GoFundMe', https://torontosun.com, 26 February 2020.

28. Stewart Bell, Andrew Russell and Catherine McDonald, 'Deadly attack at Toronto erotic spa was incel terrorism, police allege', https://globalnews.ca, 20 May 2020.

29. Amy Coles, 'Plymouth shootings: Police face scrutiny over decision to give gunman Jake Davison his shotgun licence back last month', https://news.sky.com, 14 August 2021.

30. Matthew Weaver and Steven Morris, 'Plymouth gunman: a hate-filled misogynist and "incel"', www.theguardian.com, 13 August 2021.

31. 'Plymouth shootings: Attack could be reclassified as terrorism over Jake Davison's "incel" links', https://news.sky.com, 17 August 2021.

32. Lori Hinnant, 'French child kidnapping plot shows global sway of QAnon style', www.post-gazette.com, 5 October 2021.

33. Joe Hernandez, 'A California Father Claims QAnon Conspiracy Led Him To Kill His 2 Children, FBI Says', www.npr.org, 13 August 2021.

34. 'QAnon Is Thriving in Germany. The Extreme Right Is Delighted', www.nytimes.com, 11 October 2020.

35. 'Germany coronavirus: Anger after attempt to storm parliament', www.bbc.co.uk/news, 30 August 2020.

36. This is set out nicely in this thread from two weeks after the Capitol attack: https://twitter.com/radiofreetom/status/1351011133264719 875?s=21.

37. 'Presidential Results', https://edition.cnn.com/election/2020/resu lts/president, accessed 13 October 2022.

38. Megan Graham and Salvador Rodriguez, 'Twitter and Facebook race to label a slew of posts making false election claims before all votes counted', www.cnbc.com, 4 November 2020.

39. Brandy Zadrozny, '"Carol's Journey": What Facebook knew about how it radicalized users', www.nbcnews.com, 22 October 2021.

40. There are other sources used throughout, but to give credit where it is due, the Wikipedia timeline for this day is brilliantly done: 'Timeline of the United States Capitol Attack', https://en.wikipedia.org, accessed 13 October 2022.

41. Given that Mike Pence was still in the role at the time, I am using 'his' for simplicity.

42. Jane C. Timm, 'Fact check: No, Pence can't overturn the election results', www.nbcnews.com, 5 January 2021.

43. 'Trump tried to grab steering wheel to go to U.S. Capitol Jan 6-witness', www.reuters.com, 28 June 2022.

44. McKenzie Sadeghi, 'Fact check: Trump repeats false claim that Pelosi rejected request for National Guard ahead of Jan. 6', https://eu.usatoday.com, 16 December 2021.

45. Whitney Wild, Zachary Cohen and Evan Perez, 'Exclusive: Kamala Harris drove within several yards of pipe bomb at DNC headquarters during Capitol riot', https://edition.cnn.com, 31 January 2022.

46. Nancy A. Youssef and Alexa Corse, 'Covid-19 Contracted by Scores of National Guard Members in Washington', www.wsj.com, 22 January 2021.

47. Madison Hall et al., 'At least 919 people have been charged in the Capitol insurrection so far. This searchable table shows them all', www.insider.com, 21 September 2022.

48. Ted Mann, Dustin Volz, Lindsay Wise and Chad Day, 'Lawmakers Were Feet and Seconds Away From Confrontation With the Mob in the Capitol', www.wsj.com, 12 January 2021.

49. 'Almost a year after Capitol assault, most Americans feel democracy is under threat', www.france24.com, 3 January 2022.

50. David Edwards, 'QAnon congresswoman faces calls for arrest after live-tweeting Nancy Pelosi's location to rioters', www.rawstory. com, 10 January 2021.

51. John Bowden, 'Burner phones and a seven-hour gap: What we still don't know about the Trump White House call logs from Jan 6', www.independent.co.uk, 29 March 2022.

52. At https://twitter.com/deangloster/status/1508896725330657284.

53. At https://twitter.com/oversightdems/status/1421131313319399 425?s=21.

54. Louise Hall, 'Man charged in US Capitol riot worked for FBI and held top-secret security clearance, lawyer says', www.independent. co.uk, 9 February 2021.

55. At https://twitter.com/shayan86/status/1337553661250183 169?s=21.

56. Cristina Marcos, 'Rep. Marjorie Greene files articles of impeachment against Biden', https://thehill.com, 21 January 2021.

7 #SAVETHECHILDREN

1. 'Harvey Weinstein's Stunning Downfall: 23 Years in Prison', www. nytimes.com, 11 March 2020.

2. There is something of a timeline here: 'Jimmy Savile: timeline of his sexual abuse and its uncovering', www.theguardian.com, 26 June 2014.

3. Among them my TBIJ colleague Meirion Jones; Poppy Sebag-Montefiore, 'How two BBC journalists risked their jobs to reveal the truth about Jimmy Savile', www.theguardian.com, 2 November 2021.

4. Gino Spocchia, 'Lauren Boebert accused of parroting QAnon conspiracy with tweet about missing children', www.independent. co.uk, 14 December 2021.

5. 'Fact Check-Tweet overstates number of children who went missing in the United States in 2020', www.reuters.com, 13 December 2021.

6. 'QAnon's "Save the Children" morphs into popular slogan', www.independent.co.uk, 28 October 2020.

7. Joshua Pease, 'The sin of silence: The epidemic of denial about sexual abuse in the evangelical church', www.washingtonpost.com, 31 May 2018.

8. 'How "Save the Children" Is Keeping QAnon Alive', www.nytimes.com, 28 September 2020.

9. David J. Ley, 'Forget Me Not: The Persistent Myth of Repressed Memories', www.psychologytoday.com, 6 October 2019.

10. Another one where honestly the Wikipedia article is the best primer: 'Day-care sex-abuse hysteria', https://en.wikipedia.org, accessed 13 October 2022.

11. Simon Murphy, 'Revealed: how Carl Beech, the serial child abuse accuser, became the accused', www.theguardian.com, 22 July 2019.

12. Facebook took down the group in November 2020, and suspended the accounts of both Ward and Davis. See https://twitter.com/Shayan86/status/1326276306871472133.

13. Gian M. Volpicelli, 'How QAnon took hold in the UK', www.wired.co.uk, 21 September 2020.

14. Where it remains online (as at March 2022): https://twitter.com/BreesAnna/status/1275719028766621698.

15. Nick Reilly, 'Robbie Williams suggests debunked Pizzagate conspiracy theory is true: "The right questions haven't been asked"', www.nme.com, 25 June 2020.

16. This account is largely sourced from Kaylee Fagan, '#SaveTheChildren: How a Fringe Conspiracy Theory Fueled a Massive Child Abuse Panic', https://mediamanipulation.org, 23 March 2022.

17. Alongside other subjects excised for brevity: 'About Us', https://mediamanipulation.org.

18. The post (and many like it) was removed by Twitter eventually, but has been recreated as part of this excellent *Washington Post* story: Jessica Contrera, 'A QAnon Con: A Wayfair sex trafficking lie pushed by QAnon hurt real kids', www.washingtonpost.com, 16 December 2021.

19. Daniel Funke, 'How the Wayfair child sex-trafficking conspiracy theory went viral', www.politifact.com, 15 July 2020.

20. EJ Dickson, 'A Wayfair Child-Trafficking Conspiracy Theory Is Flourishing on TikTok, Despite It Being Completely False', www.rollingstone.com, 14 July 2020.

21. Funke, 'How the Wayfair'.

22. This video is still available on Facebook, where Mumin (now an adult) still regularly posts: www.facebook.com/100011665152188/videos/1157816001283894.

23. Russell Goldman, 'Half of All Autistic Kids Will Run Away, Tragedy Often Follows', https://abcnews.go.com, 1 May 2013.

24. 'Fact check: No evidence linking Wayfair to human trafficking operation', www.reuters.com, 13 July 2020.

25. Olivia Solon, 'How A Book About Flies Came To Be Priced $24 Million On Amazon', www.wired.com, 27 April 2011.

26. At www.amazon.com/Making-Fly-Genetics-Animal-Design/dp/0632030488/ref=sr_1_1?crid=1DOJPC37GR1S4&keywords=Peter+Lawrence%E2%80%99s+The+Making+of+a+Fly&qid=1648856119&sprefix=peter+lawrence+s+the+making+of+a+fly+%2Caps%2C627&sr=8-1, accessed 13 October 2022.

27. Kimi Robinson, 'Why is Wayfair accused of trafficking children? 7 things to know about the conspiracy theory', https://eu.azcentral.com, 17 August 2020.

28. Bryan Heater and Taylor Hatmaker, 'Facebook is limiting distribution of "save our children" hashtag over QAnon ties', https://techcrunch.com, 30 October 2020.

29. Contrera, 'A QAnon Con'.

30. '#SaveTheChildren Questions and Answers', https://polarisproject.org, accessed 13 October 2022.

31. Richard Scorer, 'QAnon is undermining vital child protection work', https://newhumanist.org.uk, 25 November 2020.

32. David Smith and Julia Carrie Wong, 'Trump tacitly endorses baseless QAnon conspiracy theory linked to violence', www.theguardian.com, 19 August 2020.

33. Jessica Guynn, 'Trump believes QAnon claim it's fighting pedophiles, refuses to disavow extremist conspiracy theory', 15 October 2020.

34. 'Matt Gaetz Is Said to Face Justice Dept. Inquiry Over Sex With an Underage Girl', www.nytimes.com, 30 March 2021.

35. Eliza Relman, 'The 26 women who have accused Trump of sexual misconduct', www.businessinsider.com, 17 September 2020.

36. 'Transcript: Donald Trump's Taped Comments About Women', www.nytimes.com, 8 October 2016.

37. David Gilbert, 'QAnon Thinks Matt Gaetz Being Investigated for Sex Trafficking Is All Part of the Plan', www.vice.com, 31 March 2021.

38. At https://twitter.com/oneunderscore__/status/1377083576588587 009?s=21.

39. If you believe Dan Brown's *The Da Vinci Code* (which you shouldn't), massive conspiracies hide small clues to their existence through codes and symbols left everywhere. But you can find codes anywhere – there are several that can be found hidden in these very notes, if you want them enough.

40. At https://twitter.com/asherlangton/status/1426290185436901 377?s=21.

41. EJ Dickson, 'A $100,000 Chicken McNugget Triggered a Child-Sex-Trafficking Conspiracy Theory', www.rollingstone.com, 3 August 2021.

42. Mary-Ann Russon, 'The cost of the Suez Canal blockage', www.bbc.co.uk, 29 March 2021.

43. Manthan C., '"Evergreen" Container Ship Blocking Suez Canal Sparks Human Trafficking Conspiracy Theory Linked to Clinton, Obama', www.ibtimes.sg, 30 March 2021.

44. It really was: Philip Bump, '"Here are the 2016 candidates" Secret Service code names – and your own', www.washingtonpost.com, 28 July 2016.

45. Matthew Champion, 'A Cargo Ship Drew a Giant Dick Pic in the Ocean Then Got Stuck in the Suez Canal', www.vice.com, 24 March 2021.

46. Ibid.

8 ENOUGH IS ENOUGH

1. 'Coronavirus confirmed as pandemic by World Health Organization', www.bbc.co.uk, 11 March 2020.

2. ' Prime Minister's statement on coronavirus (COVID-19): 23 March 2020', www.gov.uk, 23 March 2020.

3. 'Preppers' are a predominantly US group who believe some form of societal-ending event is nearby, and so like to stock up on supplies and ammunition.

4. Chad P. Brown and Melina Kolb, 'Trump's Trade War Timeline: An Up-to-Date Guide', www.piie.com, 21 June 2022.

5. Amy Maxmen and Smriti Mallapaty, 'The COVID lab-leak hypothesis: what scientists do and don't know', www.nature.com, 8 June 2021.

6. 'The territorial impact of COVID-19: Managing the crisis and recovery across levels of government', www.oecd.org, 10 May 2021.

7. Axel Bruns, Stephen Harrington and Edward Hurcombe, '"Corona? 5G? or both?": the dynamics of COVID-19/5G conspiracy theories on Facebook', www.ncbi.nlm.nih.gov, November 2020.

8. Nina Burleigh, 'How The Covid-19 Vaccine Injected Billions Into Big Pharma — And Made Its Executives Very Rich', www.forbes.com, 14 May 2021.

9. As discussed in earlier chapters, even Facebook's own internal research highlighted this issue for the world's largest social network. This is a good YouTube example: Katie Dowd, 'We ran a YouTube test. The results horrified us', www.sfgate.com, 21 May 2021.

10. Or people who identified as journalists, at least.

11. 'The Truth Behind the Coronavirus Pandemic, Covid-19 Lockdown & the Economic Crash – David Icke', https://freedomplatform.tv, 18 March 2020.

12. This is in fact a paraphrase of 'Alle Dinge sind Gift, und nichts ist ohne Gift, allein die Dosis macht dass ein Ding kein Gift ist', which translates as 'All things are poison, and nothing is without poison, the dosage alone makes it so a thing is not a poison.'

13. 'Bill Gates, at Odds With Trump on Virus, Becomes a Right-Wing Target', www.nytimes.com, 17 April 2020.

14. At the time of writing, he is fourth on Forbes' rich list: www.forbes.com.

15. Klint Finley, 'Was Microsoft's Empire Built on Stolen Code? We May Never Know', www.wired.com, 7 August 2012.

16. Aditi, 'Abuse Of Dominance: The Microsoft Cases', www.lawctopus.com, 29 August 2014.

17. 'Bill Gates Met With Jeffrey Epstein Many Times, Despite His Past', www.nytimes.com, 12 October 2019.

18. Lisa Kim, 'Bill Gates Was Warned About "Inappropriate" Emails to a Female Employee At Microsoft In 2008, Report Says', www.forbes.com, 18 October 2021.

19. QAnon had some wild theories relating to the divorce, incidentally: Shweta Sharma, 'QAnon conspiracy theorists are

having a field day with Bill and Melinda Gates divorce', www.inde pendent.co.uk, 5 May 2021.

20. Matthew Brown, 'Fact check: Bill Gates has given over $50 billion to charitable causes over career', https://eu.usatoday.com, 6 November 2020.

21. The Foundation receives funding from some other sources, including philanthropy from Gates' friend and fellow multi-billionaire Warren Buffett

22. The Bureau retains full editorial independence, including the freedom to criticise the Gates Foundation and Gates-funded projects. It also discloses Gates funding to all prospective global health sources and commentators, and publishes it alongside each published story.

23. As of April 2022: 'Coronavirus death toll', at www.worldomet ers.info.

24. David Adam, '15 million people have died in the pandemic, WHO says', www.nature.com, 5 May 2022.

25. 'Bill Gates, at Odds With Trump on Virus, Becomes a Right-Wing Target', www.nytimes.com, 17 April 2020.

26. Thomas Ricker, 'Bill Gates is now the leading target for coronavirus falsehoods, says report', www.theverge.com, 17 April 2020.

27. Kristi Keck, 'Big Tobacco: A History of Its Decline', https://edit ion.cnn.com, 19 June 2009.

28. Geoffrey Supran and Naomi Oreskes, 'The forgotten oil ads that told us climate change was nothing', www.theguardian.com, 18 November 2021.

29. Dietrich Knauth, Jonathan Stempel and Tom Hals, 'Sacklers to pay $6 billion to settle Purdue opioid lawsuits', www.reuters.com, 4 March 2022.

30. You can listen to part of this interview here: David Taylor, 'Covid-19: the 5G conspiracy', www.tortoisemedia.com, 16 April 2020.

31. Rebecca Heilwell, 'How the 5G coronavirus conspiracy theory went from fringe to mainstream', www.vox.com, 4 April 2020.

32. 'Clapping, the NHS and 5G. Is this the most ridiculous coronavirus conspiracy so far?', www.thatsnonsense.com, 3 April 2020.

33. Kaitlyn Tiffany, 'Something in the Air', www.theatlantic.com, 14 May 2020.

34. Bruce Y. Lee, '5G Networks And COVID-19 Coronavirus: Here Are The Latest Conspiracy Theories', www.forbes.com, 9 April 2020.

35. Alexander Martin,' Coronavirus: 90 attacks on phone masts reported during UK's lockdown', https://news.sky.com, 25 May 2020.

36. 'Coronavirus: '"Murder threats" to telecoms engineers over 5G', www.bbc.co.uk, 23 April 2020.

37. CBS, 'Trump says coronavirus will "miraculously" be gone by April "once the weather warms up"', www.youtube.com, 11 February 2020.

38. Gabriel Sherman, '"This Is So Unfair to Me": Trump Whines About His COVID-19 Victimhood as Campaign Flails', www.vanityfair.com, 26 May 2020.

39. 'Daily new confirmed Covid-19 deaths per million people', https://ourworldindata.org, accessed 14 October 2022.

40. Martin Pengelly, 'Rush Limbaugh: coronavirus a "common cold" being "weaponised" against Trump', www.theguardian.com, 25 February 2020.

41. Ryan Broderick, 'Trump's Biggest Supporters Think The Coronavirus Is A Deep State Plot', www.buzzfeednews.com, 27 February 2020.

42. At https://twitter.com/RightWingWatch/status/1232332782401134593.

43. 'No, Dr Anthony Fauci did not fund research tied to Covid', www.politifact.com, 8 February 2021.

44. Elizabeth Dwoskin, 'Massive Facebook study on users' doubt in vaccines finds a small group appears to play a big role in pushing the skepticism', www.washingtonpost.com, 14 March 2021.

45. Renee DiRest and Isabella Garcia-Camargo, 'Virality Project (US): Marketing meets Misinformation', https://cyber.fsi.stanford.edu, 26 May 2020.

46. Samantha Walther and Andrew McCoy, 'US Extremism on Telegram: Fueling Disinformation, Conspiracy Theories, and Accelerationism', *Perspectives on Terrorism*, 15/2 (2021), at www.jstor.org.

47. Louise Hall, '"Forcing boys to wear masks is emasculating": GOP QAnon candidate defies CDC guidance on face coverings', www.independent.co.uk, 9 September 2020.

48. Timothy Caulfield, 'Covid vaccine and mask conspiracies succeed when they appeal to identity and ideology', www.nbcnews.com, 18 December 2020.

49. James Meikle, 'Thalidomide "caused up to 10,000 miscarriages and infant deaths in UK"', www.theguardian.com, 6 March 2016.

50. 'Wakefield is struck off for the "serious and wide-ranging findings against him"', www.bmj.com, at 24 May 2010.
51. Saad B. Omer, 'The discredited doctor hailed by the anti-vaccine movement', www.nature.com, 27 October 2020.
52. Karina Shah, 'CIA's hunt for Osama bin Laden fuelled vaccine hesitancy in Pakistan', www.newscientist.com, 11 May 2021.
53. Veena Raleigh and Jonathan Holmes, 'The health of people from ethnic minority groups in England', www.kingsfund.org.uk, 17 September 2021.
54. 'The Tuskegee Timeline', www.cdc.gov, accessed 17 October 2022.
55. John P. Moore and Ian A. Wilson, 'Decades of basic research paved the way for today's "warp speed" Covid-19 vaccines', www.statnews.com, 5 January 2021.
56. 'CORRECTED – Fact Check – COVID-19 vaccines are not experimental and they have not skipped trial stages', www.reuters.com, 14 April 2021.
57. Sarah R. Olutola, 'Nicki Minaj's COVID-19 vaccine tweet about swollen testicles signals the dangers of celebrity misinformation and fandom', https://theconversation.com, 20 September 2021.
58. 'No, other people's Covid vaccines can't disrupt your menstrual cycle', www.nytimes.com, 29 March 2021.
59. Angelo Fichera, 'Video Targets Gates With Old Clip, Misleading Edit', www.factcheck.org, 5 March 2021.
60. One sad example: David Gilbert, 'Of Course Anti-Vaxxers Are Spreading Lies About Betty White's Death', www.vice.com, 4 January 2022.
61. Adam Smith, 'Conspiracy theorists spread '5G Covid' mind-control chip diagram that is actually a guitar pedal', www.independent.co.uk, 5 January 2021.
62. At https://twitter.com/BadVaccineTakes/status/1509821894744326174.
63. 'FALSE: When the COVID-19 vaccine is introduced, microchips will also be introduced into the human body, then 5G networks will come into play, through which the world's elite will send various signals to nanochips that have settled in human organisms. They will want to send such a signal that only the a "Golden" billion will remain on Earth.', www.poynter.org, 1 May 2020.
64. At https://twitter.com/BadVaccineTakes/status/1502037554929053701.

65. At https://twitter.com/BadVaccineTakes/status/150192436365 8043393.

66. At https://twitter.com/BadVaccineTakes/status/150169168985 7126400.

67. Andrew Romano, 'New Yahoo News/YouGov poll shows coronavirus conspiracy theories spreading on the right may hamper vaccine efforts', https://news.yahoo.com, 22 May 2020.

68. Kathy Frankovic, 'Why won't Americans get vaccinated?', https://today.yougov.com, 15 July 2021.

69. 'Religious Identities and the Race Against the Virus: (Wave 2: June 2021)', www.prri.org, 27 July 2021.

70. Simon Childs, 'Boris Johnson's "Ex-Lover" Has Gone Down a QAnon-Inspired Rabbit Hole', www.vice.com, 21 December 2021.

71. 'Anti-vax protesters shouting false Savile slurs target Keir Starmer – video', www.theguardian.com, 7 February 2022.

72. Ibid.

73. Rob Price, 'Gaia was a wildly popular yoga brand. Now it's a publicly traded Netflix rival pushing conspiracy theories while employees fear the CEO is invading their dreams.', www.businessinsider.com, 14 February 2021.

74. Will Sommer, 'Demi Lovato Promotes Lizard-War Videos at "Hub for QAnon"', www.thedailybeast.com, 9 November 2021.

75. Anders Anglesey, 'QAnon-Friendly Event Attendees Are Coming Down Sick—They Think It's Anthrax', www.newsweek.com, 22 December 2021.

76. Justin Rohrlich, 'Wisconsin Vaccine Saboteur Steven Brandenburg Is a Flat-Earther, FBI Document Reveals', www.thedailybeast.com, 31 January 2021.

77. There is much interesting on this theme in this paper: Matteo Cinelli et al., 'The COVID-19 social media infodemic', www.nature.com, 6 October 2020.

9 NOTHING CAN STOP WHAT'S COMING

1. At https://twitter.com/_MAArgentino/status/130097436149 1406849.

2. 'A dangerous new virus threatens UK — QAnon', www.thetimes.co.uk, 27 September 2020 (okay maybe this one was me).

3. Elias Isquith, 'Alex Jones: Obama is enlisting refugees into a secret army of child soldiers!', www.salon.com, 30 July 2014.

4. 'Fact check: Men who stormed Capitol identified by Reuters are not undercover Antifa as posts claim', www.reuters.com, 9 January 2021.

5. David Schmidt, '"Won't somebody please think of the children?"', https://brooklynrail.org, December 2020.

6. At https://twitter.com/yashar/status/1352770707499831297?s=21.

7. 'On this day: JFK Jr. killed in plane crash', www.history.com, accessed 17 October 2022.

8. 'Maria Shriver Responds to the QAnon Obsession with JFK Jr', www.townandcountrymag.com, 24 November 2021.

9. He didn't say it: 'Viral Image: Says John F. Kennedy Jr. said, "If my dear friend Donald Trump ever decided to sacrifice his fabulous billionaire lifestyle to become president he would be an unstoppable force for ultimate justice that Democrats and Republicans alike would celebrate"', www.politifact.com, 8 April 2019.

10. EJ Dickson, 'QAnon Followers Think JFK Jr. Is Coming Back on the 4th of July', www.rollingstone.com, 3 July 2019.

11. VICE have a great piece on Protzman here: David Gilbert, 'Meet the Antisemitic QAnon Leader Who Led Followers to Dallas to Meet JFK', www.vice.com, 5 November 2021.

12. At https://twitter.com/stevanzetti/status/1455338895793659910?s=21.

13. At https://twitter.com/willsommer/status/1460454073291972608.

14. At https://twitter.com/Shayan86/status/1460633229862608916.

15. 'Cognitive dissonance: What to know', www.medicalnewstoday.com, accessed 17 October 2022.

16. David Gilbert, 'Roger Stone Visited the JFK-QAnon Cult In Dallas', www.vice.com, 14 December 2021.

17. World Economic Forum, 'Our Mission', www.weforum.org, accessed 17 October 2022.

18. World Economic Forum, 'Annual Report 2018–2019', https://www3.weforum.org, accessed 17 October 2022.

19. Taylor Thompson Fuller, 'False posts target World Economic Forum founder with hoax Covid-19 conspiracy', https://factcheck.afp.com, 7 July 2021.

20. Office of the Director of National Intelligence, 'Bin Laden's Bookshelf', www.dni.gov, accessed 17 October 2022.

21. H. G. Wells's *The Open Conspiracy* is available at https://gutenberg.net.au.

22. Klaus Schwab, *COVID-19: The Great Reset* (Geneva, 2020), pp. 248–50.
23. World Economic Forum, 'The Great Reset', https://www.weforum.org, accessed 17 October 2022.
24. A disclosure: before he worked at the WEF, Adrian Monck was a journalism professor and the head of the journalism department at City, University of London, where I studied. We met when I was a student and have stayed in touch intermittently since.
25. Fr Richard Heilman, 'Breaking!! Abp. Viganò open letter to the president – "children of light vs. children of darkness"', www.romancatholicman.com, 6 June 2020.
26. 'Abp. Viganò: More Reflections on the Great Reset', at https://catholicfamilynews.com, 31 May 2021.
27. All of Monck's remarks here are from author interview.
28. At www.antihate.ca/queen_of_canada_calling_us_supporters_invade_canada_execute_traitors, accessed 17 October 2022.
29. Gina Spocchia, 'Woman who claims to be secret queen of Canada develops following among QAnon devotees, report says', www.independent.co.uk, 18 June 2021.
30. At www.antihate.ca/queen_of_canada_calling_us_supporters_invade_canada_execute_traitors.
31. Ibid.
32. 'Canada's QAnon "Queen" and her escalating rhetoric', www.cbc.ca, 6 December 2021.
33. Anders Anglesey, 'QAnon Influencer Romana Didulo Detained Over Alleged "Shoot To Kill" Medics Posts', www.newsweek.com, 2 December 2021.
34. 'Queen of Canada Romana Didulo Joins the Freedom Convoy 2022', www.youtube.com, 3 February 2022.
35. Justin Ling, 'Canada was warned before protests that violent extremists infiltrated convoy', www.theguardian.com, 17 February 2022.
36. Amanda Coletta and Amy Cheng, 'Trudeau's emergency powers upheld in Canada's House amid worries "Freedom Convoy" could return', www.washingtonpost.com, 22 February 2022.
37. Tracey Lindeman, 'Maple leaf flags, conspiracy theories and The Matrix: inside the Ottawa truckers' protest', www.theguardian.com, 11 February 2022.
38. Rachelle Elsiufi, '"I regret going": Protester says he spent life savings to support Freedom Convoy', www.cbc.ca, 24 March 2022.

39. John Paul Tasker, 'Banks are moving to freeze accounts linked to convoy protests. Here's what you need to know', www.cbc.ca, 16 February 2022.

40. This video is still online as at April 2022: Glenn Beck, 'Canada just proved The Great Reset is in operation NOW', www.youtube.com, 15 February 2022.

41. 'C.W. McCall – Convoy', www.youtube.com, 8 October 2012.

42. At https://twitter.com/oneunderscore__/status/1499813393309605 897?s=21.

43. Mack Lamoureux, 'Trucker Convoy Doesn't Plan to Leave D.C. Area Anytime Soon', www.vice.com, 9 March 2022.

44. 'Police divert "People's Convoy" away from downtown D.C.', www.washingtonpost.com, 15 March 2022.

45. 'Meet the Bike Man who brought the trucker convoy to a crawl', www.washingtonpost.com, 26 March 2022.

46. Catherine Lee, ' "Don't say gay", bill: Florida should learn from the harmful legacy of Britain's section 28', https://theconversation.com, 16 February 2022.

47. At https://twitter.com/AriDrennen/status/1508976786356334593.

48. David Gilbert, 'The Right Has Gone Full QAnon on Disney', www.vice.com, 1 April 2022.

49. Joe Gould, 'After Trump impeachment, US lawmakers stress unity on Ukraine military aid', www.defensenews.com, 19 February 2020.

50. 'What We Know and Don't About Hunter Biden and a Laptop', www.nytimes.com, 22 October 2022.

51. NATO, 'Hybrid Warfare – New Threats, Complexity, and "Trust" ', www.nato.int, 30 November 2021.

52. At https://twitter.com/joshuahol/status/1507061556252655619?s=21.

53. Olga Robinson, Shayan Sardarizadeh and Jake Horton, 'Ukraine war: Fact-checking Russia's biological weapons claims', www.bbc.co.uk, 15 March 2022.

54. At https://twitter.com/oneunderscore__/status/1503437677445537 793?s=21.

55. US Department of State, 'GEC Special Report: Pillars of Russia's Disinformation and Propaganda Ecosystem', www.state.gov, 4 August 2020.

56. Liam O'Dell, 'QAnon think Trump backs Ukraine-Russia conflict to destroy "secret labs" run by Fauci', www.indy100.com, 12 March 2022.

57. Taylor Orth and Kathy Frankovic, 'Which groups of Americans believe conspiracy theories about Ukraine and Russia?', https://today.yougov.com, 30 March 2022.

58. Grant LaFleche, 'How vaccination status might predict views on the Russian invasion of Ukraine', *Toronto Star*, 19 March 2022, at https://archive.ph/a1mWC

59. David Gilbert, 'QAnon Isn't Dead. It's Growing', www.vice.com, 24 February 2022.

60. 'Extremism on the Ballot in 2022', www.adl.org, 25 January 2022.

61. Ed Pilkington, '"We have a project": QAnon followers eye swing state election official races', www.theguardian.com, 11 February 2022.

62. Annie Kelly and Mei-Ling McNamara, 'Outcry as Trump restricts funding for sex-trafficking survivors', www.theguardian.com, 6 July 2018.

10 TRUST THE PLAN

1. The thread was long ago removed by Twitter, but is archived here: https://twtext.com/article/1325124397729001472 (although a carbon copy of it is still on the site here: https://twitter.com/eredu verseau/status/1325863522924900352).

2. This time is GMT. In US Eastern, it would be 12 November, as would the following post.

3. At https://qposts.online/post/4950.

4. At https://qposts.online/post/4951.

5. Christopher Bing, 'Senior U.S. cybersecurity official asked to resign amid Trump transition tumult', www.reuters.com, 12 November 2020.

6. As covered in Chapter Six.

7. A good summary of one of the most infamous calls can be found here: 'Trump–Raffensperger phone call', https://en.wikipedia.org, accessed 17 October 2022.

8. Hugo Lowell, '"Just say the election was corrupt," Trump urged DoJ after loss to Biden', www.theguardian.com, 30 July 2021.

9. 'The president vaguely warned of a "criminal offense" as he pressured Secretary of State Brad Raffensperger in the call, according to an audio recording', www.nytimes.com, 3 January 2021.

10. Ewan Palmer, 'QAnon Couple Are Behind 3-Day Dallas Event Billing Michael Flynn and Sidney Powell', www.newsweek.com, 7 April 2021.

11. At https://twitter.com/shayan86/status/1345092143413649 409?s=21.

12. At https://twitter.com/travis_view/status/1325807371872989184/ photo/2.

13. Ibid.

14. Nathan J. Robinson, 'QAnon and the Fragility of Truth', www.cur rentaffairs.org, 30 December 2020.

15. Hunter Walker, 'NBA player turned conspiracy theorist stages one-man pro-Trump protest amid inaugural security prepared for thousands', https://news.yahoo.com, 20 January 2021.

16. All accessible from this thread: https://twitter.com/NickyWoolf/sta tus/1351936432097669123.

17. https://www.reuters.com/article/us-usa-biden-qanon-idUSKB N29P2VO

18. https://www.washingtonpost.com/technology/2021/01/20/ qanon-trump-era-ends/

19. https://abcnews.go.com/Technology/twitter-facebook-slap-labels-trumps-misleading-election-posts/story?id=74020537

20. https://about.fb.com/news/2020/08/addressing-movements-and-organizations-tied-to-violence/

21. https://www.mediamatters.org/qanon-conspiracy-theory/ang elo-carusone-speaks-bbc-news-about-impact-qanon-conspir acy-theory

22. https://www.knbr.com/2021/08/10/aubrey-huffs-twitter-account-suspended-former-giant-responds-on-instagram/

23. https://twitter.com/AdamWeinstein/status/1325258500440793095/ photo/2

24. https://twitter.com/raheemkassam/status/1347752625677217 794?s=21

25. https://twitter.com/RaheemKassam/status/1347755871145701376

26. https://brandnewtube.com/watch/qanon-is-a-psyop-wake-up-peo ple-david-icke-dot-connector-videocast_y9iqXBaVkjazpPX.html

27. https://www.nytimes.com/2021/01/20/technology/qanon-inaug uration.html?smid=tw-share

28. This is all taken from 'When Prophecy Fails', which gives Martin the pseudonym of 'Marian Keech'.

29. Knight's remarks are all from an author interview.

30. https://www.oxforddnb.com/view/10.1093/ref:odnb/9780198614
    128.001.0001/odnb-9780198614128-e-95563
31. https://www.carersuk.org/news-and-campaigns/featu
    res/10-facts-about-women-and-caring-in-the-uk-on-internatio
    nal-women-s-day
32. This is the UK figure, as an example: https://www.theguardian.com/
    business/2020/feb/18/average-uk-wages-rise-above-pre-financial-
    crisis-levels
33. https://www.vanityfair.com/news/2021/06/donald-trump-august-
    reinstatement
34. https://www.newsweek.com/qanon-theorists-
    switch-date-march-20-after-no-trump-inaugurat
    ion-call-4th-false-flag-1573871
35. https://www.reuters.com/article/factcheck-trump-reinstated-
    idUSL1N2OV1W3
36. https://www.independent.co.uk/news/world/americas/us-politics/
    mike-lindell-mypillow-trump-reinstatement-b1924336.html
37. https://www.independent.co.uk/news/world/americas/us-politics/
    republicans-trump-reinstated-president-yougov-b1957930.html
38. https://www.reuters.com/article/uk-factcheck-qanon-military-
    theories-idUSKBN29R1ZA
39. At https://twitter.com/kaleighrogers/status/1372269726995509
    251?s=21.
40. At   https://twitter.com/KaleighRogers/status/1372280139539701
    760/photo/1.
41. At https://qposts.online/post/2668.
42. At https://qposts.online/post/2352.
43. At https://qposts.online/post/4953.
44. At https://twitter.com/Shayan86/status/1379099213661937665.
45. https://www.bbc.co.uk/news/world-asia-55882489
46. At https://twitter.com/GraceSpelman/status/135626116215
    3873411.

11 THE GREAT AWAKENING

 1. Guru Jagat, 'The Great Awakening Map: Guru Jagat x Champ
    Parinya', www.youtube.com, accessed 17 October 2022.
 2. I should probably confess: I have this as a framed poster in my flat.
    But you can see it online at www.greatawakeningmap.co.

3. At www.greatawakeningmap.co/downloads.
4. 'Pepe Silvia', https://knowyourmeme.com, accessed 17 October 2022.
5. Matt Ridley, 'In Retrospect: *The Selfish Gene*', www.nature.com, 27 January 2016.
6. Richard Dawkins, *The Selfish Gene* (Oxford, 1976), p. 245.
7. Ibid., pp. 248–49.
8. Ibid., p. 251, emphasis original
9. 'Global Internet usage', https://en.wikipedia.org, accessed 18 October 2022.
10. Unless otherwise footnoted, everything from Phillips is from our interview.
11. The Church of Scientology disputes this claim, but it is a frequent one made by those who have left the church: Ryan Buxton et al., 'Inside Scientology's Auditing Process: How Members Are Pushed To Reveal Their Private "Sexual Indiscretions"', www.huffingtonp ost.co.uk, 30 March 2015.
12. Rich Haridy, 'Facebook isn't secretly listening to your conversations, but the truth is much more disturbing', https://newatlas.com, 6 September 2016.
13. Sam Levin, '"They don't care": Facebook factchecking in disarray as journalists push to cut ties', www.theguardian.com, 13 December 2018.
14. At https://twitter.com/Shayan86/status/1352242020308418560/photo/1.

12 WAKE UP, SHEEPLE

1. 'Meatspace' came to popularity as a term for the offline world (yes, really) in the online forums of the 1990s, as an alternative to 'cyberspace'.
2. CDC, 'Treatment of Malaria: Guidelines for Clinicians (United States)', www.cdc.gov, accessed 18 October 2022.
3. Sam Wassner and Sanjib Mohanty, 'Malaria and the brain – what long-term impact does malaria have on brain function?', www. lshtm.ac.uk, 15 December 2021.
4. You may see what I'm driving at here …

5. This is the genetic one, which is the most interesting: Rob Stein, 'How an Altered Strand of DNA Can Cause Malaria-Spreading Mosquitoes to Self-Destruct', www.npr.org, 28 July 2021.

6. WHO, 'WHO recommends groundbreaking malaria vaccine for children at risk', www.who.int, 6 October 2021.

7. William Dalrymple and Anita Anand, *Empire*, ep. 2: 'Company Rule in India', https://podcasts.apple.com, 16 August 2022.

8. Patrick J. Kiger, 'Did Colonists Give Infected Blankets to Native Americans as Biological Warfare?', www.history.com, 25 November 2019.

9. Heather Pringle, 'How Europeans brought sickness to the New World', www.science.org, 4 June 2015.

10. All of Marianna's comments are from author interviews.

11. Of Chapter Eleven fame.

12. 'Wake up, sheeple!' is a phrase so beloved of conspiracy movements that it's become something of an affectionate cliché.

13. It really does: Stella Talic et al., 'Effectiveness of public health measures in reducing the incidence of covid-19, SARS-CoV-2 transmission, and covid-19 mortality: systematic review and meta-analysis', www.bmj.com, 18 November 2021.

14. Patrick Saunders-Hastings, 'Effectiveness of personal protective measures in reducing pandemic influenza transmission: A systematic review and meta-analysis', *Epidemics*, 20 (September 2017), www.sciencedirect.com.

15. Correct for the UK Amazon site as at April 2022.

16. Zachary Cohen, 'China and Russia "weaponized" QAnon conspiracy around time of US Capitol attack, report says', https://edition.cnn.com, 19 April 2021.

17. Author interview, as before.

18. All author interview, as is O'Connor shortly afterwards.

19. I recommend starting here. Make sure you complete any urgent work first: 'Not Me ThisTime', https://tvtropes.org, accessed 18 October 2022.

CONCLUSION

1. This is a longstanding thought experiment, but also a genuinely fun and disturbing online game: www.decisionproblem.com.

2. Read the word backwards.

3. Samuel Butler, *Erewhon*, Penguin, 2006, p. 97.
4. Ibid., p. 199.
5. *Dune 2* is the usual go-to here, but personally I much prefer the point-and-click *Dune* adventure, in all its joyous 1980s-ness.
6. Yes, I know they're not actually nuns.
7. If it starts facing upwards.
8. 'Barack Obama Takes on a New Role: Fighting Disinformation', www.nytimes.com, 20 April 2022.

Bibliography and Further Reading

This is a selection of titles referenced through this book, and also some related to the subject. Some *are* conspiratory theories, some tackle conspiracy theories and some do a bit of both.

Butler, Samuel, *Erewhon* [1872], Penguin Classics, Harmondsworth, 2006

Butter, Michael, *The Nature of Conspiracy Theories*, Polity Press, Cambridge, 2020

Coleman, Gabriella, *Hacker, Hoaxer, Whistleblower, Spy: The Many Faces of Anonymous*, Verso Books, London, 2014

Dawkins, Richard, *The Selfish Gene*, Oxford University Press, New York, 1976

Ebner, Julia, *Going Dark: The Secret Social Lives of Extremists*, Bloomsbury Publishing, London, 2019

Festinger, Leon, *When Prophecy Fails*, Pinter & Martin Ltd, London, 1956

Jankowicz, Nina, *How to Lose the Information War: Russia, Fake News, and the Future of Conflict*, I. B. Tauris & Company, London, 2020

Johnson, Stanley, *The Marburg Virus*, William Heinemann, London, 1984

Nagle, Angela, *Kill All Normies: Online Culture Wars from 4chan and Tumblr to Trump and the Alt-Right*, Zero Books, Portland, OR, 2017

Phillips, Whitney, *You Are Here: A Field Guide for Navigating Polarized Speech, Conspiracy Theories, and Our Polluted Media Landscape*, The MIT Press, Cambridge, MA, 2021

Rebel Press Media, *The Great Reset!: The Truth about Agenda 2021–2030, New Covid Variants, Vaccines & Medical Apartheid – Mind Control – World Domination – Sterilization Exposed!*, (Anonymous Truth Leaks) self-published, 2021

Robertson, Pat, *The New World Order*, W Publishing Group, New York, 1991

Schwab, Klaus, *COVID-19: The Great Reset*, World Economic Forum, Geneva, 2020

Shea, Robert, *The Illuminatus! Trilogy*, Constable & Robinson, London, 1975

Sunstein, Cass R., *Conspiracy Theories and Other Dangerous Ideas*, Simon & Schuster, New York, 2014

Walker, Jesse, *The United States of Paranoia: A Conspiracy Theory*, Harper Perennial, London, 2012

Index

About the Author

James Ball is a Fellow at the Centre for the Analysis of Social Media, Demos and the author of multiple books, including *Post-Truth* and *The System*. He has written for the Bureau of Investigative Journalism, *BuzzFeed*, the *Guardian* and the *Washington Post* and his work has won the Pulitzer Prize for Public Service, the Scripps Howard Prize and the British Journalism Award for investigative reporting, among others. He lives in London.